# OVER
# THE
# SPECTRUM

**Melbourne House Publishers**

First Published in 1982 by Melbourne House

This Remastered Edition
Published by
**Acorn Books**
www.acornbooks.co.uk

## PUBLISHER'S NOTE
=================

We at Melbourne House are very excited to be involved
with the publication of this book, making available as it
does not only 30 interesting and varied programs for the
Sinclair ZX Spectrum - undoubtedly the most powerful and most
affordable small computer in the world - but also showing you
how to use the computer's complete facilities to its maximum.
This book offers you not only strategy, gambling and arcade
games but also utilities, business and educational programs.

We are also publishers of other titles for the
Spectrum computer, as a glance at the back pages of this book
will show, ranging from titles for the complete beginner to
titles of interest to more experienced users.

We have a commitment to providing literature and
software for the Sinclair ZX Spectrum, and as you will note
by leafing through this book, many of the programs we publish
are the result of programs that were submitted to us by ZX
Spectrum owners.

So if you have a program or article you think would be
of interest to other ZX Spectrum owners, please write to us.
We will give you a prompt assessment and reply whether the
material is something we could use.
In the meantime, happy computing.

ALFRED MILGROM
PUBLISHER

# C O N T E N T S

## UTILITIES

## BUSINESS PROGRAMS

## STRATEGY PROGRAMS

NOTES ON THE PROGRAM LISTINGS:
----------------------------------

   As you are no doubt aware, there are a
number of different modes available in
operating the Spectrum keyboard, each
resulting in a different keyword or graphic
symbol being recorded by the Spectrum.

   The program listings in this book have been
specially designed and printed to make
reading these listings easier. A few words
may be needed to explain the meaning of some
of the symbols:

   ▲         This symbol is used whenever
         a space is to be entered in the
         program. This may be in a graphics
         character string, or it may be in
         a PRINT statement.
         Spaces have been used in these
         programs to aid readability, and
         in some cases are essential to
         the proper working of the
         program.

   SHI     This symbol is used to indicate that
         the CAPS SHIFT key needs to be held
         down for the next character.

   EXT     This symbol is used to indicate that
         you need to be in EXTENDED mode to
         enter the following character.
         EXTENDED mode is obtained by pressing
         both the CAPS SHIFT and SYMBOL SHIFT
         keys together. See your Spectrum
         manual for more details.

   GRA     This symbol is used to indicate that
         you need to be in GRAPHICS mode to
         enter the following character.
         GRAPHICS mode is obtained by pressing
         the "9" key while holding down the
         CAPS SHIFT key. See your Spectrum
         manual for more details.

   INV     Indicates INVERSE VIDEO mode.
         Press "4" and CAPS SHIFT keys
         together.

   TRU     Indicates TRUE VIDEO mode.
         Press "3" and CAPS SHIFT keys
         together.

Further notes on the use of EXTENDED MODE

In this book we have made use of all the facilities
of the ZX Spectrum, inlcuding the ability to specify
the paper and ink color from within a program line or
PRINT statement.

This is achieved by entering EXTENDED MODE, and then
pressing the appropriate color key (for paper color)
or the CAPS SHIFT key and the appropriate key (for
ink color).

For example, this is shown in the book as :
        **EXT SHI** 3        (choose ink color 3)

    or      **EXT** 6        (choose paper color 6).


To demonstrate this, the following may help :
        **EXT SHI** 3 :    1. Press both the CAPS SHIFT
                              and SYMBOL SHIFT keys.
                              The "K" cursor should now
                              have changed to an "E".
                           2. Press the CAPS SHIFT key.
                              While holding this key
                              press the "3" key. The
                              cursor will now be a "K"
                              again.
        **EXT** 6      :   1. Press both the CAPS SHIFT
                              and SYMBOL SHIFT keys.
                              The "K" cursor should now
                              have changed to an "E".
                           2. Press the "6" key.
                              The cursor will now be a
                              "K" again.

# Leapfrog

Copyright (c) by Beam Software


The game of leapfrog  is a nice simple one:

  You start off with two opposing sets of frogs, and each
frog can only move to an adjacent space or leap over one
frog.

          X X X X - O O O O
          1 2 3 4 5 6 7 8 9

  So, as a first move, for example the frog at position 4 can
move to 5, or the frog at 6 can move to 5, or the frog at 3
can leap over the frog at 4 to land at 5, or the frog at 7
can leap over the frog at 6 to land at 5.

  The object of the game is to try to get all the frogs on
the left to the right, and vice versa in the least number of
moves. It's great fun!

Structure of the program:
-------------------------

The first part of any program is to initialise any variables
that might be required. In this case, we want to define the
initial position of the frogs, and set the number of moves
taken so far to zero.

  An overview of the program reveals the following structure:

                  Initialise variables
        Print     Print position of frogs
                  Check if finished
                      If yes, then go to Finish
        Input     Enter player's move
                  Check if move is allowed
                      If not, go to Input again
                  Add one to the number of moves
                  Make the move and go to Print
        Finish    Congratulate player
                  Ask player if he wants to play again
                      If yes, then RUN again

This simple "top-down" approach gives us an overview of the
program, and lets us understand the program should we wish to
make any changes at a later stage.


Structure of the variables:
---------------------------

For this program we shall be using "string variables" to
define the position of the frogs. A string variable is easy

to manipulate in this context, and makes printing very fast.

We define a$ as the original position of the frogs and b$ as the present position. We can use the same variables to check if we are finished (see line 150).

We use the variables "to" and "from" to represent the position the from is moving to and from. Because a frog can only move into an empty position we can check this easily (see line 200).

The rest of the program is very straightforward, with "count" being the number of moves taken.


Running the program:
----------------------

The program expects a 2-digit input to define the moves to and from. It will accept as a valid first move only the following inputs:

    35    45    65    75

Happy leapfrogging!

LEAPFROG

```
100 LET a$ = " GRA SHI 8▲ GRA SHI 8▲
        GRA SHI 8▲ GRA SHI 8▲▲▲
        GRA SHI 6▲ GRA SHI 6▲
        GRA SHI 6▲ GRA SHI 6"
110 LET b$ = a$
120 LET count = 0
130 CLS
140 PRINT AT 5, 3; b$; AT 6, 3;
        "1▲2▲3▲4▲5▲6▲7▲8▲9"
150 IF b$(1 TO 7) = a$(11 TO 17) AND
        b$(11 TO 17) = a$(1 TO 7) THEN GO TO 250
160 INPUT "Please▲enter▲your▲move"; k$
170 IF LEN k$ <> 2 THEN GO TO 160
180 LET from = 2*( CODE k$(1)-48)-1
190 LET to = 2*( CODE k$(2)-48)-1
200 IF b$(to) <> "▲" OR ABS (to-from) > 4
        THEN GO TO 160
210 LET count = count+1
220 LET b$(to) = b$(from)
230 LET b$(from) = "▲"
240 GO TO 140
250 PRINT "You▲did▲it▲in▲"; count; "▲moves"
260 INPUT "Another▲go?"; k$
270 IF CODE k$ = 121 THEN RUN
```

3

# Number Reversal

This is a puzzle to test your powers of logic! You start with 9 numbers, from 1 to 9, in a random order.

The aim is to get them into order in as few moves as possible. The only facility you have to change the order of the numbers is the ability to "reverse" the order of some of the elements.

For example, if you had the first three numbers "3 2 1", then reversing the first three will give you "1 2 3". If you had reversed only the first two, you would have had "3 1 2".

Note that you can specify only how many numbers you would like reversed. This program is quite short, so entering it into your computer will be easy, and it will certainly challenge your powers of logic.

Programming notes:
--------------------

This program highlights the use of arrays, and also shows how easily readable programs can be if you are prepared to take the trouble to define meaningful variable names.

Look at the program listing - there is no need for a separate program structure, because all the information you need is there.

Note also that it is possible to put spaces at the beginning of lines to make FOR-NEXT loops, etc., more obviously highlighted.

The use of variable names for line numbers in GOTOs and GOSUBs is also a very efficient way of keeping track of what is going on. It also minimises the work that has to be done if you use the RENUMBERing routines provided later in this book.

Use of arrays:
--------------

The use of arrays allows us to easily refer to a particular element without having to have a separate name for each element.

At the beginning of the program we dimension the array, and this sets each member of the array to zero. Note that the size of the array is defined in a variable, so if you want to test your logic with a longer list of numbers you can do so by simply changing that one line.

Note the way that the numbers are made to appear in random order – we take each number in turn and swap it with the number in a randomly chosen position. This algorithm is also a very useful and efficient way of shuffling cards in a card program.

## NUMBER REVERSAL

```
100 LET print = 600
110 LET reverse = 400
120 LET input = 300
130 LET size = 9
140 DIM a(size)
150 FOR c = 1 TO size
160    LET a(c) = c
170 NEXT c
180 FOR c = size TO 2 STEP -1
190    LET swap = 1+ INT (size* RND )
200    LET temp = a(c)
210    LET a(c) = a(swap)
220    LET a(swap) = temp
230 NEXT c
240 LET count = 0
250 GO SUB print
300 INPUT "How▲many▲numbers▲do▲you▲wish▲to
       ▲reverse?▲"; howmany
310 IF howmany = 0 THEN STOP
320 IF howmany <= size THEN GO TO reverse
330 PRINT size; "▲is▲maximum▲that▲can▲be
       ▲swapped"
340 GO TO input
400 PRINT "Reversing▲"; howmany; "▲numbers"
410 LET count = count+1
420 FOR d = 1 TO INT (howmany/2)
430    LET temporary = a(d)
440    LET mirror = howmany-d+1
450    LET a(d) = a(mirror)
460    LET a(mirror) = temporary
470 NEXT d
480 GO SUB print
490 FOR d = 1 TO size
500    IF a(d) <> d THEN GO TO input
510 NEXT d
520 PRINT "You▲did▲it▲in▲"; count; "▲moves."
530 STOP
600 POKE 23692, 255
610 FOR d = 1 TO size
620 PRINT a(d); "▲";
630 NEXT d
640 PRINT
650 RETURN
```

# Asteroids in Space

Copyright (c) by Neil Streeter

You are travelling through space in your spaceship, when suddenly you encounter a space storm.

You can steer your ship past the debris only by using your rudder controls (key '5' to go left, and key '8' to go right) - hyperdrive has been disabled by one of the meteors.

As if this was not bad enough, if you do survive the meteor storm, you will find you have become so disoriented that you are travelling the wrong way in the space lanes. All the space traffic is coming directly at you.

You must steer past these in the same way as before, but the space ships are bigger than the meteor debris, so it is more difficult.

Eventually, you will CRASH! When you do, you will find the survival rating on the screen of your spaceship console.

Program structure:
-------------------

This program simulates the use of the SCROLL function, which is available on most micro computers, but not on the Spectrum.

You are no doubt familiar with SCROLL already, as for example the program listing scrolls, but you may have noticed there is no command directly available to you to achieve the same result.

The same result can however be obtained by changing the value of the variable SCR-CT (this is achieved by POKEing 23692 - see Machine Code Monitor notes for more information about PEEK and POKE), and then printing two spaces at the end of the screen (ie AT 21,31).

When the display is SCROLLed, your ship will move with everything else, so it is overwritten with blanks, then printed again in the correct position. In this way, your ship stays on the same line in the screen, while everything else moves.

The asteroid debris and space ships appear randomly on the bottom of the screen, and the information about their position is kept in variables a, b, c, d, and e, with e being the closest. By comparing e with the position of your ship, the program determines whether you are about to crash.

The screen is SCROLLed two lines in each cycle, so that there are only 11 asteroid debris on the screen at any one time. You could SCROLL only once in each cycle, but this means there would be far too much asteroid debris on the screen, and you would have to keep track of twice as many variables.

Improving the program:
----------------------------

The program has been deliberately kept simple to allow you to improve it.

The first step that can be done is to use the facilities of the Spectrum's user defined graphics to define really exciting shapes for your ship and for the asteroid debris.

Secondly, you will note that there are two places in the program where sound is generated through the BEEP command. The purpose of these commands is not merely to create sound! Try deleting those lines, and I'm sure you will find the program runs much too fast for you.

You can therefore speed up or slow down the program by changing the length of the note or number of notes to be played.

There is also sufficient time in each cycle for you to write in additional ships attacking you, adding the ability for you to fire at the asteroids, and so on.

# ASTEROIDS IN SPACE

```
100 LET a$ = "*"
110 LET n = 0
120 LET a = 0
130 LET b = 0
140 LET c = 0
150 LET d = 0
160 LET t = 1
170 LET x = 12
180 LET r = INT (27* RND )
190 PRINT AT 21, r; INK (4* RND ); a$
200 POKE 23692, 255
210 PRINT AT 21, 31; "▲▲"
220 BEEP .3, 0
230 PRINT AT 10, x-2; "▲▲▲▲▲▲▲"
240 PRINT AT 11, x; " GRA 6 GRA SHI 6"
250 PRINT AT 21, 31; "▲▲"
260 LET n = n+t
270 IF n = 100 THEN
        LET a$ = " GRA SHI 6 GRA SHI 7"
280 IF n = 104 THEN LET t = 2
290 LET e = d
300 LET d = c
310 LET c = b
320 LET b = a
330 LET a = r
340 PRINT AT 10, x-2; "▲▲▲▲▲▲▲"
350 PRINT AT 11, x; " GRA 6 GRA SHI 6"
360 IF x >= e-2 AND x <= e+t THEN GO TO 410
370 BEEP .2, 5
380 IF INKEY$ = "5" THEN LET x = x-t
390 IF INKEY$ = "8" THEN LET x = x+t
400 GO TO 180
410 PRINT AT 11, x-1; "CRASH"
420 PRINT AT 0, 0; "SCORE = "; n
430 BEEP 2, -12
440 PRINT AT 21, 0; "Press▲any▲key▲to▲try
        ▲again"
450 IF INKEY$ = "" THEN GO TO 450
460 RUN
```

# Spectrum Clock

## DESCRIPTION

This program is a simulation of a REAL-TIME CLOCK; both normal clock and digital clock are implemented and displayed on the screen. You will be amazed at the accuracy of the SPECTRUM CLOCK; not only that, you can also set the ALARM and the SPECTRUM CLOCK will remind you by generating alarm tone.

## HOW TO RUN THE PROGRAM

Type RUN followed by (ENTER) to start the program.

You will need to enter the HOUR, MINUTE, SECOND which you want the clock to start. Note that HOUR is entered in a 24 hour basis; it means that you have to type in 13th hour instead of 1 PM.

The program checks the validity of the input, so you can't type a negative number or any number greater than 60 for minutes and seconds; they won't be accepted.

You will have to input in a similar way if you want to set the alarm.

One method of using this alarm effectively is as an EARLY MORNING ALARM : Run the program at night, setting the correct time and the alarm, then turn the TV off to save electricity.

The SPECTRUM will continue running the program until the alarm time is reached, and the sound of the internal beeper may wake you up.

## PROGRAM STRUCTURE

The program uses the SPECTRUM frame-counter as its internal clock. The frame-counter is stored in three bytes starting at memory location 23672 with least significant bytes first. Every 20 ms, the frame-counter is increased by 1; in other word, the total of counter divided by fifty will give the number of seconds from start of count.

The structure of the program is as follow :

## INITIALISATION

```
INPUT HOUR MINUTE and SECOND
IF SET-ALARM
    INPUT ALARM HOUR MINUTE and SECOND
    DISPLAY ALARM TIME
```

```
        DRAW CLOCK FACE
        CALCULATES INITIAL VALUE OF FRAME COUNTER BYTES
        POKE VALUE INTO FRAME COUNTER WHEN ANY KEY PRESSED
        DEFINE FUNCTION : no. of seconds since start
        INITIALIZE STARTING TIME
```

MAIN LOOP
---------

```
H:  DETERMINE HOUR HAND POSITION
M:  DETERMINE MINUTE HAND POSITION
S:  DETERMINE SECOND HAND POSITION
    DRAW SECOND HAND
    DRAW MINUTE HAND
    DRAW HOUR HAND
    CALCULATE AND DISPLAY DIGITAL CLOCK
        determine hour minute second digits
        adjust for cross noon boundary
        IF ALARM TIME MATCHES WITH DIGITS
            FLASH CLOCK and GENERATE ALARM
    FETCH FRAME COUNTER UNTIL ONE SECOND HAS PASSED
    DRAW OVER SECOND HAND
    IF SAME MINUTE THEN GO TO S:
    DRAW OVER MINUTE HAND
    IF SAME HOUR THEN GO TO M:
    DRAW OVER HOUR HAND
    GO TO H:
```

SPECIAL FEATURES
----------------

DEF FN t() is used to facilitate frequent
referencing of FRAME COUNTER.

SIN and COS functions are used to draw clock hands.

SECOND hand is moved every second; MINUTE hand is
moved every minute; HOUR hand is moved every 12 minutes.

Program takes care of AM/PM setting.

Checking is built into the program to ensure validity
of time input.

SPECIAL NOTES
-------------

The SPECTRUM CLOCK is accurate up to 10 seconds
deviation per day provided that the computer is only
running this program without generating any INPUT/OUTPUT
including sound.  Note that the frame counter is no
longer an accurate clock once any input/output is
performed because the frame counter is not incremented
during that time.

Once Alarm is reached, the clock will need to be
reset; that is, if you want to use the clock again you
will need to RUN the program again .

SPECTRUM CLOCK

```
100 GO SUB 360
110 LET c = PI /30
120 DEF FN t() = INT ((65536* PEEK 23674+256*
        PEEK 23673+ PEEK 23672)/50)
        *REM no.of.second.since.start
130 REM Now.we.start.the.clock
140 LET t1 = FN t()
150 LET hi = INT (t1/720)
160 LET h = hi*c
170 LET hx = 50* SIN h * LET hy = 50* COS h
180 LET mi = INT (t1/60)
190 LET m = mi*c
200 LET mx = 60* SIN m * LET my = 60* COS m
210 LET a = t1*c
        * REM a.is.angle.of.second.hand
                in.radian
220 LET sx = 72* SIN a * LET sy = 72* COS a
230 PLOT 131, 91 * DRAW sx, sy
        * REM Draw.second.hand
240 PLOT 131, 91 * DRAW mx, my
250 PLOT 131, 91 * DRAW hx, hy
260 GO SUB 740
270 LET t = FN t()
280 IF t <= t1 THEN GO TO 270
        * REM wait.until.time.next.hand
290 LET t1 = t
300 PLOT 131, 91 * DRAW OVER 1; sx, sy
        * REM .erase.second.hand
310 IF INT (t1/60) <= mi THEN GO TO 210
320 PLOT 131, 91 * DRAW mx, my * PLOT 131, 91
        * DRAW OVER 1; mx, my
330 IF INT (t1/720) <= hi THEN GO TO 180
340 PLOT 131, 91 * DRAW hx, hy * PLOT 131, 91
        * DRAW OVER 1; hx, hy
350 GO TO 150
360 EXI SHI 0 BORDER 7 * PAPER 7 * INK 0 * OVER (
        * FLASH 0 * CLS
        * PRINT "Please.input.which.hour?"
        * PRINT "(0.-.23)"
370 INPUT H * IF H < 0 OR H > 23 THEN GO TO 370
380 PRINT FLASH 1; INK 2; H
390 LET D = 0 * IF H >= 12 THEN LET D = 1
        * LET H = H-12*(H <> 12)
400 PRINT "Which.MINUTE?" * PRINT "(0.-.59)"
410 INPUT M * IF M < 0 OR M > 59 THEN GO TO 410
420 PRINT FLASH 1; INK 1; M
430 PRINT "Which.SECOND?" * PRINT "(0.-59)"
440 INPUT S * IF S < 0 OR S > 59 THEN GO TO 440
450 PRINT FLASH 1; INK 3; S
460 PAUSE 50 * CLS
470 PRINT "Do.you.want.to.set.the.ALARM.?"
        * PRINT "(y.or.n)"
480 INPUT a$
        * IF a$ <> "y" AND a$ <> "n" THEN GO TO 480
```

```
490 IF a$ = "n" THEN LET al = 0
      : BORDER 0 : PAPER 0 : INK 7 : CLS
      : GO TO 630
500 LET al = 1 : PRINT : PRINT "Hour?.";
510 INPUT ah : IF ah < 0 OR ah > 24 THEN GO TO 510
520 PRINT ah : LET ad = 0
      : IF ah > 11 THEN LET ad = 1
      : LET ah = ah-(ah <> 12)*12
530 PRINT : PRINT "Minutes?.";
540 INPUT am
      : IF am < 0 OR am > 59 THEN GO TO 540
550 PRINT am
560 PRINT : PRINT "Second?.";
570 INPUT as
      : IF as < 0 OR as > 59 THEN GO TO 570
580 PRINT as : PAUSE 50
590 REM Draw.clock.face
600 PAPER 0 : EXI SHI 0 BORDER 0 : INK 7 : CLS
      : PRINT AT 20, 0; "ALARM"
      : PRINT ah; " :"; am; " :"; as; ".";
610 IF ad = 0 THEN PRINT "AM" : GO TO 630
620 IF ad = 1 THEN PRINT "PM"
630 FOR n = 1 TO 12
640 PRINT AT 10-10* COS (n/6* PI )
         10+10* SIN (n/6* PI ); n
650 NEXT n
660 LET dh = H : LET dm = M : LET ds = S
670 LET T = (H*3600+M*60+S)*50
680 LET b1 = T- INT (T/256)*256
690 LET b2 = INT (T/256)- INT (T/256^2)*256
700 LET b3 = INT (T/256^2)- INT (T/256^3)*256
710 IF INKEY$ = "" THEN GO TO 710
720 POKE 23674, b3 : POKE 23673, b2
      : POKE 23672, b1
730 RETURN
740 LET ds = t1- INT (t1/60)*60
      : LET dm = INT (t1/60)- INT (t1/3600)*60
      : LET dh = INT (t1/3600)
750 IF ds = 0 THEN PRINT AT 0, 0;
      ".........."
760 IF dh >= 13 THEN LET dh = dh-12
770 IF dh <> 12 OR ds <> 0 OR dm <> 0
      THEN GO TO 810
780 IF D = 0 THEN LET D = 1 : LET dh = 12
      : GO TO 810
790 IF D = 1 THEN LET D = 0 : LET dh = 0
800 LET dh = dh-(dh = 12 AND D = 0)*12
810 PRINT AT 0, 0; dh; " :"; dm; " :"; FLASH 1
      : ds
820 PRINT AT 0, 8; ".";
830 IF D = 0 THEN PRINT "AM"
840 IF D = 1 THEN PRINT "PM"
850 IF al = 0 THEN RETURN
860 IF ah <> dh OR am <> dm OR as <> ds OR ad <> D
      THEN RETURN
870 PRINT AT 0, 0; dh; " :"; dm; " :"; ds
```

```
       : FOR s = 22528 TO 23231
       : POKE s, 128+ PEEK s : NEXT s
880 BEEP 0.5, 27 : BEEP 0.5, 20
       : IF INKEY$ = "" THEN GO TO 870
890 RETURN
```

# 3-D Mazeman

Copyright (c) by Beam Software

You are trapped in a maze. You must get out! The pressure is getting to you.

You move forward, a doorway appears on the left, quick! Oh no, . . . another dead end!

Will you ever get out of here alive?
This amazing 3-dimensional simulation places you right in the maze, with the task of getting out. The only thing to be thankful for is that there are no monsters here!! Yet!!

You can take as long as you like, but the time you take is being measured. At each position you will see a realistic perspective view. You can turn left or right (using the "o" and "p" keys respectively), move forward (using the space bar) or turn around (using the "r" key).

If you get really lost, it might be a good idea to draw a map.


Program structure:
--------------------

This program uses the PLOT and DRAW functions of the Spectrum.

At each point down the corridor, there is the option of the doorway being open or the doorway being closed. This program uses a different subroutine to draw the doorway depending on its distance from the observer and depending on whether it's open or not.

This explains all the different subroutines from 6000 to 8508.

A separate data table (lines 9100 - 9208) defines the particular maze you are in.


Defining your own maze:
------------------------

The maze used here is drawn on a 9 x 9 grid, somewhat like a Chess board, and each position in the maze is represented by a square on the board.

Obviously each square can have walls in any of the four directions. This program uses two arrays to keep track of walls, one array for the walls found looking up the board, and one array looking across.

15

A total of 18 lines need to be defined, 9 looking up at the board, and 9 looking across. For each line, we put a 0 down if there is no wall blocking our path, and a 1 if there is a wall there. There are always walls on the outside perimeter, and these do not need ot be defined.

This information is stored in the DATA statements 9100 – 9108 and 9200 – 9208.

For example, looking up the board from the bottom left corner, we see a wall. If we were able to break through that wall, there would be another one, and the another. Finally we would see a corridor stretching four squares before the last wall. This is the information contained in line 9100.

The exit is defined by line 156. It says that if you are in the 9th row, and facing backwards, and less than 5 from the end you will see the EXIT sign. The requirement of 5 from the end is because there is a wall in the current maze blocking the view if you are say 6 from the end.

You can easily adapt the program to show your own maze, but remember to change the conditions for EXIT.

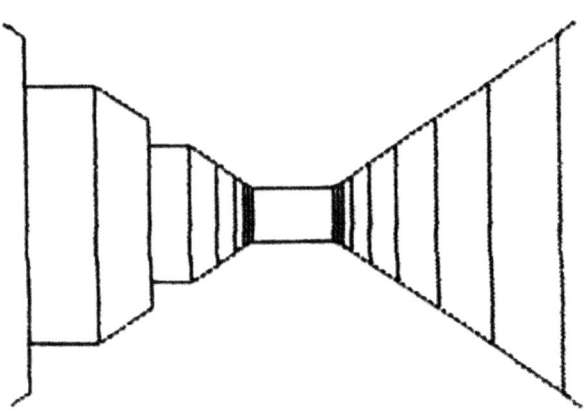

# 3-D MAZEMAN

```
 100 DIM v(10, 10) : DIM h(10, 10)
 110 GO SUB 9000
 120 LCT x = 1 : LET y = 1 : IFT dx = 1 :
        LET dy = 0
 125 LET ti = PEEK 23672+256* PEEK 23673+4096*
        PEEK 23674
 130 LET L = 9 : LET Lx = x+(dx = -1) :
        LET Ly = y+(dy = -1)
 132 LET L = L-1 : LET Lx = Lx+dx : LET Ly = Ly+dy
 134 IF dx <> 0 AND v(Lx, Ly) = 0 THEN GO TO 132
 136 IF dy <> 0 AND h(Lx, Ly) = 0 THEN GO TO 132
 140 CLS : GO SUB 6000+L
 145 LET Lx = Lx-(dx = -1) : LET Ly = Ly-(dy = -1)
 150 FOR i = L TO 8
 155 LET Lx = Lx-dx : LET Ly = Ly-dy : GO SUB 1000
        : NEXT i
 156 IF dx = -1 AND y = 9 AND x < 5 THEN PRINT
        AT 10, 14; " EXI SHI 2EXIT
         EXI SHI 0"
 158 LET a$ = INKEY$ : IF a$ = "" THEN GO TO 158
 160 IF a$ <> "." THEN GO TO 190
 170 IF (dx = 1 AND v(x+1, y) = 0) OR
        (dx = -1 AND v(x, y) = 0) OR
        (dy = 1 AND h(x, y+1) = 0) OR
        (dy = -1 AND h(x, y) = 0) THEN
        LET x = x+dx : LET y = y+dy
 190 IF x = 1 AND y = 9 THEN GO TO 9990
 200 IF a$ = "r" THEN LET dx = -dx : LET dy = -dy
        : GO TO 130
 210 IF a$ = "o" THEN GO TO 300
 215 IF a$ <> "p" THEN GO TO 130
 220 IF ABS dx = 1 THEN LET dy = -dx : LET dx = 0
        : GO TO 130
 230 LET dx = dy : LET dy = 0 : GO TO 130
 300 IF ABS dx = 1 THEN LET dy = dx : LET dx = 0
        : GO TO 130
 310 LET dx = -dy : LET dy = 0 : GO TO 130
1000 IF dx <> 1 THEN GO TO 1100
1010 IF h(Lx, Ly+1) = 0 THEN GO SUB 7500+i
        : GO TO 1050
1020 GO SUB 7000+i
1050 IF h(Lx, Ly) = 0 THEN GO TO 8500+i
1060 GO TO 8000+i
1100 IF dx <> -1 THEN GO TO 1200
1110 IF h(Lx, Ly) = 0 THEN GO SUB 7500+i : GO TO 1150
1120 GO SUB 7000+i
1150 IF h(Lx, Ly+1) = 0 THEN GO TO 8500+i
1160 GO TO 8000+i
1200 IF dy <> -1 THEN GO TO 1300
1210 IF v(Lx+1, Ly) = 0 THEN GO SUB 7500+i
        : GO TO 1250
1220 GO SUB 7000+i
1250 IF v(Lx, Ly) = 0 THEN GO TO 8500+i
```

```
1260 GO TO 8000+i
1300 IF v(Lx, Ly) = 0 THEN GO SUB 7500+i
      : GO TO 1350
1310 GO SUB 7000+i
1350 IF v(Lx+1, Ly) = 0 THEN GO TO 8500+i
1360 GO TO 8000+i
6000 PLOT 110, 76 : DRAW 0, 24 : DRAW 36, 0
      : DRAW 0, -24 : DRAW -36, 0 : RETURN
6001 PLOT 108, 75 : DRAW 0, 26 : DRAW 40, 0
      : DRAW 0, -26 : DRAW -40, 0 : RETURN
6002 PLOT 106, 74 : DRAW 0, 28 : DRAW 44, 0
      : DRAW 0, -28 : DRAW -44, 0 : RETURN
6003 PLOT 102, 71 : DRAW 0, 34 : DRAW 52, 0
      : DRAW 0, -34 : DRAW -52, 0 : RETURN
6004 PLOT 94, 65 : DRAW 0, 46 : DRAW 68, 0
      : DRAW 0, -46 : DRAW -68, 0 : RETURN
6005 PLOT 82, 57 : DRAW 0, 62 : DRAW 92, 0
      : DRAW 0, -62 : DRAW -92, 0 : RETURN
6006 PLOT 64, 45 : DRAW 0, 86 : DRAW 128, 0
      : DRAW 0, -86 : DRAW -128, 0 : RETURN
6007 PLOT 40, 29 : DRAW 0, 118 : DRAW 176, 0
      : DRAW 0, -118 : DRAW -176, 0 : RETURN
6008 PLOT 8, 7 : DRAW 0, 162 : DRAW 240, 0
      : DRAW 0, -162 : DRAW -240, 0 : RETURN
7000 PLOT 108, 75 : DRAW 2, 1 : DRAW 0, 24
      : DRAW -2, 1 : RETURN
7001 PLOT 106, 74 : DRAW 2, 1 : DRAW 0, 26
      : DRAW -2, 1 : RETURN
7002 PLOT 102, 71 : DRAW 4, 3 : DRAW 0, 28
      : DRAW -4, 3 : RETURN
7003 PLOT 94, 65 : DRAW 8, 6 : DRAW 0, 34
      : DRAW -8, 6 : RETURN
7004 PLOT 82, 57 : DRAW 12, 8 : DRAW 0, 46
      : DRAW -12, 8 : RETURN
7005 PLOT 64, 45 : DRAW 18, 12 : DRAW 0, 62
      : DRAW -18, 12 : RETURN
7006 PLOT 40, 29 : DRAW 24, 16 : DRAW 0, 86
      : DRAW -24, 16 : RETURN
7007 PLOT 8, 7 : DRAW 32, 22 : DRAW 0, 118
      : DRAW -32, 22 : RETURN
7008 PLOT 0, 1 : DRAW 8, 6 : DRAW 0, 162
      : DRAW -8, 6 : RETURN
7500 PLOT 108, 76 : DRAW 2, 0 : DRAW 0, 24
      : DRAW -2, 0 : RETURN
7501 PLOT 106, 75 : DRAW 2, 0 : DRAW 0, 26
      : DRAW -2, 0 : RETURN
7502 PLOT 102, 74 : DRAW 4, 0 : DRAW 0, 28
      : DRAW -4, 0 : RETURN
7503 PLOT 94, 71 : DRAW 8, 0 : DRAW 0, 34
      : DRAW -8, 0 : RETURN
7504 PLOT 82, 65 : DRAW 12, 0 : DRAW 0, 46
      : DRAW -12, 0 : RETURN
7505 PLOT 64, 57 : DRAW 18, 0 : DRAW 0, 62
      : DRAW -18, 0 : RETURN
7506 PLOT 40, 45 : DRAW 24, 0 : DRAW 0, 86
      : DRAW -24, 0 : RETURN
```

```
7507 PLOT 8, 29 : DRAW 32, 0 : DRAW 0, 118
        : DRAW -32, 0 : RETURN
7508 PLOT 0, 7 : DRAW 8, 0 : DRAW 0, 162
        : DRAW -8, 0 : RETURN
8000 PLOT 148, 75 : DRAW -2, 1 : DRAW 0, 24
        : DRAW 2, 1 : RETURN
8001 PLOT 150, 74 : DRAW -2, 1 : DRAW 0, 26
        : DRAW 2, 1 : RETURN
8002 PLOT 154, 71 : DRAW -4, 3 : DRAW 0, 28
        : DRAW 4, 3 : RETURN
8003 PLOT 162, 65 : DRAW -8, 6 : DRAW 0, 34
        : DRAW 8, 6 : RETURN
8004 PLOT 174, 57 : DRAW -12, 8 : DRAW 0, 46
        : DRAW 12, 8 : RETURN
8005 PLOT 192, 45 : DRAW -18, 12 : DRAW 0, 62
        : DRAW 18, 12 : RETURN
8006 PLOT 216, 29 : DRAW -24, 16 : DRAW 0, 86
        : DRAW 24, 16 : RETURN
8007 PLOT 248, 7 : DRAW -32, 22 : DRAW 0, 118
        : DRAW 32, 22 : RETURN
8008 PLOT 255, 1 : DRAW -8, 6 : DRAW 0, 162
        : DRAW 8, 6 : RETURN
8500 PLOT 148, 76 : DRAW -2, 0 : DRAW 0, 24
        : DRAW 2, 0 : RETURN
8501 PLOT 150, 75 : DRAW -2, 0 : DRAW 0, 26
        : DRAW 2, 0 : RETURN
8502 PLOT 154, 74 : DRAW -4, 0 : DRAW 0, 28
        : DRAW 4, 0 : RETURN
8503 PLOT 162, 71 : DRAW -8, 0 : DRAW 0, 34
        : DRAW 8, 0 : RETURN
8504 PLOT 174, 65 : DRAW -12, 0 : DRAW 0, 46
        : DRAW 12, 0 : RETURN
8505 PLOT 192, 57 : DRAW -18, 0 : DRAW 0, 62
        : DRAW 18, 0 : RETURN
8506 PLOT 216, 45 : DRAW -24, 0 : DRAW 0, 86
        : DRAW 24, 0 : RETURN
8507 PLOT 248, 29 : DRAW -32, 0 : DRAW 0, 118
        : DRAW 32, 0 : RETURN
8508 PLOT 255, 7 : DRAW -7, 0 : DRAW 0, 162
        : DRAW 7, 0 : RETURN
9000 FOR i = 1 TO 9 : LET h(i, 1) = 1 :
        LET h(i, 10) = 1 : FOR j = 2 TO 9 : READ a :
        LET h(i, j) = a : NEXT j : NEXT i
9010 FOR i = 1 TO 9 : LET v(1, i) = 1 :
        LET v(10, 1) = 1 : FOR j = 2 TO 9 : READ a :
        LET v(j, i) = a : NEXT j : NEXT i
9020 RETURN
9100 DATA 1, 1, 1, 0, 0, 0, 0, 1
9101 DATA 0, 0, 1, 0, 0, 1, 0, 1
9102 DATA 1, 1, 0, 0, 0, 0, 1, 1
9103 DATA 0, 0, 1, 1, 0, 0, 1, 0
9104 DATA 1, 1, 1, 0, 0, 1, 1, 0
9105 DATA 1, 0, 0, 0, 0, 0, 0, 1
9106 DATA 1, 1, 1, 0, 1, 0, 0, 1
9107 DATA 1, 1, 1, 0, 0, 1, 1, 0
9108 DATA 1, 0, 0, 0, 0, 0, 0, 0
```

```
9200 DATA 0, 0, 0, 0, 0, 0, 0, 0
9201 DATA 1, 1, 1, 1, 0, 1, 0, 0
9202 DATA 0, 0, 0, 0, 0, 0, 0, 1
9203 DATA 0, 1, 0, 0, 1, 0, 0, 0
9204 DATA 1, 1, 0, 1, 1, 1, 1, 1
9205 DATA 1, 1, 1, 1, 1, 1, 0, 1
9206 DATA 0, 0, 0, 0, 0, 0, 1, 0
9207 DATA 1, 1, 0, 0, 1, 1, 0, 0
9208 DATA 0, 0, 0, 1, 0, 0, 0, 1
9990 LET te = PEEK 23672+256* PEEK 23673+4096*
     PEEK 23674
9991 LET t = te-ti
9992 PRINT AT 0, 4; "WELL▲DONE!!▲You▲got▲out"
9993 PRINT AT 1, 4; "in▲"; t/50; "▲seconds"
9994 STOP
```

# Geometry Test

Copyright (c) by Beam Software

The particular test questions included in this program
happen to be those of geometry, but the program design is
more general than that.

This program can be used in any situation where a multiple
question/answer series is desired.

One very interesting facet of the Spectrum in a
mathematical test is that either a number answer or a formula
answer can be given. In other words to the question "What is
the area of a circle radius 2?", either the answer "4 * PI"
or the answer " 12.75 " would be acceptable. (The latter
answer although not exactly correct would be accepted, as
this program accepts as correct replies within .5 of the
correct answer).

Program structure:
--------------------

A short control loop from lines 100 - 260 chooses the
question, compares the answer given with that it expects and
prints the appropriate message.

Each question is contained within a subroutine that not
only prints the question but specifies the answer it will
accept.

Obviously the number and range of questions is limited only
by your imagination.

## GEOMETRY TEST

```
100 CLS
110 LET q = 1+ INT (4* RND )
120 LET m = 2+ INT (20* RND )
130 GO SUB q*1000
200 INPUT r : PRINT r
210 IF ABS (r-a) > .5 THEN GO TO 240
220 PRINT "YES, ▴the▴answer▴is▴"; a
230 GO TO 250
240 PRINT "SORRY, ▴the▴answer▴was▴"; a
250 INPUT "Press▴ < ENTER > ▴when▴ready"; y$
260 RUN
1000 PRINT "What▴is▴the▴circumference▴of▴a
        ▴▴circle▴with▴radius▴"; m
1010 LET a = 2* PI *m
1020 RETURN
2000 PRINT "What▴is▴the▴area▴of▴a▴circle
        ▴▴▴▴with▴radius▴"; m
2010 LET a = PI *m*m
2020 RETURN
3000 PRINT "What▴is▴the▴surface▴area▴of▴a
        ▴▴▴sphere▴with▴radius▴"; m
3010 LET a = (4/3)* PI *m*m
3020 RETURN
4000 PRINT "What▴is▴the▴volume▴of▴a▴sphere
        ▴▴with▴radius▴"; m
4010 LET a = PI *m*m*m/3
4020 RETURN
```

# Kings and Queens

Copyright (c) by Beam Software

This program uses a multiple choice format to test your
knowledge of English history.

The computer chooses a year from 1066 to 1461, and asks
you who was reigning in that particular year. You will be
given a choice of three names. If the year given is one
where there was a changeover, the correct answer is the
monarch reigning at the beginning of that year. Type in
the answer - only the computer knows for sure if you're
right or not.

At the end of 25 questions, you will be given your result
as a percentage. Since the probability of getting the
right answer by just guessing randomly is 1 in 3, you
would need to work pretty hard to get less than 30%!

Program structure:
--------------------


The structure of this program is pretty simple, but what
makes it interesting is the way in which the information
about the monarchs is stored in the program.

As there is only one right answer for any given year
(because of the way we have framed the question), this
program uses the special ability of Spectrum subroutine
calls to be specified by a variable and for subroutine
calls to fall through to the next line number that
actually exists.

Look at the program listing - you will see that, for
example there are no line numbers between 1088 and 1100.
If you entered the instruction GOSUB 1090, the computer
would go to line 1090, find it wasn't there, try 1091,
and so on, until it finally reached line 1100. In other
words, any number from 1089 to 1100 will come back with
the result

               a$ = William 2

This is a pretty good start, as William 2 reigned from
1087 to 1100, and as for the purposes of this test, any
year from 1088 to 1100 would be accepted as correct.

Let's look at what happens if we were to enter GOSUB
1088:
the program would come back with no particular
information about a$ as all it would encounter would be
the RETURN instruction.

We can take care of this as, for example, this program
does in line 530, by saying that if we get no answer, go
to the subroutine on the next highest line! ie. if 1088

23

gives you no answer, try 1089, which will return William
2.

This means that all number within the range of this test
will return the correct answer.

The same program structure can be used for any other test
where a range of non-overlapping values is correct in
different situations.

Kings and Queens of England Part 1:
----------------------------------------

```
1066 - 1087    William 1        Norman
1087 - 1100    William 2
1100 - 1135    Henry 1
1135 - 1154    Stephen
1154 - 1189    Henry 2          Plantaganet
1189 - 1199    Richard 1
1199 - 1216    John
1216 - 1272    Henry 3
1272 - 1307    Edward 1
1307 - 1327    Edward 2
1327 - 1377    Edward 3
1377 - 1399    Richard 2
1399 - 1413    Henry 4          Lancaster
1413 - 1422    Henry 5
1422 - 1461    Henry 6
```

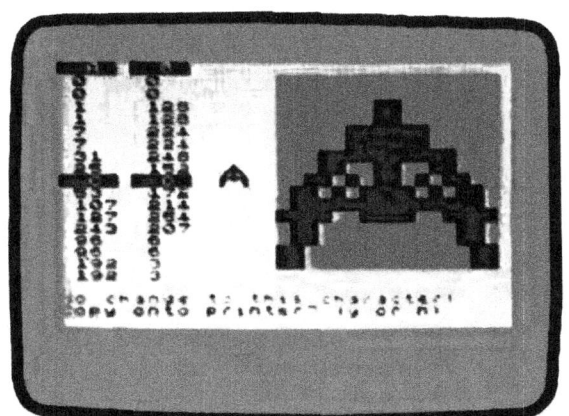

High Resolution
Graphics

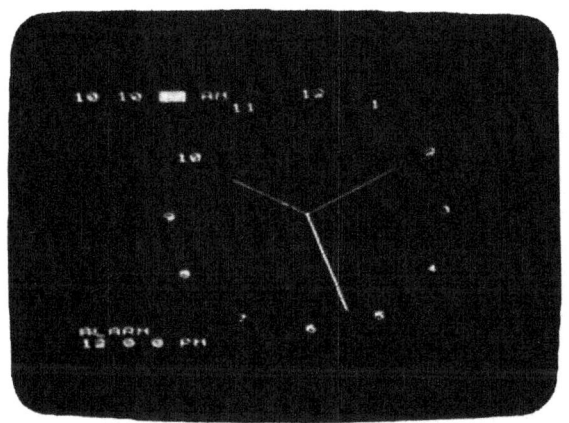

Spectrum Clock

**Spectrum Invaders**

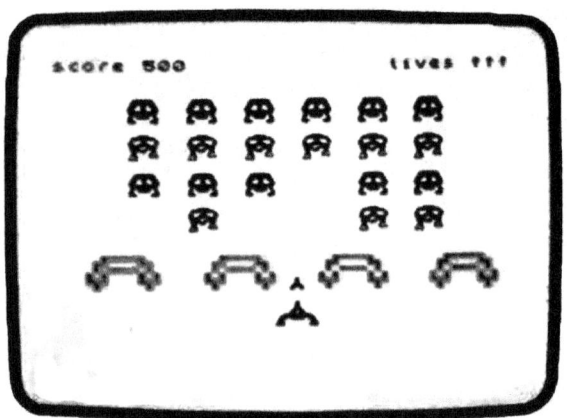

**Freeway Frog**

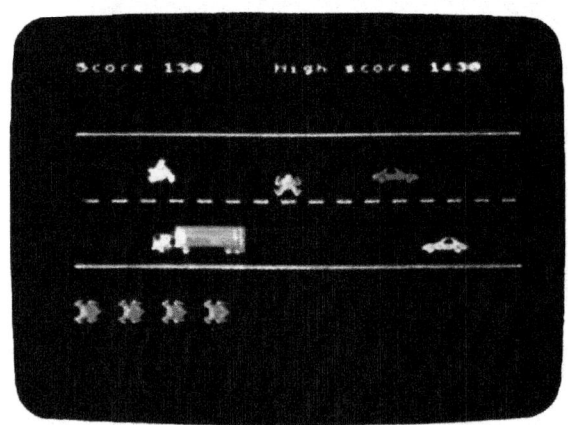

KINGS AND QUEENS OF ENGLAND

```
 100 DIM p(3)
 110 RANDOMIZE
 120 LET s = 0
 130 FOR i = 1 TO 25
 140 GO SUB 500
 150 LET c$ = a$
 160 GO SUB 500
 170 LET b$ = a$
 180 IF b$ = c$ THEN GO TO 160
 190 GO SUB 500
 200 IF a$ = b$ OR a$ = c$ THEN GO TO 190
 210 PRINT i; ".▲Who▲was▲monarch▲in▲"; ▲n;
     "▲?"
 220 LET p(1) = INT (3* RND )+1
 230 LET p(2) = INT (3* RND )+1
 240 IF p(2) = p(1) THEN GO TO 230
 250 LET p(3) = 6-p(1)-p(2)
 260 FOR t = 1 TO 3
 270 PRINT AT 5+t, 5; t; ".▲";
 280 IF t = p(1) THEN PRINT a$
 290 IF t = p(2) THEN PRINT b$
 300 IF t = p(3) THEN PRINT c$
 310 NEXT t
 320 PRINT AT 12, 0;
 330 LET x$ = ▲ INKEY$ : IF x$ < "1" OR x$ > "3"
     THEN GO TO 330
 340 IF VAL x$ = p(1) THEN PRINT "GREAT" :
     LET s = s+1 : BEEP .5, 2 : BEEP .2, 5 :
     BEEP .2, 7 : GO TO 370
 350 PRINT "NO▲-▲it▲was▲"; a$
 360 FOR j = 1 TO 8 : BEEP RND /4, 10* RND -30 :
     NEXT j : BEEP 1, -25
 370 PRINT FLASH 1; AT 20, 0; "Press▲any▲key▲for
     ▲the▲next▲one"
 380 LET x$ = INKEY$
 390 IF x$ = "" THEN GO TO 380
 400 CLS
 410 NEXT i
 420 PRINT "YOU▲SCORED▲"; 4*s; "▲PERCENT"
 430 STOP
 500 LET n = INT (396* RND )+1066
 510 LET a$ = "▲"
 520 GO SUB n
 530 IF a$ = "▲" THEN GO SUB n+1
 540 RETURN
1087 LET a$ = "William▲1"
1088 RETURN
1100 LET a$ = "William▲2"
1101 RETURN
1135 LET a$ = "Henry▲1"
1136 RETURN
1154 LET a$ = "Stephen"
1155 RETURN
```

```basic
1189 LET a$ = "Henry▲2"
1190 RETURN
1199 LET a$ = "Richard▲1"
1200 RETURN
1216 LET a$ = "John"
1217 RETURN
1272 LET a$ = "Henry▲3"
1273 RETURN
1307 LET a$ = "Edward▲1"
1308 RETURN
1327 LET a$ = "Edward▲2"
1328 RETURN
1377 LET a$ = "Edward▲3"
1378 RETURN
1399 LET a$ = "Richard▲2"
1400 RETURN
1413 LET a$ = "Henry▲4"
1414 RETURN
1422 LET a$ = "Henry▲5"
1423 RETURN
1461 LET a$ = "Henry▲6"
1462 RETURN
```

# Blackjack

Copyright (c) by Beam Software


This is the traditional casino game at the Club ZX
Spectrum. Welcome! As a special greeting to all our
guests, we will give you a voucher for $100 valid only at
our blackjack tables.

Step right up. The rules of the house are:
- before any cards are dealt you must decide how
  much you are prepared to bet. Note that the
  Club ZX Spectrum does not extend credit.
- the dealer deals himself one card face up, then
  deals you one card face up. You can then choose
  as many additional cards as you desire.
- if you have not gone bust (that is, your total
  has not exceeded 21) then the dealer will deal
  himself additional cards. The dealer always draws
  on 16 or below, always sits on 17 and above.

If you should win a hand, you win the amount you have
bet. If you and the dealer have the same total, the
dealer wins. Five cards under 21 will win for you
provided the dealer does not have blackjack. If you have
BLACKJACK (a total of 21 in only two cards) then you will
win twice the amount bet, again provided the dealer does
not have blackjack himself.

Step right up ladies and gentlemen.

Structure of the program:
--------------------------

The structure of the program is as follows:

NEW BET        INPUT PLAYER'S BET
                 IF NO MONEY LEFT, STOP
               DEAL FIRST CARD TO DEALER AND PLAYER

               FOR PLAYER AND DEALER
                 IF PLAYER ASK IF CARD WANTED
                   IF NOT SWITCH TO DEALER
               DEAL THE CARD AND PRINT IT
               CALCULATE VALUE OF HAND AND PRINT IT
               IF OVER 21 GO TO PAYOUT
               IF DEALER AND OVER 16 GO TO PAYOUT

PAYOUT         IF PLAYER BUST, OR IF DEALER TOTAL
                 GREATER THAN OR EQUAL TO PLAYER
                 THEN MONEY WON = 0
               IF BLACKJACK THEN MONEY WON DOUBLED
               KITTY = KITTY + MONEY WON
               GO TO NEW BET AGAIN

The structure of this program is therefore fairly simple, and you should have little trouble changing the program if you wished to change the 'house rules'.

Graphics display:
-------------------

The subroutine at line 8000 defines a one character design for the four card suits. This subroutine obviously is only called once at the beginning of the program.

Each card is printed by the subroutine at line 8500. The card outline, which is light blue, is printed first, and then the one character suit is printed in the appropriate colour (black or red).

The problem of how to print the cards themselves then comes up. As you know there are only 21 graphics characters easily accessible for use. We have already used up 4 of them for the suits, leaving only 17.

There are 13 cards possible, but using only a one character display would make this only as big as the normal printed characters themselves. The solution employed in this program is to look up the standard shape of each character in the ROM where its shape is stored, blow it up to double size (that is two characters wide, and two characters high), and store this in the special graphics character set, as ABCD. Because there is no standard character for '10' a one-character version of this is defined in subroutine 8000.

This method is a little slow, but in the program itself this is acceptable as it adds to the mounting tension of discovering what card has been dealt.

As you are no doubt aware each character is displayed on the Spectrum screen as a collection of 8 bytes, and the definition for the standard character set is stored in the ROM starting at location 15616. The starting address of each character can be determined from its code by the formula 15360 + 8 * code of character (see line 9020).

The program then has to work to determine how to blow this up to twice the size, and stores it in the UDG area.

Special notes:
------------------

You will notice a strange notation in line 270
$$\text{LET } a = p(i) = 11$$

30

In this program the variable 'a' is being used to keep
track of the number of aces in the hand. What this line
says is

             LET a = 0
             IF p(i) = 11 THEN LET a = 1
where p(i) is the card total for player i.

The expression could have been written as just above, or
we could have written as
             LET a = ( p(i) = 11 )

because we know that on the ZX Spectrum an expression
will be set equal to 0 if it is false and equal to 1 if
it is true. As it turns out we can leave out the bracket
without any possibility of error, and so we have the
strange but very compact expression found in line 270.

The other expression that you might find odd is in line
530, where the value of p(i) is calculated. We have just
chosen a card number from 2 to 14, represented by
variable 'c', and we want to add the value of c if it
less than or equal to 10 (ie a number card), add 10 if c
is a suit card (12, 13 or 14) and add 1 or 11 if it is an
ace ( c=11 ).

We could do it as
             IF c =( 10 THEN ...
             IF c ) 11 THEN ...
             IF c = 11 THEN ...
but that one line does it almost all. What it says is add
the value of the card if the value is less than 12, and
add 10 if the value is over 11. Simple, isn't it!

Lines 540 - 560 take care of the ace being counted as 11
or 1, greatly simplifying the program.

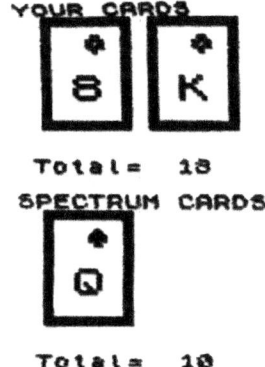

YOUR CARDS

Total=   18

SPECTRUM CARDS

Total=   10

BLACKJACK

```
100 BORDER 7 : PAPER 7 : INK 0 : OVER 0 : CLS
110 LET b$ = "N23456789TAJQK"
120 LET a = 0 : LET m = 100
130 GO SUB 8000
140 DIM p(4)
150 IF m = 0 THEN PRINT AT 10, 1; "Kitty▲stands
    ▲at▲$0"; AT 19, 1; "Sory, ▲your▲credit
    ▲has▲run▲out.▲▲Come▲again▲when▲you
    ▲have▲more▲▲▲money." : STOP
160 PRINT AT 10, 1; "Kitty▲stands▲at▲$"; m :
    PRINT "How▲much▲do▲you▲want▲to▲bet?"
170 INPUT b
180 CLS
190 IF b > m THEN GO TO 160
200 LET m = m-b
210 PRINT INK 0; AT 0, 0; "YOUR▲CARDS"; AT 11, 0;
    "SPECTRUM▲CARDS"
220 PRINT AT 9, 1; "Total = "; AT 20, 1; "Total = "
230 FOR i = 2 TO 1 STEP -1
240 GO SUB 500
250 NEXT i
260 FOR i = 1 TO 2
270 LET a = p(i) = 11
280 IF i = 1 THEN INPUT FLASH 1; PAPER 2; INK 7;
    "Do▲you▲want▲another▲card?▲"; a$ :
    LET a$ = a$+"▲" : IF a$(1) = "n" THEN
    GO TO 340
290 GO SUB 500
300 IF p(i) > 21 THEN LET i = 2 : GO TO 340
310 IF p(i+2) = 5 THEN GO TO 340
320 IF i = 2 AND p(i) > 16 THEN GO TO 340
330 GO TO 280
340 NEXT i
350 IF p(1) <= 21 AND p(3) = 5 AND (p(2) <> 21 OR
    p(4) <> 2) THEN GO TO 380
360 IF p(1) = 21 AND p(3) = 2 AND (p(2 <> 21 OR
    p(4) <> 2)) THEN LET b = b*1.5 : PRINT
    FLASH 1; AT 5, 18; "BLACKJACK" : GO TO 380
370 IF (p(2) <= 21 AND p(2) >= p(1)) OR p(1) > 21
    THEN LET b = 0
380 LET m = m+2*b
390 GO TO 130
500 LET p(i+2) = p(i+2)+1
510 LET c = INT (13* RND )+2
520 IF c = 11 THEN LET a = a+1
530 LET p(i) = p(i)+c*(c < 12)+10*(c > 11)
540 IF p(i) < 22 OR a = 0 THEN GO TO 570
550 LET a = a-1
560 LET p(i) = p(i)-10
570 GO SUB 8500
580 GO SUB 9000
590 PRINT INK 0; AT 11*i-2, 9; p(i)
600 RETURN
```

32

```
8000 DATA 0, 78, 209, 81, 81, 81, 78, 0
8010 DATA 102, 255, 255, 255, 126, 60, 24, 24
8020 DATA 24, 60, 126, 255, 255, 126, 60, 24
8030 DATA 24, 60, 126, 255, 255, 219, 24, 60
8040 DATA 60, 60, 219, 231, 231, 219, 24, 24
8050 RESTORE 8000
8060 FOR k = USR "e" TO USR "e"+39 : READ x :
     POKE k, x : NEXT k
8070 RETURN
8500 LET p = 11*i-7 : LET q = 6*p(i+2)-5
8510 INK 5 : PRINT AT p-3, q;
     " GBA 5 GBA 3 GBA 3 GBA 3 GBA 3
     GBA SHI 5" : FOR k = 1 TO 5 :
     PRINT AT p-3+k, q; " GBA 5
     ▲▲▲▲ GBA SHI 5" : NEXT k :
     PRINT AT p+3, q; " GBA 1 GBA 3
     GBA 3 GBA 3 GBA 3 GBA 2" : INK 0
8520 LET suit = 1+ INT (4* RND ) : INK 2*(suit < 3)
     : PRINT AT p-2, q+3; CHR$ (148+suit)
8530 RETURN
9000 LET x = USR "a"
9010 FOR k = 0 TO 31 : POKE x+k, 0 : NEXT k
9020 LET s = 8* CODE b$(c)+15360 : IF b$(c) = "T"
     THEN LET s = USR "e"
9030 FOR j = 0 TO 7 : LET v = PEEK (s+j) : LET c = 0
     : LET d = 256
9040 FOR k = 8 TO 1 STEP -1 : LET d = d/2 : IF v >= d
     THEN LET c = c+3*d*d : LET v = v-d
9050 NEXT k
9060 LET h = INT (c/256) : LET L = c-256*h
9070 POKE x, h : POKE x+1, h : POKE x+8, L :
     POKE x+9, L
9080 LET x = x+2+8*(j = 3)
9090 PRINT AT p, q+2; " GBA A GBA B"; AT p+1, q+2;
     " GBA C GBA D"
9100 NEXT j
9110 RETURN
```

33

# Fruit Machine

Copyright (c) by Beam Software

This program simulates the fruit machines to be found in pubs and gambling parlours.

The main benefit of gambling here of course is that if you should lose the 10 pounds you came in with, it doesn't matter too much. Of course the main drawback is similar - you can't take your winnings with you.

This program of FRUIT MACHINE will extend the concepts you may have about the applications of the user defined graphics. In this program we will define 60 user defined characters for the 16K version, and an additional 40 for those with more memory. In fact on a 48K machine many more graphic characters could be defined with no additional programming required.

So step right up, ladies and gentlemen, and try your luck! At the very least, you'll be amazed at the graphics of this program.

You obviously win if you get all three windows showing the same picture, with different amount depending on the picture. If you get two adjacent windows with the same picture, you also win, except if it's two lemons.

Programming considerations:
-----------------------------

The design of this program is for a fruit machine with three cylinders, each rotating independently. Each "window" is comprised of 20 characters (4 across, 5 deep), each possibly showing the picture of a different symbol - lemon, bell, cherry, etc.

As only 21 graphic characters are allowed, this immediately places restrictions on what we can do. Fortunately for us, we do not need to have all 60 (or 100 or whatever) characters specially defined at the same time.

Once a graphic character has been written to the screen, the memory locations corresponding to that position on the screen will keep that shape, and not lose it until you overwrite it. What you do with the graphic character you defined is not important.

As an example, let's assume we define A as BIN 01010101, BIN 10101010, BIN 01010101, etc., and that we said
        PRINT AT 0,0; "A"
then the eight memory locations corresponding to (0,0) would remembered this as BIN 01010101, BIN 10101010, etc., and not as "A". We can change the definition of A and it will have no effect on the screen. This is not the case with all computers.

This program therefore draws shapes, then redefines the characters, draws again, and so on.

Program structure:
-------------------

| | |
|---|---|
| 100 - 200 | Define variables |
| 950 - 1810 | Draw fruit machine<br>    and check that player is solvent |
| 2000 - 2230 | Main loop<br>    ---------<br>For each window<br>  For each of 3 to 6 displays<br>    Choose a picture<br>    For each of five lines<br>      Redefine character set<br>      Print up each block<br>    Next line<br>  Next display<br>  Redefine character set<br>Next window |
| 2500 - 2560 | Calculate winnings if any |

The program gets all its information from DATA statements, including which ink and paper colour to use in drawing the next block.


Fitting the program in 16K:
-------------------------------

The program as it stands will NOT fit into 16K. DATA statements are not a particularly efficient way of storing information (see notes in METEOR STORM), and no steps have been taken to minimise memory usage.

The version included here has 4 different pictures possible: Cherry, Lemon, Bell and Pineapple. As well, at the beginning of each pull of the lever, all windows are reset to show a large question mark.

The program can be modified to fit into 16K very easily with the following changes:

>    Only 3 pictures are possible: Cherry, Lemon and
>        Bell.
>    At the beginning of each pull of the lever, each
>        window will show a cherry.

To effect these alterations, the following is required:

* Delete lines 8000 - 8053 (defining the question mark)
* Delete lines 8400 - 8453 (defining the pineapple)
* Delete lines 9010 and 9400 (defining ink and paper for question mark and pineapple)
* Change line 2040 to read
        LET picture = 1 + INT ( 3 * RND )
This limits the choice to 3 pictures
* Change lines 5510, 5520, 5530 to read
        LET pattern = 1
        LET picture = 1
        LET oldpict = 1
This sets up the cherries instead of the question marks.

Using some of the space saving techniques described elsewhere in the book, it should be possible for you to fit all of the program within 16K. (Try it as a programming exercise!)

You have £9.5 left
Press <ENTER> to play

36

FRUIT MACHINE

```
 100 LET fillhires = 5300
 110 LET drawblock = 5100
 120 LET first = 5
 130 LET resethires = 5500
 140 LET blankwindow = 5700
 150 LET money = 10
 160 DIM r(3)
 170 DIM s(4)
 180 RESTORE 7000
 190 FOR k = 1 TO 4 : READ s(k) : NEXT k
 200 INK 7 : PAPER 5 : BORDER 5 : CLS
 950 REM draw.fruit.machine
 980 LET c$ =
        " GRA SHI 8 GRA SHI 8 GRA SHI 8 GRA SHI 8
         GRA SHI 8 GRA SHI 8 GRA SHI 8 GRA SHI 8
         GRA SHI 8 GRA SHI 8 GRA SHI 8 GRA SHI 8
         GRA SHI 8 GRA SHI 8 GRA SHI 8 GRA SHI 8"
1000 PRINT AT 1, 5; " GRA 4"; c$; " GRA SHI 7"
1010 PRINT AT 2, 4; " GRA 4 GRA SHI 8";
        c$; " GRA SHI 8 GRA SHI 7"
1020 PRINT AT 3, 3; " GRA 4 GRA SHI 8 GRA SHI 8";
        c$;
        " GRA SHI 8 GRA SHI 8 GRA SHI 7.. GRA 4"
1030 PRINT AT 4, 3;
        " GRA SHI 8 GRA SHI 8 GRA SHI 8";
        c$; " GRA SHI 8 GRA SHI 8 GRA SHI 8
        .. GRA SHI 8 GRA SHI 5"
1040 PRINT AT 5, 3;
        " GRA SHI 8 GRA SHI 8 GRA SHI 8";
        c$; " GRA SHI 8 GRA SHI 8 GRA SHI 8
        .. GRA SHI 8 GRA SHI 5"
1050 PRINT AT 6, 3; " GRA SHI 8 GRA SHI 8
        .... GRA SHI 8 GRA SHI 8 GRA SHI 8
        .... GRA SHI 8 GRA SHI 8 GRA SHI 8
        .... GRA SHI 8 GRA SHI 8
        .. GRA SHI 8 GRA SHI 5"
1060 PRINT AT 7, 3; " GRA SHI 8 GRA SHI 8
        .... GRA SHI 8 GRA SHI 8 GRA SHI 8
        .... GRA SHI 8 GRA SHI 8 GRA SHI 8
        .... GRA SHI 8 GRA SHI 8
        .. GRA SHI 8 GRA SHI 5"
1070 PRINT AT 8, 3; " GRA SHI 8 GRA SHI 8
        .... GRA SHI 8 GRA SHI 8 GRA SHI 8
        .... GRA SHI 8 GRA SHI 8 GRA SHI 8
        .... GRA SHI 8 GRA SHI 8
        .. GRA 5"
1080 PRINT AT 9, 3; " GRA SHI 8 GRA SHI 8
        .... GRA SHI 8 GRA SHI 8 GRA SHI 8
        .... GRA SHI 8 GRA SHI 8 GRA SHI 8
        .... GRA SHI 8 GRA SHI 8
        .. GRA 5"
1090 PRINT AT 10, 3; " GRA SHI 8 GRA SHI 8
        .... GRA SHI 8 GRA SHI 8 GRA SHI 8
```

```
         ▲▲▲▲ GRA SHI 8 GRA SHI 8 GRA SHI 8
         ▲▲▲▲ GRA SHI 8 GRA SHI 8
         ▲▲ GRA 5"
1100 PRINT AT 11, 3; " GRA SHI 8 GRA SHI 8";
     c$; " GRA SHI 8 GRA SHI 8 GRA SHI 8
      GRA SHI 8 GRA SHI 3 GRA SHI 3 GRA SHI 2"
1110 PRINT AT 12, 3; " GRA SHI 8 GRA SHI 8"; c$;
     " GRA SHI 8 GRA SHI 8 GRA SHI 8 GRA SHI 8"
1120 PRINT AT 13, 3;
     " GRA SHI 8 GRA SHI 8 GRA SHI 8 GRA SHI 8
      GRA SHI 8 GRA SHI 8 GRA SHI 8 EXI SHI 0
      GRA SHI 8 GRA SHI 8 GRA SHI 8 GRA SHI 8
      GRA SHI 8 GRA SHI 8 GRA SHI 8 GRA SHI 8
      EXI SHI 7 GRA SHI 8 GRA SHI 8 GRA SHI 8
      GRA SHI 8 GRA SHI 8 GRA SHI 8 GRA SHI 8"
1130 PRINT AT 14, 3;
     " GRA SHI 8 GRA SHI 8 GRA SHI 8 GRA SHI 8
      GRA SHI 8 GRA SHI 8 GRA SHI 8 EXI SHI 0
      GRA SHI 8 GRA SHI 8 GRA SHI 8 GRA SHI 8
      EXI SHI 7 GRA SHI 8 GRA SHI 8 GRA SHI 8
      GRA SHI 8 GRA SHI 8 GRA SHI 8 GRA SHI 8"
1140 PRINT AT 15, 3;
     " GRA SHI 8 GRA SHI 8 GRA SHI 8 GRA SHI 8
      GRA SHI 8 GRA SHI 8 EXI SHI 0 GRA SHI 8
      GRA SHI 8 GRA SHI 8 GRA SHI 8 GRA SHI 8
      GRA SHI 8 GRA SHI 8 GRA SHI 8 GRA SHI 8
      GRA SHI 8 EXI SHI 7 GRA SHI 8 GRA SHI 8
      GRA SHI 8 GRA SHI 8 GRA SHI 8 GRA SHI 8
      EXI SHI 0"
1150 PRINT AT 16, 3;
     " GRA SHI 8 GRA SHI 8 GRA SHI 8 GRA SHI 8
      GRA SHI 8 GRA SHI 8 GRA SHI 8 GRA SHI 8
      GRA SHI 8 GRA SHI 8 GRA SHI 8 GRA SHI 8
      GRA SHI 8 GRA SHI 8 GRA SHI 8 GRA SHI 8
      GRA SHI 8 GRA SHI 8"
1160 PRINT AT 17, 3; " GRA SHI 8 GRA SHI 8"; c$;
     " GRA SHI 8 GRA SHI 8 GRA SHI 8 GRA SHI 8"
1500 GO SUB blankwindow
1750 IF money > 0 THEN GO TO 1780
1760 PRINT INK 0; AT 20, 0; "Sorry▲-▲all▲your
     ▲money▲is▲gone"
1770 STOP
1780 PRINT INK 0; AT 20, 0; "You▲have▲`"; money;
     "▲left"; AT 21, 0; "Press
     ▲ < ENTER > ▲to▲play"
1790 INPUT k$
1800 PRINT AT 20, 0; "▲▲▲▲▲▲▲▲▲▲▲▲▲▲▲▲▲▲
     ▲▲▲▲▲▲▲▲▲▲▲▲▲▲▲▲▲▲▲▲▲▲▲▲
     ▲▲▲▲▲▲▲▲▲▲▲▲▲▲▲▲▲▲▲▲▲▲▲▲
     ▲▲▲▲"
1810 LET money = money-.5
1820 PRINT INK 0; PAPER 0; AT 13, 13; "▲▲▲";
     AT 14, 13; "▲▲▲"; AT 15, 13; "▲▲▲"
1830 GO SUB blankwindow
```

```
2000 REM display_all_windows
2010 FOR w = 1 TO 3
2020 FOR d = 1 TO 3+3* RND
2030 LET oldpict = picture
2040 LET picture = 1+ INT (4* RND )
2050 IF picture = oldpict THEN GO TO 2040
2060 FOR L = 5 TO 1 STEP -1
2070 GO SUB fillhires
2080 LET p = 0
2090 LET pattern = picture
2100 FOR b = L TO 5
2110 LET p = p+1
2120 GO SUB drawblock
2130 NEXT b
2140 LET pattern = oldpict
2150 FOR b = 1 TO L-1
2160 LET p = p+1
2170 GO SUB drawblock
2180 NEXT b
2190 NEXT L
2200 NEXT d
2210 LET r(w) = picture
2220 GO SUB resethires
2230 NEXT w
2500 IF r(1) <> r(2) AND r(2) <> r(3) THEN GO TO 1750
2510 IF r(2) = 2 THEN GO TO 1750
2520 LET win = 1
2530 IF r(1) = r(2) AND r(2) = r(3) THEN
     LET win = s(r(1))
2540 PRINT PAPER 0; AT 13, 13; "YOU"; AT 14, 13;
     "WON"; AT 15, 13; "`"; win
2550 LET money = money+win
2560 GO TO 1750
5100 REM get_correct_colours_for_block
5110 RESTORE 9000+100*pattern
5120 FOR c = 1 TO b-1
5130 READ ink, paper
5140 NEXT c
5150 READ ink, paper
5200 REM print_one_block
5210 PRINT AT first+p, 7*w-2;
5220 FOR c = 1 TO 4
5230 PRINT INK ink; PAPER paper; CHR$ (144+4*b-5+c);
5240 NEXT c
5250 RETURN
5300 REM redefine_hi_resolution_characters
5310 RESTORE 8000+100*picture+10*L
5320 FOR h = _ USR "a"+32*L-32 TO USR "a"+32*L-1
5330 READ byte : POKE h, byte
5340 NEXT h
5350 RETURN
5500 REM define_hires_as_"?"
5510 LET pattern = 0
5520 LET picture = 0
5530 LET oldpict = 0
5540 FOR L = 5 TO 1 STEP -1
```

```
5550 GO SUB fillhires : IF handle = 0 THEN
     GO TO 5590
5560 IF L = 5 THEN PRINT AT 3, 27; "▲▲";
     AT 4, 27; "▲▲"; AT 5, 27; " GRA 4▲";
     AT 8, 27; " GRA SHI 8 GRA SHI 5";
     AT 9, 27; " GRA SHI 8 GRA SHI 5"
5570 IF L = 3 THEN PRINT AT 5, 27; "▲▲";
     AT 6, 27; "▲▲"; AT 10, 27;
     " GRA SHI 8 GRA SHI 5"
5580 IF L = 1 THEN PRINT AT 7, 27; "▲▲";
     AT 8, 27; "▲▲"; AT 9, 27; "▲▲";
     AT 11, 27; " GRA SHI 8 GRA SHI 5"
5590 NEXT L
5600 RETURN
5700 REM fill▲all▲windows▲with▲?
5710 LET handle = 1 : GO SUB resethires :
     LET handle = 0
5720 FOR w = 1 TO 3
5730 LET d = 1
5740 FOR b = 1 TO 5
5750 LET p = b
5760 GO SUB drawblock
5770 NEXT b
5780 IF w = 1 THEN PRINT AT 7, 27;
     " GRA SHI 8 GRA SHI 5"; AT 8, 27;
     " GRA SHI 8 GRA SHI 5"; AT 9, 27;
     " GRA SHI 8 GRA SHI 5"; AT 11, 27;
     " GRA SHI 2▲"
5790 IF w = 2 THEN PRINT AT 5, 27; " GRA 4▲";
     AT 6, 27; " GRA SHI 8 GRA SHI 5";
     AT 10, 27; " GRA 5▲"
5800 IF w = 3 THEN PRINT AT 3, 27; " GRA 4▲";
     AT 4, 27; " GRA SHI 8 GRA SHI 5";
     AT 5, 27; " GRA SHI 8 GRA SHI 5";
     AT 8, 27; " GRA 5▲"; AT 9, 27;
     " GRA 5▲"
5810 NEXT w
5820 RETURN
7000 DATA 15, 3, 12, 7
8000 REM Data▲for▲high▲resolution▲pictures▲-
     ▲first▲one▲is▲question▲mark
8010 DATA 0, 0, 0, 0, 0, 0, 0, 0
8011 DATA 0, 0, 0, 3, 15, 60, 112, 112
8012 DATA 0, 0, 0, 248, 252, 62, 14, 7
8013 DATA 0, 0, 0, 0, 0, 0, 0, 0
8020 DATA 0, 0, 0, 0, 0, 0, 0, 0
8021 DATA 224, 224, 224, 240, 248, 248, 240, 96
8022 DATA 3, 3, 3, 3, 3, 7, 6, 14
8023 DATA 0, 128, 128, 128, 128, 0, 0, 0
8030 DATA 0, 0, 0, 0, 0, 0, 0, 0
8031 DATA 0, 0, 0, 0, 1, 1, 3, 3
8032 DATA 28, 56, 112, 224, 192, 128, 0, 0
8033 DATA 0, 0, 0, 0, 0, 0, 0, 0
8040 DATA 0, 0, 0, 0, 0, 0, 0, 0
8041 DATA 7, 7, 7, 3, 3, 1, 0, 0
8042 DATA 0, 0, 128, 192, 192, 128, 0, 0
```

```
8043 DATA 0, 0, 0, 0, 0, 0, 0, 0
8050 DATA 0, 0, 0, 0, 0, 0, 0, 0
8051 DATA 3, 15, 15, 15, 3, 0, 0, 0
8052 DATA 0, 192, 192, 192, 0, 0, 0, 0
8053 DATA 0, 0, 0, 0, 0, 0, 0, 0
8100 REM Cherry
8110 DATA 0, 0, 0, 0, 0, 0, 0, 0
8111 DATA 0, 0, 0, 0, 0, 0, 0, 0
8112 DATA 0, 6, 6, 14, 30, 30, 62, 126
8113 DATA 0, 0, 0, 0, 0, 0, 0, 0
8120 DATA 0, 0, 0, 0, 0, 0, 0, 0
8121 DATA 0, 0, 1, 1, 1, 2, 2, 2
8122 DATA 127, 191, 31, 3, 0, 0, 0, 0
8123 DATA 0, 0, 0, 128, 128, 0, 0, 0
8130 DATA 0, 0, 0, 0, 0, 0, 0, 0
8131 DATA 4, 4, 4, 4, 4, 4, 2, 2
8132 DATA 0, 0, 0, 0, 0, 0, 0, 0
8133 DATA 0, 0, 0, 0, 0, 0, 0, 0
8140 DATA 0, 0, 0, 0, 1, 1, 1, 1
8141 DATA 29, 60, 126, 255, 255, 255, 255, 255
8142 DATA 224, 240, 120, 124, 252, 254, 254, 254
8143 DATA 0, 0, 0, 0, 0, 0, 0, 0
8150 DATA 1, 1, 0, 0, 0, 0, 0, 0
8151 DATA 255, 255, 255, 127, 63, 31, 7, 0
8152 DATA 254, 254, 252, 252, 248, 224, 128, 0
8153 DATA 0, 0, 0, 0, 0, 0, 0, 0
8200 REM Lemon
8210 DATA 0, 0, 0, 0, 0, 0, 0, 0
8211 DATA 0, 0, 0, 0, 0, 0, 0, 1
8212 DATA 0, 0, 0, 0, 0, 0, 127, 255
8213 DATA 0, 0, 0, 0, 0, 0, 16, 188
8220 DATA 0, 0, 0, 0, 1, 1, 3, 7
8221 DATA 7, 31, 127, 255, 254, 248, 240, 224
8222 DATA 255, 255, 255, 255, 15, 15, 31, 63
8223 DATA 254, 254, 126, 60, 196, 246, 254, 254
8230 DATA 7, 15, 31, 31, 63, 63, 63, 63
8231 DATA 192, 193, 199, 255, 255, 255, 255, 255
8232 DATA 127, 255, 255, 255, 255, 255, 255, 255
8233 DATA 254, 254, 254, 254, 254, 252, 252, 252
8240 DATA 63, 63, 63, 63, 63, 63, 31, 31
8241 DATA 255, 255, 255, 255, 255, 255, 255, 255
8242 DATA 255, 255, 255, 255, 255, 255, 255, 255
8243 DATA 248, 248, 240, 224, 224, 192, 128, 0
8250 DATA 63, 63, 63, 63, 31, 0, 0, 0
8251 DATA 255, 255, 255, 255, 0, 0, 0, 0
8252 DATA 254, 248, 224, 128, 0, 0, 0, 0
8253 DATA 0, 0, 0, 0, 0, 0, 0, 0
8300 REM Bell
8310 DATA 0, 0, 0, 0, 0, 0, 0, 0
8311 DATA 0, 0, 3, 14, 8, 8, 12, 6
8312 DATA 0, 0, 192, 112, 16, 16, 48, 96
8313 DATA 0, 0, 0, 0, 0, 0, 0, 0
8320 DATA 0, 0, 0, 0, 0, 0, 0, 0
8321 DATA 3, 15, 63, 127, 127, 255, 255, 255
8322 DATA 192, 240, 252, 254, 254, 255, 255, 255
8323 DATA 0, 0, 0, 0, 0, 0, 0, 0
```

```
8330 DATA 0, 1, 1, 1, 1, 1, 1, 1
8331 DATA 255, 255, 255, 255, 255, 255, 255, 255
8332 DATA 255, 255, 255, 255, 255, 255, 255, 255
8333 DATA 0, 128, 128, 128, 128, 128, 128, 128
8340 DATA 1, 3, 3, 3, 3, 7, 14, 56
8341 DATA 255, 255, 255, 255, 127, 127, 127, 255
8342 DATA 255, 255, 255, 255, 255, 255, 255, 255
8343 DATA 128, 192, 192, 192, 192, 224, 240, 252
8350 DATA 31, 3, 0, 0, 0, 0, 0, 0
8351 DATA 255, 255, 3, 3, 1, 0, 0, 0
8352 DATA 255, 255, 128, 128, 0, 0, 0, 0
8353 DATA 252, 192, 0, 0, 0, 0, 0, 0
8400 REM pineapple
8410 DATA 0, 0, 0, 1, 1, 9, 13, 7
8411 DATA 0, 4, 4, 14, 142, 158, 254, 189
8412 DATA 0, 64, 68, 196, 220, 221, 247, 245
8413 DATA 0, 0, 16, 112, 224, 192, 128, 184
8420 DATA 7, 3, 3, 1, 1, 0, 0, 0
8421 DATA 187, 221, 219, 235, 247, 251, 253, 255
8422 DATA 245, 250, 253, 251, 247, 239, 223, 223
8423 DATA 240, 224, 192, 128, 128, 0, 0, 0
8430 DATA 0, 0, 0, 0, 1, 1, 3, 3
8431 DATA 127, 127, 80, 219, 219, 219, 39, 178
8432 DATA 254, 254, 46, 111, 227, 29, 93, 125
8433 DATA 0, 0, 0, 128, 128, 128, 192
8440 DATA 3, 3, 3, 3, 3, 3, 1, 1
8441 DATA 182, 183, 70, 57, 53, 53, 174, 209
8442 DATA 200, 215, 27, 187, 145, 183, 119, 191
8443 DATA 192, 192, 192, 192, 128, 128, 128, 128
8450 DATA 1, 1, 0, 0, 0, 0, 0, 0
8451 DATA 219, 255, 197, 237, 237, 127, 31, 0
8452 DATA 147, 187, 27, 218, 198, 252, 248, 0
8453 DATA 0, 0, 0, 0, 0, 0, 0, 0
9000 REM ink, paper▲data▲for▲each▲block
9010 DATA 0, 5, 0, 5, 0, 5, 0, 5, 0, 5
9100 DATA 4, 1, 4, 1, 4, 1, 2, 1, 2, 1
9200 DATA 6, 4, 6, 4, 6, 4, 6, 4, 6, 4
9300 DATA 7, 2, 7, 2, 7, 2, 7, 2, 7, 2
9400 DATA 4, 3, 4, 3, 6, 3, 6, 3, 6, 3
```

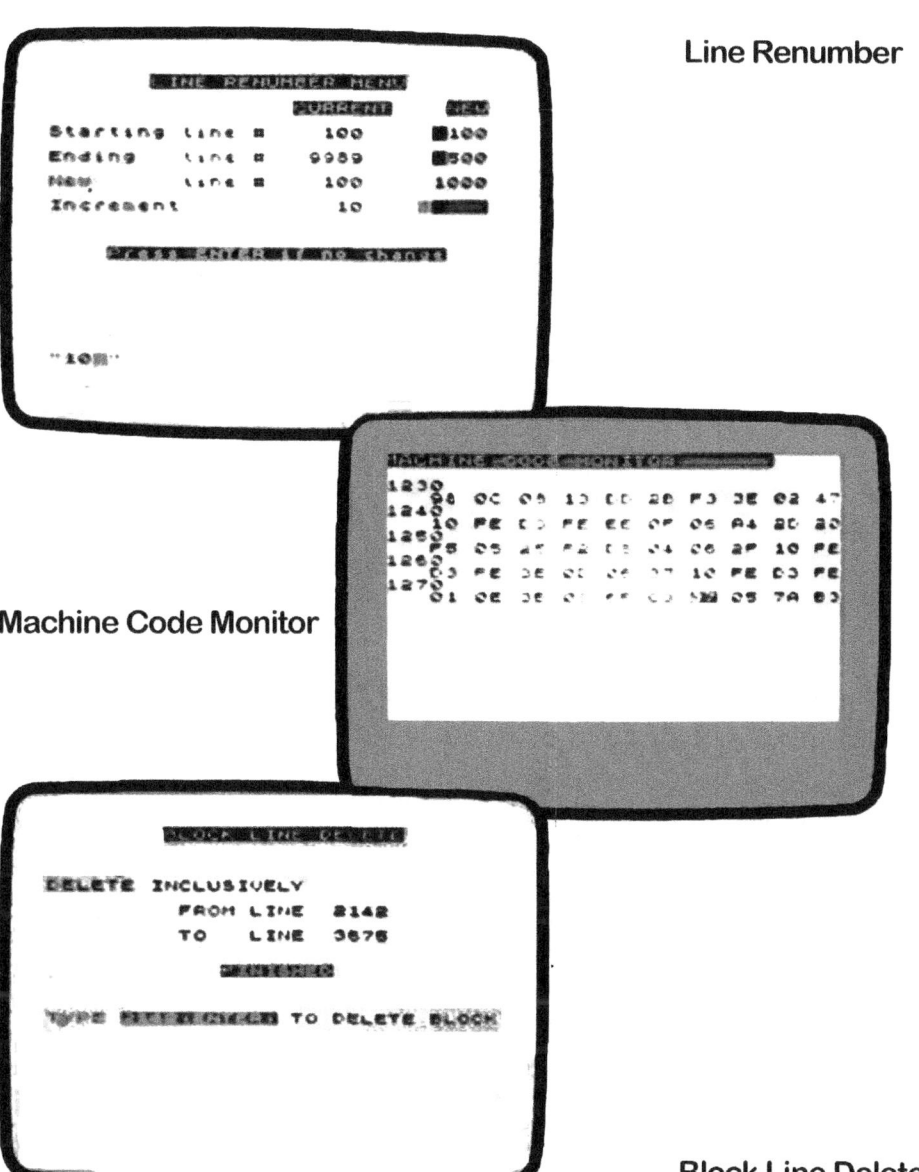

**Line Renumber**

**Machine Code Monitor**

**Block Line Delete**

**Eliminator**

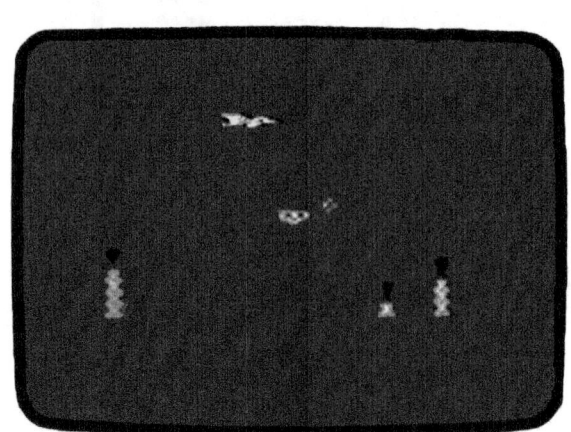

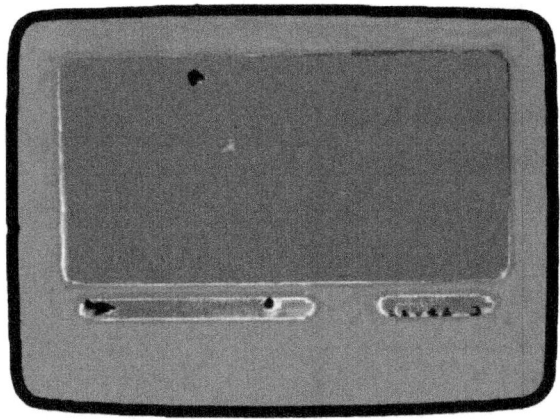

**Meteor Storm**

# Bubble Sort

There are all sorts of people interested in computing,
but in mathematics the word 'sort' has a different
meaning. There are indeed many different sorts of sorts.

A sort is a process by which you can create order out of
chaos, and usually the sorting process is applied to a
large number of names or an array of numbers.

The program given here serves as both a demonstration of
the processes involved in the sorting process, as well as
being the basis for a compact subroutine you can use in
your own programs — for example to sort a list of names
and addresses, or to sort a hand of cards in a bridge
game.

The demonstration of these sorts given here is
graphically very enjoyable as well as being slow enough
to allow a good understanding of the sorting process.

The bubble sort:
-----------------

The first program given here is a traditional bubble
sort. What the program does is that it compares two
numbers adjacent in a list: if the numbers are the wrong
way round (in other words the larger number comes before
the smaller number) then it swaps them around.

If you run this program, you will soon realise why it is
called a bubble sort — the smaller numbers seem to bubble
to the top and the larger ones bubble to the bottom.

The program will keep on swapping adjacent numbers, over
and over again, each time getting the list of numbers a
little bit more sorted than before until finally there is
no more sorting to be done.

The program is very cute in its execution, and you can
see how hard the dumper truck has to work to sort the
mess out.
You will soon realise that there must be a better way to
sort things.

Modified bubble sort:
---------------------

The second program listing is a modified bubble sort. Now
the program is no longer concerned to swap merely
adjacent numbers — it is prepared to roam much further
afield.

This cuts the number of swaps to be done to about half those on a traditional bubble sort.

You can either enter the second program as listed, or if you have already entered program 1, all that is needed is to change lines 320, 330, 340, 500 and 510.

Sort subroutine:
------------------

Aside from its demonstration purposes, you can use sorts in your own programs. Program 3 gives the listing of the modified bubble sort in subroutine form (lines 8000 - 8030) which you can use in your own programs.

This subroutine assumes the numbers to be sorted are in an array p(n), and that n is the number of elements to be sorted.

Program 3 can be obtained from Program 2 by deleting lines 110 - 130 and lines 280 onwards, and then inserting new lines 280 - 300, 1000 - 1040, and 8000 - 8030.

As you can see from this program, 15 numbers can be sorted in about 3 seconds, including the time required to print the 15 numbers twice.

```
6.3883362
15.1362
11.215912
2.1986542
15.914856
9.6141956
2.8718536
6.4046157          1.3719334

13.911662
9.3784465
14.39119
15.341049
11.679376
14.456252
```

SORT VERSION 1

```
100 BORDER 7 : PAPER 7 : INK 0 : OVER 0 : CLS
110 RESTORE 600
120 FOR i = USR "a" TO USR "d"-1
130 READ x : POKE i, x : NEXT i
140 LET n = 15
150 DIM p(n)
160 PRINT "Do▲you▲want▲to▲choose▲your▲own
    ▲▲numbers▲(y▲or▲n)?"
170 LET b$ = INKEY$ : IF b$ = "" THEN GO TO 170
180 IF b$ = "n" OR b$ = "N" THEN GO TO 240
190 PRINT "Enter▲15▲numbers▲to▲be▲sorted"
200 FOR y = 1 TO n
210 INPUT p(y) : PRINT p(y)
220 NEXT y
230 GO TO 270
240 FOR x = 1 TO n
250 LET p(x) = 15* RND +1
260 NEXT x
270 CLS
280 FOR x = 1 TO n
290 PRINT AT x, 0; p(x)
300 NEXT x
310 LET m = 18
320 FOR i = n-1 TO 1 STEP -1
330 FOR j = 1 TO i
340 LET L = j+1
350 IF p(j) <= p(L) THEN GO TO 500
360 LET b$ = "▲▲▲▲▲▲▲▲▲▲"( TO LEN STR$ p(j))
    : PRINT AT j, 0; OVER 1; PAPER 5; b$
370 IF L = m THEN GO TO 390
380 FOR x = m TO L STEP SGN (L-m) : PRINT INK 2;
    AT x, 18; " GRA A GRA B GRA C";
    AT x+ SGN (m-L), 18; "▲▲▲" : NEXT x
390 LET y = LEN STR$ p(L) : FOR x = 17 TO y STEP -:
    : PRINT INK 2; AT L, x;
    " GRA A GRA B GRA C▲" : NEXT x
400 FOR x = 0 TO 10 : PRINT AT L, x; "▲"; p(L);
    INK 2; " GRA A GRA B GRA C" : NEXT x
410 FOR x = L TO j STEP -1 : PRINT AT x, 11; p(L);
    INK 2; " GRA A GRA B GRA C"; AT x+1, 11;
    "▲▲▲▲▲▲▲▲▲▲▲▲▲▲▲" : NEXT x
420 PRINT OVER 1; AT j, 0; p(j)
430 FOR x = j TO L : PRINT OVER 1; AT x, 0; p(j);
    AT x, 0; p(j) : NEXT x : PRINT AT L, 0; p(j)
440 FOR x = 10 TO 0 STEP -1 : PRINT AT j, x; p(L);
    INK 2; " GRA A GRA B GRA C"; "▲" : NEXT x
450 FOR x = y TO 17 : PRINT AT j, x; INK 2;
    "▲ GRA A GRA B GRA C" : NEXT x
460 LET m = j
470 LET t = p(L)
480 LET p(L) = p(j)
490 LET p(j) = t
500 NEXT j
```

```
510 NEXT i
520 FOR x = m TO 18 : PRINT AT x, 18; INK 2;
    " GRA A GRA B GRA C"; AT x-1, 18; "▲▲▲" :
    NEXT x
530 PRINT AT 21, 0; "Do▲you▲want▲to▲sort
    ▲again?▲"
540 LET b$ = INKEY$ : IF b$ = "" THEN GO TO 540
550 IF b$ = "y" OR b$ = "Y" THEN RUN 100
560 IF b$ = "y" OR b$ = "Y" THEN RUN 100
600 DATA 0, 0, 2, 6, 15, 30, 63, 254
610 DATA 0, 0, 63, 127, 241, 100, 238, 4
620 DATA 63, 255, 241, 228, 158, 223, 14, 4
SORT VERSION 2

100 BORDER 7 : PAPER 7 : INK 0 : OVER 0 : CLS
110 RESTORE 600
120 FOR i = USR "a" TO USR "d"-1
130 READ x : POKE i, x : NEXT i
140 LET n = 15
150 DIM p(n)
160 PRINT "Do▲you▲want▲to▲choose▲your▲own
    ▲▲numbers▲(y▲or▲n)?"
170 LET b$ = INKEY$ : IF b$ = "" THEN GO TO 170
180 IF b$ = "n" OR b$ = "N" THEN GO TO 240
190 PRINT "Enter▲15▲numbers▲to▲be▲sorted"
200 FOR y = 1 TO n
210 INPUT p(y) : PRINT p(y)
220 NEXT y
230 GO TO 270
240 FOR x = 1 TO n
250 LET p(x) = 15* RND +1
260 NEXT x
270 CLS
280 FOR x = 1 TO n
290 PRINT AT x, 0; p(x)
300 NEXT x
310 LET m = 18
320 FOR j = 1 TO n-1
330 FOR i = j+1 TO n
340 LET L = n+j-i+1
350 IF p(j) <= p(L) THEN GO TO 500
360 LET b$ = "▲▲▲▲▲▲▲▲▲▲"( TO LEN STR$ p(j))
    : PRINT AT j, 0; OVER 1; PAPER 5; b$
370 IF L = m THEN GO TO 390
380 FOR x = m TO L STEP SGN (L-m) : PRINT INK 2;
    AT x, 18; " GRA A GRA B GRA C";
    AT x+ SGN (m-L), 18; "▲▲▲" : NEXT x
390 LET y = LEN STR$ p(L) : FOR x = 17 TO y STEP -1
    : PRINT INK 2; AT L, x;
    " GRA A GRA B GRA C▲" : NEXT x
400 FOR x = 0 TO 10 : PRINT AT L, x; "▲"; p(L);
    INK 2; " GRA A GRA B GRA C" : NEXT x
410 FOR x = L TO j STEP -1 : PRINT AT x, 11; p(L);
    INK 2; " GRA A GRA B GRA C"; AT x+1, 11;
    "▲▲▲▲▲▲▲▲▲▲▲▲" : NEXT x
```

```
420 PRINT OVER 1; AT j, 0; p(j)
430 FOR x = j TO L : PRINT OVER 1; AT x, 0; p(j);
    AT x, 0; p(j) : NEXT x : PRINT AT L, 0; p(j)
440 FOR x = 10 TO 0 STEP -1 : PRINT AT j, x; p(L);
    INK 2; " GRA A GRA B GRA C"; "▲" : NEXT x
450 FOR x = y TO 17 : PRINT AT j, x; INK 2;
    "▲ GRA A GRA B GRA C" : NEXT x
460 LET m = j
470 LET t = p(L)
480 LET p(L) = p(j)
490 LET p(j) = t
500 NEXT i
510 NEXT j
520 FOR x = m TO 18 : PRINT AT x, 18; INK 2;
    " GRA A GRA B GRA C"; AT x-1, 18; "▲▲▲" :
    NEXT x
530 PRINT AT 21, 0; "Do▲you▲want▲to▲sort
    ▲again?▲"
540 LET b$ = INKEY$ : IF b$ = "" THEN GO TO 540
550 IF b$ = "y" OR b$ = "Y" THEN RUN 100
560 IF b$ = "y" OR b$ = "Y" THEN RUN 100
600 DATA 0, 0, 2, 6, 15, 30, 63, 254
610 DATA 0, 0, 63, 127, 241, 100, 238, 4
620 DATA 63, 255, 241, 228, 158, 223, 14, 4
```

SORT VERSION 3

```
 100 BORDER 7 : PAPER 7 : INK 0 : OVER 0 : CLS
 140 LET n = 15
 150 DIM p(n)
 160 PRINT "Do▴you▴want▴to▴choose▴your▴own
        ▴▴numbers▴(y▴or▴n)?"
 170 LET b$ = INKEY$ : IF b$ = "" THEN GO TO 170
 180 IF b$ = "n" OR b$ = "N" THEN GO TO 240
 190 PRINT "Enter▴15▴numbers▴to▴be▴sorted"
 200 FOR y = 1 TO n
 210 INPUT p(y) : PRINT p(y)
 220 NEXT y
 230 GO TO 270
 240 FOR x = 1 TO n
 250 LET p(x) = 15* RND +1
 260 NEXT x
 270 CLS
 280 GO SUB 1000 : GO SUB 8000
 290 GO SUB 1000
 300 STOP
1010 FOR x = 1 TO n
1020 PRINT AT x, 0; p(x)
1030 NEXT x
1040 RETURN
8000 REM sort▴subroutine
8010 FOR j = 1 TO n-1 : FOR i = j+1 TO n :
        LET L = n+j-i+1
8020 IF p(L) <= p(j) THEN LET t = p(L) :
        LET p(L) = p(j) : LET p(j) = t
8030 NEXT i : NEXT j : RETURN
```

# Simultaneous Equations

Copyright (c) by Beam Software

This program solves two simultaneous equations of the type
$$ax + by + c = 0$$

This equation is the general form of equation for a straight line, and the 'solution' of two such lines is the mathematical term for the point where the two lines cross.

You will be asked by the program to enter the values of a, b and c for each of the two equations, and the program will find out for what values of x and y the lines meet.

If there is no solution – in other words the two lines are parallel and do not meet – the program will tell you so.

The program will then draw for you each of the two lines and show you where they cross.

Program structure:
--------------------

The actual calculation part of the program is fairly small – most of the program consist of getting the correct information from you, and then displaying the results to you (including the graph).

Line 830 calculates the determinant D. If D is zero, no solution exists.

The block from 900 – 990 determines in which quadrant the intersection of the two lines occurs, and in which direction the graphs should be plotted.

## SIMULTANEOUS EQUATIONS

```
100 REM EQUATION
101 REM
110 REM simultaneous.equation
120 BORDER 7 : INK 1 : PAPER 7 : FLASH 0 : INVERSE 0
    : CLS
130 PRINT AT 0, 5; INVERSE 1;
    "SIMULTANEOUS.EQUATIONS"
140 PRINT AT 2, 0; INK 2; INVERSE 1;
    "a1X+b1Y+c1 = 0"
150 PRINT AT 2, 16; PAPER 6; INK 0; "a2X+b2Y+c2 = 0"
160 PRINT AT 4, 0; "a1 = "; AT 4, 16; "a2 = ";
    AT 5, 0; "b1 = "; AT 5, 16; "b2 = "; AT 6, 0;
    "c1 = "; AT 6, 16; "c2 = "
170 DIM C(6) : REM coeficient.array
180 DIM S$(7)
190 DIM X$(7)
200 DIM Y$(7)
500 REM
510 REM input.first.equation
520 FOR I = 1 TO 3
530 PRINT AT I+3, 3; FLASH 1; " > "; FLASH 0; INK 2;
    INVERSE 1; "▲▲▲▲▲▲▲▲▲▲▲"
540 INPUT S$ : LET C(I) = VAL S$
550 PRINT AT I+3, 3; "▲▲▲▲▲▲▲▲▲▲▲▲▲▲";
    AT I+3, 4; ABS C(I)
560 IF SGN C(I) = -1 THEN PRINT AT I+3, 3; "-"
570 NEXT I
600 REM
610 REM input.second.equation
620 FOR I = 4 TO 6
630 PRINT AT I, 19; FLASH 1; " > "; FLASH 0;
    PAPER 6; "▲▲▲▲▲▲▲▲▲▲▲"
640 INPUT S$ : LET C(I) = VAL S$
650 PRINT AT I, 19; "▲▲▲▲▲▲▲▲▲▲▲▲▲▲";
    AT I, 20; ABS C(I)
660 IF SGN C(I) = -1 THEN PRINT AT I, 19; "-"
670 NEXT I
800 REM
810 REM calculates.solution
820 PRINT AT 7, 0;
830 LET D = C(2)*C(4)-C(1)*C(5)
840 IF D = 0 THEN PRINT INVERSE 1; "DEGENERATE :";
    INVERSE 0; "▲"; FLASH 1; "NO.SOLUTIONS" :
    RUN
850 LET A = (C(3)*C(5)-C(2)*C(6))/D
860 LET X$ = STR$ A : LET A = VAL X$
870 LET B = (C(1)*C(6)-C(3)*C(4))/D
880 LET Y$ = STR$ B : LET B = VAL Y$
890 PRINT INVERSE 1; "SOLUTIONS": INVERSE 0;
    "▲X = ▲"; X$; "▲▲Y = ▲"; Y$
900 REM
910 REM plot.axis
920 IF A >= 0 AND B >= 0 THEN LET ox = 72 :
```

```
          LET oy = 0 : PRINT AT 21, 8; "O"; AT 8, 8;
          "Y"; AT 21, 23; "X"
 930 IF A >= 0 AND B < 0 THEN LET ox = 72 :
          LET oy = 111 : PRINT AT 8, 8; "O"; AT 21, 8;
          "Y"; AT 8, 23; "X"
 940 IF A < 0 AND B >= 0 THEN LET ox = 183 :
          LET oy = 0 : PRINT AT 21, 23; "O"; AT 21, 8;
          "X"; AT 8, 23; "Y"
 950 IF A < 0 AND B < 0 THEN LET ox = 183 :
          LET oy = 111 : PRINT AT 8, 23; "O"; AT 8, 8;
          "X"; AT 21, 23; "Y"
 960 LET dx = ( SGN A >= 0)-( SGN A < 0)
 970 LET dy = ( SGN B >= 0)-( SGN B < 0)
 980 PLOT ox, oy : DRAW INK 0; dx*111, 0 :
          PLOT ox, oy : DRAW INK 0; 0, dy*111
 990 GO SUB 1500 : REM plot.lines
1000 INPUT "More.equation?(y.or.n)"; k$
1100 IF k$ = "n" OR k$ = "N" THEN STOP
1110 IF k$ = "y" OR k$ = "Y" THEN RUN
1120 GO TO 1000
1500 REM
1510 LET rx = ABS (55/A) : LET ry = ABS (55/B)
1520 REM draw.first.line
1530 PRINT AT 2, 0; INK 2; OVER 1; FLASH 1;
          "▲▲▲▲▲▲▲▲▲▲▲▲▲"
1540 IF C(1) = 0 THEN LET ix1 = 0 :
          LET iy1 = -C(3)/C(2) : LET ix2 = 2*A :
          LET iy2 = iy1 : GO TO 1620
1550 IF C(2) = 0 THEN LET iy1 = 0 :
          LET ix1 = -C(3)/C(1) :  LET iy2 = 2*B :
          LET ix2 = ix1 : GO TO 1620
1560 LET ix1 = 2*A : LET iy1 = -(C(3)+C(1)*ix1)/C(2)
1570 IF dy*iy1 < 0 THEN LET iy1 = 0 : GO TO 1590
1580 IF ( ABS iy1- ABS (2*B)) > 0 THEN LET iy1 = 2*B
1590 LET ix2 = 0 : LET iy2 = -C(3)/C(2)
1600 IF dy*iy2 < 0 THEN LET iy2 = 0 : GO TO 1620
1610 IF ( ABS iy2- ABS (2*B)) > 0 THEN LET iy2 = 2*B
1620 PLOT ox+rx*ix1, oy+ry*iy1
1630 DRAW (ix2-ix1)*rx, (iy2-iy1)*ry
1640 PAUSE 100
1650 PRINT AT 2, 0; INK 2; INVERSE 1;
          "a1X+b1Y+c1 = 0"
1800 REM
1810 REM draw.second.line
1820 PRINT AT 2, 16; OVER 1; FLASH 1; PAPER 6;
          INK 0; "▲▲▲▲▲▲▲▲▲▲▲▲"
1830 PLOT OVER 1; ox+rx*ix1, oy+ry*iy1
1840 DRAW OVER 1; (ix2-ix1)*rx, (iy2-iy1)*ry
1850 IF C(4) = 0 THEN LET ix3 = 0 :
          LET iy3 = -C(6)/C(5) : LET ix4 = 2*A :
          LET iy4 = iy3 : GO TO 1930
1860 IF C(5) = 0 THEN LET iy3 = 0 :
          LET ix3 = -C(6)/C(4) : LET iy4 = 2*B :
          LET ix4 = ix3 : GO TO 1930
1870 LET ix3 = 2*A : LET iy3 = -(C(6)+C(4)*ix3)/C(5)
1880 IF dy*iy3 < 0 THEN LET iy3 = 0 : GO TO 1900
```

53

```
1890 IF ( ABS iy3- ABS (2*B)) > 0 THEN LET iy3 = 2*B
1900 LET ix4 = 0 : LET iy4 = -C(6)/C(5)
1910 IF dy*iy4 < 0 THEN LET iy4 = 0 : GO TO 1930
1920 IF ( ABS iy4- ABS (2*B)) > 0 THEN LET iy4 = 2*B
1930 PLOT ox+ix3*rx, oy+iy3*ry
1940 DRAW (ix4-ix3)*rx, (iy4-iy3)*ry
1950 PAUSE 100
1960 PRINT AT 2, 16; INK 0; PAPER 6; "a2X+b2Y+c2 = 0"
1970 PLOT ox+ix1*rx, oy+iy1*ry
1980 DRAW (ix2-ix1)*rx, (iy2-iy1)*ry
1990 RETURN
```

# Space Escape

Copyright (c) Clifford Ramshaw

DESCRIPTION
------------

You have been captured by the ALIEN and you are
stranded in a tower guarded by an ALIEN ROBOT.
You have to contend with the force of gravity
dragging you to the ground and the ALIEN's powerful
tractor pulling you back towards the tower.
More than that, once the ALIEN ROBOT discovers that
you are escaping, it will then shoot at you with the high
power suction laser beam. Once you are shot, you will
then be sucked back and put into the prisoner tower
again.

GOOD LUCK IN YOUR ESCAPE PLAN !!

HOW TO RUN THE PROGRAM
-----------------------

To start the program, type RUN (ENTER).

Use 'w' key to move up, 'd' key to move forward.

You have to move above the prisoner cell level before
you can move forward. Unless you move forward, you will
be continually sucked backward until you are back to the
tower again.  Similarly, you will be falling down back to
the cell level if you don't press 'w'.

The game will halt every time you are shot or you
escape successfully.

Press any key to start another game.


PROGRAM STRUCTURE
------------------

This program uses special USER DEFINED GRAPHIC
characters to draw the ALIEN ROBOT and your space-craft
shape.
A close to real-time counter is maintained by using
the frame counter to record the time you lasted before
being re-captured by the ROBOT or if you are lucky, the
time you took to escape.

The structure of the program is as follows:

INTIALISATION
-------------
    SET SCREEN VARIABLES
    SET USER DEFINED GRAPHIC CHARACTERS

55

MAIN LOOP

```
      DRAW TOWER SHAPE AND SAFETY MARGIN LINE
      INITIALISE VARIABLES
L1:   STORE OLD POSITION
      CALCULATES NEW POSITION
      IF NOT MOVING FORWARD
           generate sound tone
      DRAW ALTERNATE SHAPE OF SPACE CRAFT
      IF REACHES MARGIN LINE
           prepare message
           goto    T1:
      IF NOT FIRE AND RND(.9
           goto    L1:
      IF FIRE-FLAG NOT ON
           set fire-flag
           calculates final position for ROBOT
      BLANK OLD ROBOT
      MOVE ROBOT TOWARDS FINAL POSITION
      DRAW NEW ROBOT
      IF FINAL POSITION NOT REACHED
           goto    L1:
      FIRE LASER BEAM ( PLOT & PLOT OVER )
      IF NOT HIT SPACE CRAFT
           goto    L1:
      PERFORM DRAW BACK ROUTINE
      PREPARE MESSAGE
T1:   CALCULATE TIME LAPSE
      PRINT FINAL MESSAGE
```

SPECIAL NOTE
-------------

The TIME LAPSE before the game ended successfully or
tragically is affected by the time taken up by any sound
generation within the program; but it is close to
real-time.

At the end of the game, any key pressed will restart
the game.

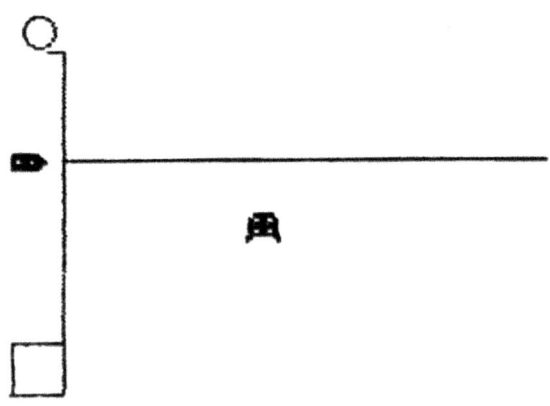

SPACE ESCAPE

```
100 REM ESCAPE
110 REM SPACE.ESCAPE
120 GO TO 8000
500 REM
510 REM define.ship.shape
520 FOR I = USR "A" TO ( USR "J"+7)
550 READ m : POKE I, m
570 NEXT I
580 DATA 0, 0, 0, 30, 30, 49, 61, 61,
       0, 0, 0, 60, 60, 198, 246, 246,
       63, 49, 49, 63, 14, 14, 2, 0,
       254, 198, 198, 254, 56, 56, 32, 0
590 DATA 0, 0, 0, 15, 15, 49, 49, 55,
       0, 0, 0, 248, 248, 198, 198, 222,
       55, 63, 49, 49, 63, 112, 96, 64,
       222, 254, 198, 198, 254, 7, 3, 1
600 DATA 255, 255, 255, 207, 207, 255, 255, 255,
       240, 248, 252, 63, 63, 252, 248, 240
1000 REM
1010 REM draw.tower.routine
1020 CIRCLE INK 0; 12, 167, 7
1030 INK 0 : PLOT 16, 158 : DRAW 7, 0
       : DRAW 0, -158 : DRAW -23, 0 : DRAW 0, 23
       : DRAW 23, 0
1040 PLOT 255, 23 : DRAW 0, -23
1050 FOR I = 23672 TO 23674
       : REM init.time.count
1060 POKE I, 0
1070 NEXT I
1080 RETURN
2000 REM
2010 REM trap.back
2020 PLOT 24, (21-ng)*8+4
       : DRAW INK 2; (D-3)*8-1, 0
2030 FOR I = (ID+(D > ID)) TO 0 STEP -1
2050 PRINT AT H, I; " GBA A GBA B."
       : PRINT AT H+1, I; " GBA C GBA D."
2060 BEEP .05, (36+I)
2070 NEXT I
2090 FOR J = RH TO 18
2100 PRINT AT J, 0; "▲▲"
       : PRINT AT J+1, 0; "▲▲"
2110 PRINT AT J+1, 0; " GBA A GBA B"
       : PRINT AT J+2, 0; " GBA C GBA D"
2120 BEEP .05, (24+J)
2130 NEXT J
2140 RETURN
8000 REM
8010 REM main.loop
8020 BORDER 6 : PAPER 6 : INK 0 : OVER 0 : FLASH 0
       : CLS
8030 RESTORE : GO SUB 500
       : REM define.user.graphic.for.ship
8040 GO SUB 1000 : REM draw.tower
```

```
8050 LET S = 30 : LET H = 20 : LET D = 3
     : LET sh = 0
     : LET og = .. INT ( RND *17)+2
     : LET fr = sn
8060 LET OH = H : LET OD = D
8070 LET k$ = INKEY$
8080 LET H = H+(H < 19)-(k$ = "w" AND H > 1)*1.5
     : LET IH = INT H
8090 LET D = D+(k$ = "d" AND H < 19)*1.5-(D > 3)*.3
     : LET ID = INT D
8100 IF k$ <> "d" THEN BEEP .0125, -24
8110 IF D > 30 THEN LET D = 30
8120 IF sh = 0 THEN GO TO 8170
8130 LET sh = 0
8140 PRINT AT OH, OD; ".."
     : PRINT AT OH+1, OD; ".."
8150 PRINT AT H, D; " GAB E GAB F"
     : PRINT AT H+1, D; " GAB G GAB H"
8160 GO TO 8200
8170 LET sh = 1
8180 PRINT AT OH, OD; ".."
     : PRINT AT OH+1, OD; ".."
8190 PRINT AT H, D; " GAB A GAB B"
     : PRINT AT H+1, D; " GAB C GAB D"
8200 IF D = 30 THEN PRINT AT 21, 0;
     "YOU.ESCAPED.IN."; : GO TO 8370
8210 IF fr = 0 AND RND < .9 OR H > 19
     THEN GO TO 8060
8220 IF fr = 1 THEN GO TO 8270
8230 LET ng = INT ( INT ( RND *2)+H)-1
     : LET ng = ng-(ng > 18)
8240 IF ng < 2 THEN LET ng = 2
8250 LET gm = (ng > og)-(ng < og)
8260 LET fr = 1
8270 IF ng = og THEN GO TO 8310
8280 PRINT AT og, 0; ".." : LET og = og+gm
8290 PRINT AT og, 0; INK 2; " GAB I GAB J"
8300 GO TO 8060
8310 PLOT 24, (21-ng)*8+4 : DRAW INK 2; 214, 0
     : BEEP .2, 20
8320 PLOT OVER 1; 24, (21-ng)*8+4
     : DRAW INK 2; OVER 1; 214, 0 : BEEP .1, 0
8330 LET RH = (IH+(H > IH))
     : IF ng <> RH AND ng <> RH+1 OR RH > 19
     THEN LET fr = 0 : GO TO 8060
8340 GO SUB 2000
8350 PRINT AT 21, 0; "YOU.LASTED.";
8370 LET T = INT (((65536* PEEK 23674+256*
     PEEK 23673+ PEEK 23672)/(50*60))*100)/100
8380 PRINT T; ".MINUTES"
8390 IF INKEY$ = "w" OR INKEY$ = "d"
     THEN GO TO 8390
8400 IF INKEY$ = "" THEN GO TO 8400
8410 CLS : GO TO 8040
```

# Lunar Lander

Copyright (c) Clifford Ramshaw

## DESCRIPTION

-----------

You are the pilot of a remote-control space capsule to be landed on the rough moon surface.

Every time you land unsuccessfully, you will destroy the capsule and also make the landing site impossible to be used again. You have to use another landing site and try again with another capsule.

On successful landing a flag will be raised to signify your claim of territory.

The capsule has a constant momentum build up moving towards the right. At the same time, it is dragged down by the moon gravity.

GOOD LUCK !!

## HOW TO RUN THE PROGRAM

-------------------------

To start the program, type RUN (ENTER).

Use '5' to move to the left, '7' to increase your height.

The space capsule will be moving constantly forwards and at the same time be dragged down by the moon gravity.

You need to land with the two legs of your space capsule exactly on the BLUE CYAN land site to be successful .

## PROGRAM STRUCTURE

-------------------

The program uses the PLOT and DRAW facilities to RANDOMLY draw the landscape for each game.

Special USER DEFINED GRAPHIC CHARACTERs are used to draw the space capsule.

The crashing test of the capsule is based on colour attribute testing.

The structure of the program is as follows:

## INITIALISATION

----------------

```
    SET USER DEFINED GRAPHIC CHARACTERS
11: SET LANDING FLAG TO 0
    GOTO MAIN LOOP
```

MAIN LOOP
---------
```
     SET SCREEN CONTROL VARIABLES
     DRAW LANDSCAPE AND LANDING SITE
     INITIALISE CAPSULE POSITION
L1:  STORE OLD POSITION
     CALCULATE NEW POSITION
     BLANK OLD SHAPE, DRAW NEW SHAPE
     IF CRASH
         draw explosion ( GOSUB 2000 )
         generate sound
         goto     E1:
     IF NOT LANDED
         goto     L1:
     FLASH BORDER, DRAW FLAG, GENERATE SOUND TONE
E1:  PAUSE
     GOTO        I1:
```

SPECIAL NOTES
-------------

     The timing between blanking and drawing of capsule
has to be short in order that the capsule will not be
flashing.
     The paper colour of the display is WHITE (7) and the
ink colour of display is BLACK (0).
     Crash testing of the capsule is based on colour
attributes; for landscape, the attributes are INK RED (2)
PAPER WHITE (7); for landing site, INK BLUE (1) PAPER
CYAN (5).
     Thus, for perfect landing of two legs of the capsule,
the correct testing will be (41+41) on attributes of new
positions for the two bottom legs.
     So, if you want to change the colour attribute of the
landscape or the landing site or the background, then you
will need to adjust the testing value in line 8100 &
8150.

LUNAR LANDER

```
 100 REM LUNAR
 110 REM Lunar▲Lander
 120 RESTORE : ▲ FOR I = 1 TO 16
       : REM initialise▲GRAPHIC
 130 LET S = USR ( CHR$ (144+I-1))
 140 FOR J = 1 TO 8
 150 READ g : POKE (S+J-1), g
 160 NEXT J
 170 NEXT I
 180 DATA 0, 0, 1, 1, 7, 7, 31, 25,
       0, 0, 128, 128, 224, 224, 248, 152,
       53, 107, 127, 243, 96, 96, 192, 192,
       172, 214, 254, 207, 6, 6, 3, 3
 190 DATA 1, 1, 1, 1, 1, 1, 1, 1,
       224, 176, 140, 134, 129, 135, 140, 176,
       1, 1, 7, 1, 7, 7, 31, 25,
       224, 128, 224, 128, 224, 224, 248, 152
 200 DATA 0, 0, 0, 4, 5, 15, 6, 15,
       0, 0, 0, 0, 96, 192, 224, 248,
       27, 7, 3, 6, 0, 0, 0, 0,
       120, 168, 112, 32, 0, 0, 0, 0
 210 DATA 160, 67, 38, 60, 24, 48, 96, 97,
       4, 154, 244, 124, 6, 4, 4, 6,
       194, 96, 32, 36, 104, 120, 79, 193,
       130, 14, 12, 36, 124, 78, 195, 2
 220 LET Ld = 0
 230 GO TO 8000
1000 REM
1010 REM draw▲base▲and▲landshape
1020 LET bx = INT ( RND *21)
       : IF bx < 11 THEN GO TO 1020
1030 LET Lt = bx*8 : LET rt = (bx+4)*8
1040 PRINT AT 21, bx; " GRA SHI 8"
       : PRINT AT 21, bx+1; PAPER 5; INK 1
       ; " GRA SHI 6 INV   GRA SHI 6 IRU "
       : PRINT AT 21, bx+3; " GRA SHI 8"
1050 LET di = -1 : GO SUB 1500
       : REM draw▲left▲of▲landshape
1060 LET di = 1 : GO SUB 1500
       : REM draw▲right▲of▲landshape
1070 RETURN
1500 REM
1510 REM draw▲landshape
1520 REM input▲di
1530 LET Ly = 8+(di = 1)*16
1540 LET Lx = ((rt+24)*(di = 1))+(Lt*(di = -1))
1550 LET up = 255-(di = -1)*255
1560 IF di = 1 THEN PLOT rt, 8
       : DRAW INK 2; 24, 16
1570 PLOT Lx, Ly
1580 LET a = RND
       : LET ry = ((a <= .6)-(a > .6))*
       ( INT ( RND *48)+1)
1590 LET rx = di*( INT ( RND *16)+1)
```

```
1600 IF di*(Lx+rx) > up*di THEN LET rx = up-Lx
1610 IF Ly+ry > 144 OR Ly+ry < 0
       THEN LET ry = 0-ry
1620 LET Lx = Lx+rx : LET Ly = Ly+ry
1630 DRAW INK 2; rx, ry
1640 IF Lx <> up THEN GO TO 1550
1650 RETURN
2000 REM
2010 REM Explosion▴routine
2020 PRINT AT H, X; "▴▴"
2030 FOR J = 1 TO 5
2040 PRINT AT H+1, X; " GRA A GRA B"
       : PRINT AT H+2, X; " GRA C GRA D"
2050 BEEP .05, -( RND *48)
2060 FOR I = 1 TO 10 : NEXT I
2070 PRINT AT H+1, X; " GRA I GRA J"
       : PRINT AT H+2, X; " GRA K GRA L"
2080 BEEP .05, -( RND *48)
2090 FOR I = 1 TO 10 : NEXT I
2100 PRINT AT H+1, X; " GRA M GRA N"
       : PRINT AT H+2, X; " GRA O GRA P"
2110 BEEP .05, -( RND *48)
2120 FOR I = 1 TO 10 : NEXT I
2130 NEXT J
2140 FOR i = h+1 TO 20
       : PRINT AT i-1, x; "▴▴"
       ; AT i, x; " GRA D GRA C"; AT i+1, x; " GRA A GRA B"
       : NEXT i
2150 RETURN
8000 REM
8010 REM MAIN▴control▴loop
8020 BORDER 3 : INK 0 : PAPER 7 : OVER 0 : FLASH 0
       : CLS
8030 GO SUB 1000 : REM draw▴land
8040 LET X = 0 : LET H = X
8050 LET OH = H : LET OX = X
8060 LET X = X+0.5*(X < 30)-( INKEY$ = "5")
8070 LET H = H+0.5-( INKEY$ = "7")*(H > 0)
8080 PRINT AT OH, OX; "▴▴"
       : PRINT AT OH+1, OX; "▴▴"
8090 PRINT AT H, X; " GRA A GRA B"
       : PRINT AT H+1, X; " GRA C GRA D"
8100 LET cr = ATTR (H+2, X)+ ATTR (H+2, X+1)
8110 IF cr < 58 OR cr = 82 OR cr = 112
       THEN GO TO 8140
8120 GO SUB 2000 : REM explode
8130 BEEP .5, 17 : BEEP .5, 15 : BEEP .25, 13
       : BEEP .25, 12 : BEEP .5, 10 : BEEP .25, 13
       : BEEP .25, 12 : GO TO 8210
8140 IF H >= 20 THEN GO TO 8120
8150 IF cr = 82 THEN LET Ld = 1 : GO TO 8170
8160 IF Ld = 0 THEN GO TO 8050
8170 FOR I = 1 TO 6 : PAUSE 25 : BORDER I : NEXT I
       : BORDER 3
8180 PRINT AT 18, bx+1; " GRA E GRA F"
       : PRINT AT 19, bx+1; " GRA G GRA H"
```

62

```
8190 BEEP .125, 12 : BEEP .25, 19 : PAUSE 10
     : BEEP .125, 12 : BEEP .25, 19 : PAUSE 10
     : BEEP .125, 12 : BEEP .25, 19 : PAUSE 10
     : BEEP .125, 12 : BEEP .25, 19 : PAUSE 10
8200 BEEP .25, 12 : BEEP .125, 14 : BEEP .125, 15
     : BEEP .125, 22 : BEEP .125, 22
     : BEEP .125, 15 : BEEP .125, 14
     : BEEP .125, 19 : BEEP .125, 14
     : BEEP .25, 12
8210 FOR I = 1 TO 100 : NEXT I : CLS : GO TO 220
```

# Alien Blitz

Copyright (c) by Clifford Ramshaw

You are the sole defender of the space station. Suddenly
overhead you see them - a convoy of enemy aliens. They must
know of your power because they stay safely out of your
tractor beam reach.

What's this? - slowly one of them separates itself from the
rest of the fleet and swoops down on your position. Is it
possible that it's flapping its wings, or is that a space
illusion?

No time to worry about that - there are missiles falling.
Got to get them, those guys are fast; quick; get out the
tractor beam and pull him in. Got him. But wait - another
alien is detaching himself from the convoy . . .


Programming considerations:
-------------------------------

This program is an arcade game for the Spectrum loosely
based on similar games to be found on video machines.

As such the main programming considerations are speed and
visual effects. Sound is only used when necessary, as it would
slow things down too much otherwise.

Therefore a minimum of work is to be done in each cycle, to
keep speed at a maximum. Only 3 variables are to be updated
each cycle:
        coordinates of swooping alien
        column position of player

The main loop is divided into two cycles, one for wings up
shape and one for wings down shape. This allows the player and
alien to move faster as no decision needs to be made within
the main cycle as to the shape to be drawn.

Colour control codes are used within PRINT strings rather
than separately specifying INK 4, etc., to speed things as
well.


Program Structure:
------------------

| | |
|---|---|
| 100 -340 | Define shapes, draw convoy |
| 500 - 630 | First part of cycle |
| | update all positions |
| 650 - 790 | Second part of cycle |
| 1000 - 1440 | Successful hits by player or alien |
| 1500 - 1540 | Destruction of enemy convoy |

ALIEN BLITZ

```
100 DATA 14, 31, 28, 24, 16, 16, 16, 16, 112, 248,
    56, 24, 8, 8, 8, 8 :
    REM wings▲resting▲shape▲-AB
110 DATA 3, 15, 63, 127, 127, 127, 255, 227, 192,
    240, 252, 254, 254, 254, 255, 199 :
    REM top▲half▲body▲shape▲-▲CD
120 DATA 227, 227, 99, 99, 127, 63, 7, 0, 199, 199,
    198, 198, 254, 252, 224, 0 :
    REM bottom▲half▲body▲shape▲-▲EF
130 DATA 240, 112, 56, 248, 124, 62, 255, 30, 15,
    14, 28, 31, 62, 124, 255, 120, 7, 0, 0, 0, 0,
    0, 0, 0, 224, 0, 0, 0, 0, 0, 0, 0 :
    REM wings▲up▲shape▲-GHIJ
140 DATA 0, 0, 0, 0, 0, 0, 0, 7, 0, 0, 0, 0, 0, 0,
    0, 224, 30, 255, 62, 124, 248, 56, 112, 240,
    120, 255, 124, 62, 31, 28, 14, 15 :
    REM wings▲down▲shape▲-▲KLMN
150 DATA 16, 16, 16, 16, 24, 28, 31, 14, 8, 8, 8,
    8, 24, 56, 248, 112 :
    REM shape▲of▲falling▲wings▲-▲OP
160 DATA 0, 0, 12, 15, 31, 63, 127, 255, 24, 60,
    60, 255, 255, 255, 231, 129, 0, 0, 48, 240,
    248, 252, 254, 255 :
    REM shape▲of▲laser▲base▲-QRS
170 DATA 66, 66, 38, 27, 15, 7, 3, 1, 66, 66, 100,
    216, 240, 224, 192, 128 :
    REM shape▲of▲enemy▲bullets▲-▲TU
180 FOR i = USR " GRA A" TO USR " GRA A"+167
190 READ x : POKE i, x
200 NEXT i
210 BORDER 7 : PAPER 7 : INK 0 : OVER 0 : CLS
220 LET v = 21
230 LET s = 1
240 LET g = 5
250 LET x = 3+4*s
260 LET y = 0
270 PRINT TAB x;
280 FOR i = 1 TO 5-s
290 PRINT "▲ EXI SHI 2 GRA C GRA D▲▲";
300 NEXT i
310 PRINT : PRINT TAB x;
320 FOR i = 1 TO 5-s
330 PRINT " EXI SHI 4 GRA A EXI SHI 2 GRA E
    GRA F EXI SHI 4 GRA B▲";
340 NEXT i
500 LET g = g+(g < 27)*( INKEY$ = "c")-(g > 1)*
    ( INKEY$ = "z")
510 PRINT AT v, g; "▲ EXI SHI 2 GRA Q GRA R
    GRA S▲"; AT y, x; "▲▲▲▲";
    AT y+1, x; "▲▲▲▲";
520 LET x = x+(y > 3)-(y < 4)+2*
    SGN (g-x)*( RND > .5) : IF x > 28 THEN
    LET x = 0
```

65

```
530 LET y = y+1
540 PRINT AT y, x; " EXI SHI O GRA G EXI SHI 1
    GRA C GRA D EXI SHI O GRA H"; AT y+1, x;
    " GRA I EXI SHI 1 GRA E GRA F EXI SHI O
    GRA J"
550 IF y = v-2 THEN GO TO 1400
560 IF RND > .15 THEN GO TO 600
570 FOR i = y+2 TO v-1 : BEEP .02, v-i :
    PRINT AT i, x+1; "▲▲"; AT i+1, x+1;
    " GRA T GRA U" : NEXT i
580 PRINT AT i, x+1; "▲▲"
590 IF g = x OR g = x-1 THEN GO TO 1300
600 IF INKEY$ <> "m" THEN GO TO 650
610 LET m = 150 : IF g = x OR g = x-1 THEN
    LET m = 157-8*y
620 PLOT 19+8*g, 8 : DRAW 0, m : BEEP .1, 0 :
    IF m < 150 THEN GO TO 1000
630 DRAW INVERSE 1; 0, 1 : DRAW INVERSE 1; 0, -m-1
640 REM second▲cycle
650 LET g = g+(g < 27)*( INKEY$ = "c")-(g > 1)*
    ( INKEY$ = "z")
660 PRINT AT v, g; "▲ EXI SHI 2 GRA Q GRA R
    GRA S▲"; AT y, x; "▲▲▲▲";
    AT y+1, x; "▲▲▲▲"
670 LET x = x+(y > 3)-(y < 4)+2*
    SGN (g-x)*( RND > .5) : IF x > 28 THEN
    LET x = 0
680 LET y = y+1
690 PRINT AT y, x; " EXI SHI O GRA K EXI SHI 1
    GRA C GRA D EXI SHI O GRA L"; AT y+1, x;
    " GRA M EXI SHI 1 GRA E GRA F
    EXI SHI O GRA N"
700 IF y = v-2 THEN GO TO 1400
710 IF RND > .15 THEN GO TO 750
720 FOR i = y+2 TO v-1 : BEEP .01, v-i :
    PRINT AT i, x+1; "▲▲"; AT i+1, x+1;
    " GRA T GRA U" : NEXT i
730 PRINT AT i, x+1; "▲▲"
740 IF g = x OR g = x-1 THEN GO TO 1300
750 IF INKEY$ <> "m" THEN GO TO 500
760 LET m = 150 : IF g = x OR g = x-1 THEN
    LET m = 157-8*y
770 PLOT 19+8*g, 8 : DRAW 0, m : BEEP .1, 0 :
    IF m < 150 THEN GO TO 1000
780 DRAW INVERSE 1; 0, 1 : DRAW INVERSE 1; 0, -m-1
790 GO TO 500
1000 FOR y = y+1 TO v-2
1005 BEEP .02, y/2
1010 PRINT AT y-1, x; "▲▲▲▲"; AT y, x;
     " EXI SHI 2 GRA O EXI SHI 6 GRA C GRA D
     EXI SHI 2 GRA P EXI SHI O"; AT y+1, x;
     "▲ EXI SHI 6 GRA E GRA F EXI SHI O▲"
1015 NEXT y
1020 PRINT AT y-1, x; "▲▲▲▲"
1200 LET s = s+1
1210 PRINT AT y. x; "▲▲▲▲"; AT y+1, x;
```

```
          "▲▲▲▲"; AT 0, 0;   : IF s < 5 THEN
          GO TO 250
1220 IF s = 5 THEN GO TO 1500
1300 PRINT AT v, g+1; " GRA Q GRA R GRA S"; OVER 1;
          AT v, x+1; " GRA T GRA U" : FOR i = 1 TO 11 :
          BEEP .1, -10 : PRINT OVER 1; AT v, g;
          "▲ GRA Q GRA R GRA S" : BEEP .02, 4 : NEXT i
1310 PAUSE 50
1320 CLS
1330 RUN 220
1400 PRINT AT y, x; "▲▲▲▲"; AT y+1, x;
          "▲▲▲▲"; AT 0, 0;
1410 IF ABS (x-g) > 1 THEN GO TO 250
1420 PRINT AT v, g+1; " EXI SHI 2 GRA Q GRA R
          GRA S"; OVER 1; AT y+1, x; " EXI SHI O
          GRA G EXI SHI 1 GRA C GRA D EXI SHI O
          GRA H"; AT y+2, x; " EXI SHI 1 GRA I GRA E
          GRA F GRA J" : FOR i = 1 TO 11 :
          BEEP .1, -10 : PRINT OVER 1; AT v, g;
          " EXI SHI ▲ GRA Q GRA R GRA S" :
          BEEP .02, 4 : NEXT i
1430 PAUSE 50
1440 RUN 100
1500 PRINT AT 5, 0; "Congratulations▲-▲you▲have
          ▲▲▲▲▲▲destroyed▲the▲entire▲enemy
          ▲fleet"
1510 BEEP .3, 1 : BEEP .05, 0 : BEEP .05, -1 :
          BEEP .5, 9 : BEEP .05, 0 : BEEP .05, -1 :
          BEEP .6, 1 : BEEP .5, 10
1520 PRINT FLASH 1; PAPER 2; INK 7; AT 10, 0;
          "WATCH▲OUT▲-▲HERE▲THEY▲COME▲AGAIN"
1530 FOR i = 1 TO 3 : BEEP 1, 20 : BEEP .1, 0 :
          NEXT i
1540 RUN 100
```

# Spectrum Invaders

Copyright (c) by Beam Software

It's hard to believe, but the all-time favourite arcade game, the one that started the whole concept of arcade games, and is still one of the most popular around the world is available right here on your Spectrum.

This version of Spectrum Invaders features
* 24 invaders moving from side to side
* animated invaders – watch them move!
* shields to hide behind
* dangerous enemy bombs
* laser fire power
* continuous score update
* sound effects
* increasing difficulty with each wave

To play the program, use the "X" and "C" keys to move the laser base left and right, and the "M" key to fire your missile.

It is your responsibility to defend the planet, earthling!

Programming considerations:
----------------------------

One of the problems with trying to write a BASIC program for this type of arcade game are the very high number of variables required, together with the demands of fast action.

It would not be possible to write a BASIC program of this type, keeping track of 27 pairs of variables (x,y coordinates of 24 invaders, laser base, enemy bomb and laser blast) and still have a reasonable arcade game. It would be doubly difficult to have them animated as well, and to keep track of which invader had been hit, for example.

This program makes use of two features of the Spectrum, which together make this amazing program possible:
* Printing a very long string is not much slower than printing a shorter string. It is certainly much faster than printing a number of strings.
* It is possible to use the unique string slicing facility on the Spectrum to assign part of a string. ie one can say, for example:
LET a$ (2 TO 6) = "HELLO"

The core of the program therefore lies in two strings, and the manipulation of these two strings, a$ and b$. the string a$ is used to keep all 24 invaders, print them, etc. For all intents and purposes, b$ is the same as a$, in that it will always be the same length as a$, have as many invaders in it, etc., but b$ contains the same invaders in a slightly different posture. By alternating rapidly between a$ and b$, the invaders appear to move their arms in and out, move their legs, and so on.

By printing a$ (and b$) in various positions, we can print in one hit all the invaders, and automatically take care of the undrawing problems (as the new printing will overwrite the old positions).

Should an invader get hit by a laser blast, the invader is replaced by blanks within the string using the string slicing technique described above. Regularly as well, the end of the string is checked to see if contains all blanks (ie all invaders in the bottom row have been killed). If that is the case, string slicing is used again to shorten the string to its new maximum length.

This not only prevents any potential problems with printing beyond the bottom of the screen, but give an immediate test as to whether the laser base has been overrun. A small by-product is that as the string gets smaller, it takes less time to print and the game speeds up a little towards the end!


Program structure:
-------------------

| | |
|---|---|
| 100 -160 | Define graphic characters |
| 200 -625 | Initialisation<br>The main task is to build up a$ and b$<br>using subroutine at 9000 - 9030 |
| 1000 -1200 | First part of main loop<br>a$ is printed, laser blast is updated,<br>laser base position unpdated if required<br>enemy bomb position updated |
| 2000 - 2999 | Second part of main loop<br>same as first part but with b$<br>also new enemy bomb creation |
| 3000 - 3530 | Change of direction for invaders<br>a$ checked for possible slicing |
| 5000 - 5220 | Effect of laser blast hit |
| 6000 - 6530 | Effect of enemy bomb hit |
| 8500 - 8550 | End of game |

```
100 DATA 0, 31, 63, 63, 123, 113, 225, 225, 0, 248,
      252, 252, 222, 142, 135, 135, 255, 127, 111,
      111, 199, 192, 240, 240, 255, 254, 246, 246,
      227, 3, 15, 15
110 DATA 7, 63, 127, 65, 193, 199, 255, 124, 224,
      252, 254, 131, 131, 227, 254, 62, 124, 127,
      51, 48, 112, 88, 136, 248, 254, 204, 142, 26,
      17, 31, 0, 0
120 DATA 31, 63, 63, 115, 113, 225, 225, 255, 248,
      252, 252, 206, 142, 135, 135, 255, 127, 111,
      103, 103, 96, 48, 60, 60, 254, 246, 230, 230,
      6, 12, 60, 60
130 DATA 7, 63, 127, 193, 193, 199, 127, 124, 224,
      252, 254, 130, 131, 227, 255, 62, 127, 51,
      113, 88, 136, 248, 0, 0, 62, 254, 204, 12, 14,
      26, 17, 31
140 DATA 24, 24, 24, 24, 60, 126, 231, 231, 7, 31,
      63, 60, 112, 112, 248, 248, 224, 248, 252, 60,
      14, 14, 31, 31
150 DATA 18, 26, 14, 14, 7, 3, 1, 0, 36, 44, 56, 56,
      112, 96, 192, 128
160 FOR i = USR "a" TO USR "a"+167 : READ x :
      POKE i, x : NEXT i
200 BORDER 7 : PAPER 7 : INK 0 : CLS
210 PRINT AT 0, 0; "score"; AT 0, 23; "lives.^^^"
220 LET f = 2
230 LET sc = 0
250 LET q = f : LET f = f+1 : IF f = 11 THEN STOP
300 LET c$ = ".▲▲▲▲▲▲▲▲▲▲▲▲▲▲▲▲▲▲
      ▲▲▲▲▲▲▲▲▲▲▲▲▲▲▲"
310 LET s = 144
320 GO SUB 9000
330 LET k$ = a$+b$+c$
340 GO SUB 9000
350 LET l$ = a$+b$+c$
360 GO SUB 9000
370 LET m$ = a$+b$+c$
380 GO SUB 9000
390 LET n$ = a$+b$+c$
400 LET a$ = k$+l$+k$+l$ : LET a$ = a$( TO 343)
410 LET b$ = m$+n$+m$+n$ : LET b$ = b$( TO 343)
500 LET k$ = " GRA 4 GRA SHI 4 GRA 3
      GRA 7 GRA SHI 7▲▲▲" :
      LET l$ = " GRA SHI 6 GRA SHI 6 GRA 3
      GRA 6 GRA 6▲▲▲" :
      LET m$ = " GRA 7 GRA 2. GRA 1
      GRA SHI 4▲▲▲" : LET n$ = ""
510 PRINT INK 4; AT 16, 2; k$; k$; k$; k$; l$; l$;
      l$; l$; m$; m$; m$; m$
590 LET L = 0
600 LET r = 0 : LET s = 10 : LET t = 1
610 LET u = 0 : LET v = 0 : LET x = 0 : LET y = 0
615 LET d = 21 : LET e = 12
```

```
 620 PRINT AT 20, 30; c$
 625 LET Li = 3
1000 FOR p = r TO s STEP t
1010 BEEP .005, 1 : PRINT AT q, 0; c$( TO p); a$;
     AT 20, L; ". GRA Q
     ▲▲▲▲▲▲▲▲▲▲▲▲▲▲▲▲▲▲▲▲▲
     ▲▲▲▲▲▲▲▲▲ GRA R GRA 3 GRA S▲"
1020 IF u < q THEN GO TO 1050
1035 IF SCREEN$ (u, v) <> "▲" THEN GO SUB 5000
1040 IF u >= q THEN PRINT AT u, v; " GRA Q";
     AT u+1, v; "▲"
1050 LET L = L+(L < 28)*( INKEY$ = "c")-(L > 0)
     *( INKEY$ = "z")
1060 IF u > q-1 OR INKEY$ <> "m" THEN GO TO 1100
1070 LET u = 20 : LET v = L+1
1100 IF d > 20 THEN GO TO 1200
1110 IF SCREEN$ (d, e) <> "▲" THEN GO SUB 6000
1115 IF SCREEN$ (d, e+1) <> "▲" THEN GO SUB 6000
1120 IF d <= 20 THEN PRINT AT d-1, e; "▲▲"; INK 2;
     AT d, e; " GRA T GRA U"
1200 LET u = u-1
2010 PRINT AT q, 0; c$( TO p); b$; AT 20, L;
     ". GRA Q▲▲▲▲▲▲▲▲▲▲▲▲▲▲▲▲▲▲▲▲
     ▲▲▲▲▲▲▲▲▲▲▲▲▲▲
     GRA R GRA 3 GRA S▲"
2020 IF u < q THEN GO TO 2050
2035 IF SCREEN$ (u, v) <> "▲" THEN GO SUB 5000
2040 IF u >= q THEN PRINT AT u, v; " GRA Q";
     AT u+1, v; "▲"
2050 LET L = L+(L < 28)*( INKEY$ = "c")-(L > 0)
     *( INKEY$ = "z")
2060 IF u > q-1 OR INKEY$ <> "m" THEN GO TO 2100
2070 LET u = 20 : LET v = L+1
2100 IF d <= 20 THEN GO TO 2130
2110 LET w = INT (6* RND ) :
     LET x$ = a$( LEN a$-4*w-2) :
     IF x$ <> " GRA C" AND x$ <> " GRA G" THEN
     GO TO 2130
2120 LET d = q+1+ INT ( LEN a$/32) :
     LET e = p-4*w+20+t
2125 IF e = 31 THEN LET e = 30
2130 IF d = 20 THEN PRINT AT 20, e; "▲▲"
2200 LET u = u-1
2210 LET d = d+1
2999 NEXT p
3000 IF t = -1 THEN GO TO 3500
3010 LET t = -1 : LET r = 9 : LET s = 0
3020 GO TO 1000
3500 IF LEN a$ > 55 THEN GO TO 3510
3505 IF a$(23 TO ) = c$ THEN GO TO 250
3510 IF a$( LEN a$-32 TO ) = c$ THEN
     LET a$ = a$( TO LEN a$-96) :
     LET b$ = b$( TO LEN a$)
3520 IF 32*q+ LEN a$ > 609 THEN GO TO 8500
3525 LET r = 0 : LET s = 10 : LET t = 1
3530 PRINT AT q, 0; c$ : LET q = q+1 : GO TO 1000
```

```
5000 IF ATTR (u, v) = 60 THEN GO TO 5100
5005 IF ATTR (u, v) = 58 THEN GO TO 6000
5010 LET h = v-p+32*(u-q-1)
5015 BEEP .05, 8
5020 IF h >= 0 THEN GO SUB 5200
5030 LET h = h+32 : IF h < LEN a$ THEN GO SUB 5200
5040 LET h = h+32 : IF h < LEN a$ THEN GO SUB 5200
5050 LET h = 4- INT (h/96)
5060 LET sc = sc+100*h : PRINT AT 0, 6; sc
5100 REM create▲an▲explosion
5110 PRINT INK 6; AT u, v; " GRA B GRA A";
        AT u+1, v; " GRA S GRA R" : BEEP .05, 10 :
        PRINT AT u, v; "▲▲"; AT u+1, v; "▲▲"
5120 LET u = 0
5130 RETURN
5200 IF h = 0 THEN LET h = 1
5205 LET a$(h TO h+2) = "▲▲▲"
5210 LET b$(h TO h+2) = "▲▲▲"
5220 RETURN
6000 REM look▲where▲alien▲bullet▲hit
6005 IF d = 20 THEN GO TO 6018
6010 PRINT AT d-1, e; "▲▲"; INK 2; AT d, e;
        " GRA A GRA B" : BEEP .05, -10 :
        PRINT AT d, e; "▲▲"
6012 IF (v = e OR v = e+1) AND d = u THEN
        PRINT AT u, v; "▲"; AT u+1, v; "▲" :
        LET u = 0
6015 LET d = 21 : RETURN
6020 PRINT AT d-1, e; "▲▲"; INK 2; AT d, e;
        " GRA A GRA B" : BEEP .05, 10 :
        PRINT AT d, e; "▲▲"
6030 FOR k = 1 TO 10 : PRINT OVER 1; AT 21, L;
        " GRA R GRA 3 GRA S" : BEEP .1, 0 : NEXT k
6040 LET Li = Li-1
6050 PRINT AT 0, 29; "▲▲▲"; AT 0, 29;
        "^^^"( TO Li)
6060 IF Li = 0 THEN GO TO 8510
6500 REM missiles▲hit▲each▲other
6510 IF d <= 20 THEN PRINT INK 6; AT d, e;
        " GRA B GRA A"; AT d+1, e; " GRA S GRA R" :
        BEEP .05, 10 : PRINT AT d, e; "▲▲";
        AT d+1, e; "▲▲"
6520 LET u = 0 : LET d = 21
6530 RETURN
8500 PRINT AT q, 0; c$; a$
8510 PRINT AT 5, 0; "▲▲The▲aliens▲have▲overrun
        ▲you." : PRINT "▲▲All▲is▲lost."
8520 INPUT "Do▲you▲want▲to▲try▲again?"; n$
8530 IF LEN n$ = 0 THEN GO TO 8520
8540 IF n$(1) = "y" OR n$(1) = "Y" THEN RUN 200
8550 STOP
9000 LET a$ = CHR$ (s)+ CHR$ (s+1)+"▲▲" :
        LET a$ = a$+a$+a$+a$+"▲▲▲▲▲▲▲▲"
9010 LET b$ = CHR$ (s+2)+ CHR$ (s+3)+"▲▲" :
        LET b$ = b$+b$+b$+b$+b$+b$+"▲▲▲▲▲▲▲▲"
9020 LET s = s+4
9030 RETURN
```

# Meteor Storm

Copyright (c) by Beam Software

METEOR STORM places you at the controls of a space craft hurtling through the asteroid belt. On your display you see the pleasant view of the solar system as seen from mid space.

In the distance, you can see Saturn with its rings, and beyond that the many stars of nearby galaxies.

Suddenly command control warns you of a METEOR STORM! Before your very eyes, you see a meteor growing in size as it heads directly for your ship! To confirm the desparate situation, your on-board radar shows the approach of the asteroid.

METEOR STORM is 3-Dimensional computer gaming at its most exciting.

Running the program:
--------------------

After you press (RUN) (ENTER), you will see the familiar console display come to life.

A cross hair in the middle of the screen marks the direction your laser beam is aimed at. To manipulate the beam, use the following controls:
    "I" and "P" to move left or right
    "W" and "X" to move up and down
    "O" to fire
Note that as with most BASIC programs, only one key can be pressed at a time.

The cross hair control features full wrap-around - in other words, going too far to the right will bring you to the left of the screen, and so on.

You can fire at any time, but missing the asteroid results only in the dull sound of the laser hurtling into the void. A hit on any part of the asteroid however will see it being thrown back beyond danger.

As you penetrate deeper into the METEOR STORM, they start coming at you faster and faster. How many can you shoot with only three lives?

Programming considerations:
---------------------------

This program makes extensive use of the OVER facility of the Spectrum, as well as demonstrating the re-useability of the user defined graphics characters.

At the beginning of the program, user defined graphics are used to draw the shape of the spaceship console, the radar display ship and the planet Saturn. This is the only time in the entire program they are drawn! In fact, immediately afterwards, the user defined graphics characters which made up the picture are re-used to define the asteroid shapes!

This works because the display on the screen is not dependent on those characters - once anything is written onto the screen memory, by whatever means, it will stay there until something overwrites it.

The immense advantage of the OVER facility now becomes obvious. By keeping very clear controls on what has been written, and making sure to erase it only by overwriting exactly the same thing at the same spot again, we can keep all the original information on the screen in its original format.

(The way OVER works is that by writing the same thing OVER a second time, it will become erased, leaving whatever was underneath it originally intact - try it!)


Structure of the program:
-------------------------------

| | |
|---|---|
| 100 - 200 | Definition of characters, as follows: |
| | Round corners |
| | Spaceship as seen on radar |
| | Saturn |
| | Shapes for small meteors I (ABCD) |
| | Shapes for small meteors II (EFG) |
| | Shapes for meteors III (HIJK) |
| | Shapes for meteors IV (LM) |
| | Shape for explosion I (NOP) |
| | Shape for explosion II (QRS) |
| | |
| 200 - 340 | Set up console screen |
| | |
| 400 - 590 | Define characters again and initialisation. FLash message |
| | The main time consuming task is taken up with defining b$, an array with random meteor shape used in final collision explosion display. |
| | Useful variables are: |

| | | |
|---|---|---|
| | x, y | position of crosshair |
| | ox, oy | old position of crosshair |
| | li | number of lives |
| | ms | meteor stage (range 0 - 9) |
| | di | difficulty level |
| | mx, my | position of meteor |
| | v | ink colour under crosshair |

| | |
|---|---|
| 900 - 1100 | Main loop |

Test keyboard, move crosshair

1200 - 1500    Laser blast

3000 - 3100    Subroutine to update radar

4000 - 4880    Subroutines to print meteor in various
               sizes

5000 - end     Routine to handle collision with meteor


Special notes:
---------------

   The extensive use of DATA statements that this program
makes is very expensive on memory, and this program would not
fit within a 16K Spectrum if we did not take special steps to
reduce the memory usage of this program.

   For example, each number in a DATA statement is stored in
memory not only as the characters you type in but ALSO as a
6-byte sequence which is in a format suitable for the
Spectrum ROM to operate. In other words, a DATA string with
32 numbers takes up 6 bytes for the line number, etc
information, about 100 bytes for the characters typed in, and
a further 200 bytes because of the way the computer stores
this information.

   This 6 byte cost of entering numbers is present in all
BASIC statements, not just DATA statements. You will
therefore note that this program defines the two most
commonly used numbers, 0 and 1, right at the beginning as
variables, and these are used throughout the program.

   The saving in memory is enormous - each number now only
requires two bytes, including the comma separating numbers.

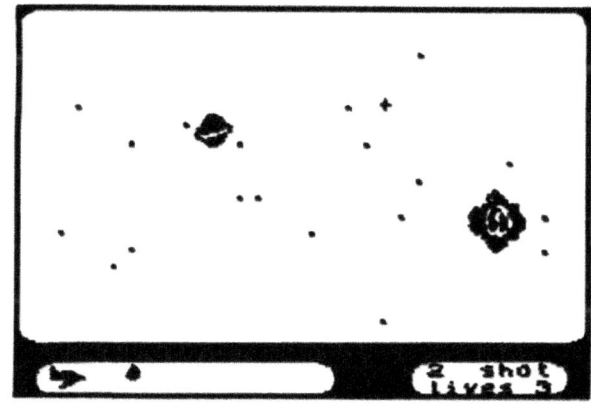

METEOR

```
  90 LET z = 0 : LET u = 1
 100 DATA 255, 248, 224, 192, 192, 128, 128, 128,
     255, 31, 7, 3, 3, u, u, u, 128, 128, 128,
     192, 192, 224, 248, 255, u, u, u, 3, 3, 7, 31,
     255
 110 DATA z, z, 128, 192, 231, 255, 255, 255, z, z,
     z, z, 192, 240, 60, 255, u, 3, 7, 14, z, z,
     z, z, 240, 224, 128, z, z, z, z, z
 120 DATA z, 3, 7, 15, 15, 31, 31, 127, z, 192, 240,
     248, 248, 254, 253, 249, 127, 220, 192, 115,
     31, 7, 3, z, 195, 4, 60, 248, 248, 240, 192, z
 130 DATA z, z, u, 3, 7, 7, 7, 2, z, 4, 6, 15, 31,
     31, 63, 14, z, 4, 14, 31, 63, 63, 63, 31, 30,
     30, 28, 12, z, z, z, z
 140 DATA 31, 63, 31, 31, 15, 6, z, z, z, z, z, z,
     128, 192, 224, 224, 224, 224, 224, 192, z, z,
     z, z
 150 DATA 3, 23, 55, 63, 127, 127, 127, 127, 128,
     224, 240, 240, 224, 248, 248, 252, 127, 63,
     63, 127, 63, 31, 11, z, 252, 252, 248, 224,
     240, 224, 128, z
 160 DATA 63, 127, 255, 127, 255, 255, 127, 63, 252,
     248, 252, 254, 254, 248, 248, 252
 170 DATA 195, 153, 60, 102, 102, 60, 153, 195, 195,
     99, 39, 60, 60, 180, 231, 231, 128, 60, 230,
     255, 91, 200, 221, 119
 180 DATA 38, 62, 246, 254, 108, 71, 227, 62, 115,
     55, 246, 180, 28, 188, 246, 99, 221, 118,
     103, 238, 184, 115, 255, 128
 200 BORDER 5 : INK 5 : PAPER 6 : CLS
 210 RESTORE 100
 220 FOR i = USR "a" TO USR "m"-u
 230 READ x : POKE i, x : NEXT i
 240 DIM s(10)
 300 PRINT AT z, z; " GRA A"; AT z, 31; " GRA B";
     AT 18, z; " GRA C"; AT 18, 31; " GRA D"
 310 PRINT
     " GRA SHI 8 GRA SHI 8 GRA SHI 8 GRA SHI 8
     GRA SHI 8 GRA SHI 8 GRA SHI 8 GRA SHI 8
     GRA SHI 8 GRA SHI 8 GRA SHI 8 GRA SHI 8
     GRA SHI 8 GRA SHI 8 GRA SHI 8 GRA SHI 8
     GRA SHI 8 GRA SHI 8 GRA SHI 8 GRA SHI 8
     GRA SHI 8 GRA SHI 8 GRA SHI 8 GRA SHI 8
     GRA SHI 8 GRA SHI 8 GRA SHI 8 GRA SHI 8
     GRA SHI 8 GRA SHI 8 GRA SHI 8 GRA SHI 8"
     : PRINT " GRA SHI 8 GRA A▲▲▲▲▲▲▲▲▲▲
     ▲▲▲▲▲▲ GRA B GRA SHI 8
     GRA SHI 8 GRA SHI 8 GRA SHI 8 GRA A
     ▲▲▲▲▲▲▲▲ GRA B GRA SHI 8
     GRA SHI 8 GRA C▲▲▲▲▲▲▲▲▲▲
     ▲▲▲▲▲▲ GRA D GRA SHI 8
     GRA SHI 8 GRA SHI 8 GRA SHI 8 GRA C
     ▲▲▲▲▲▲▲▲ GRA D GRA SHI 8"
```

```
320 PRINT INK z; AT 20, 2; " GRA E GRA F";
    AT 21, 2; " GRA G GRA H"; AT 21, 23;
    "lives.3"
330 FOR i = u TO 20 : PRINT INK 2;
    AT u+16* RND , u+29* RND ; "." : NEXT i
340 PRINT INK 3; AT 6, 10; " GRA I GRA J";
    AT 7, 10; " GRA K GRA L"
400 FOR i = USR "a" TO USR "t"-u
410 READ x : POKE i, x : NEXT i
420 PRINT OVER u; FLASH u; INK 2; AT 10, 4;
    "PREPARE.FOR.FLIGHT.INTO"; AT 11, 10;
    "METEOR.STORM"
430 LET b$ = "" : FOR j = u TO 17
435 BEEP .05, z
440 LET a$ = ".."
450 FOR i = u TO 15
460 IF RND > .6 THEN
    LET a$ = a$+ CHR$ (144+12* RND )
470 LET a$ = a$+".."
475 BEEP .005, 10
480 NEXT i
490 LET b$ = b$+a$( TO 29)+"." : NEXT j
500 PRINT OVER u; FLASH z; AT 10, 4;
    "PREPARE.FOR.FLIGHT.INTO"; AT 11, 10;
    "METEOR.STORM"
520 LET ox = 9 : LET oy = 15 : LET ov = 5
530 LET x = 9 : LET y = 15 : LET v = 7
540 INK z : PRINT AT x, y; "+"
550 LET Li = 3 : LET di = u : LET nm = z
560 LET ms = z : LET nm = nm+u
580 LET mx = u+ RND *17 : LET my = u+ RND *29
590 LET mi = u
900 LET a$ = INKEY$
910 LET ms = ms+di /7+nm/50
920 IF INT ms = 9 THEN GO TO 5000
930 GO SUB 3000
940 GO SUB 4000+100* INT ms
950 LET w = ATTR (x, y)-8* INT ( ATTR (x, y)/8) :
    IF w <> 0 THEN LET v = w
960 IF a$ = "" OR a$ = "0" THEN GO TO 1070
1000 LET y = oy+(a$ = "p")-(a$ = "i")
1010 IF y < u THEN LET y = 30
1020 IF y > 30 THEN LET y = u
1030 LET x = ox+(a$ = "x")-(a$ = "w")
1040 IF x < u THEN LET x = 17
1050 IF x > 17 THEN LET x = u
1060 LET v = ATTR (x, y)-8* INT ( ATTR (x, y)/8)
1070 PRINT OVER u; INK ov; AT ox, oy; "+"; INK z;
    AT x, y; "+"
1090 LET ox = x : LET oy = y : LET ov = v
1100 IF a$ <> "0" THEN GO TO 900
1200 FOR i = u TO 6 : BEEP i*i/100, 10/i : NEXT i
1250 IF v <> u THEN GO TO 900
1260 LET x1 = x-u : IF x1 < z THEN LET x1 = z
1270 LET y1 = y-u : IF y1 < z THEN LET y1 = z
1275 LET x2 = x+u : IF x2 > 18 THEN LET x2 = 18
```

```
1280 OVER u : FOR i = u TO 10 : BEEP .03, 3 :
      PRINT AT x, y; " GRA N" : BEEP .01, u :
      PRINT AT x1, y1; " GRA O GRA P GRA O";
      AT x, y1; " GRA Q GRA N GRA Q"; AT x2, y1;
      " GRA R GRA S GRA R" : NEXT i : OVER z
1290 DIM s(10) : LET mi = 2
1300 FOR i = INT ms TO z STEP -u
1310 LET ms = i : GO SUB 4000+100*i : GO SUB 3000
1320 NEXT i
1340 DIM s(10)
1360 LET ov = z : LET v = z
1370 PRINT INK z; OVER z; AT 20, 23; nm+Li-3;
      AT 20, 26; "shot"
1380 PRINT OVER u; INK 3; AT 6, 10; "▲▲";
      AT 7, 10; "▲▲"
1500 GO TO 560
3000 IF INT ms < 4 THEN PRINT INK u; AT 20, 14-ms;
      "▲ GRA B▲"
3010 IF INT ms = 4 THEN PRINT INK u; AT 20, 9;
      "▲▲ GRA B▲▲"
3020 IF INT ms > 4 AND INT ms < 8 THEN PRINT INK u;
      AT 20, 18-2* INT ms; "▲▲ GRA B▲▲"
3030 IF INT ms = 8 THEN PRINT INK u; AT 20, 4;
      " GRA B▲▲"
3040 RETURN
4000 IF s(1) = u THEN RETURN
4010 PRINT OVER u; INK mi; AT mx, my; " GRA A"
4020 LET s(1) = u
4030 RETURN
4100 IF s(2) = u THEN RETURN
4110 PRINT OVER u; INK mi; AT mx, my; " GRA B"
4120 LET s(2) = u
4130 RETURN
4200 IF s(3) = u THEN RETURN
4210 PRINT OVER u; INK mi; AT mx, my;
      " GRA B GRA F"
4220 LET s(3) = u
4230 RETURN
4300 IF s(4) = u THEN RETURN
4310 LET mx4 = mx+u
4320 PRINT OVER u; INK mi; AT mx, my;
      " GRA B GRA F"; AT mx4, my; " GRA D"
4330 LET s(4) = u
4340 RETURN
4400 IF s(5) = u THEN RETURN
4410 PRINT OVER u; INK mi; AT mx, my; " GRA C";
      AT mx4, my; " GRA E"
4420 LET s(5) = u
4430 RETURN
4500 IF s(6) = u THEN RETURN
4510 PRINT OVER u; INK mi; AT mx, my;
      " GRA C GRA F"; AT mx4, my; " GRA E GRA G"
4520 LET s(6) = u
4530 RETURN
4600 IF s(7) = u THEN RETURN
4610 PRINT OVER u; INK mi; AT mx, my;
```

```
          "  GRA H GRA I"; AT mx4, my; "  GRA J GRA K"
4620 LET s(7) = u
4630 RETURN
4700 IF s(8) = u THEN RETURN
4710 LET mx2 = mx-u
4720 LET my6 = my+2 : IF my6 > 31 THEN LET my6 = 31
4730 LET mx5 = mx+2 : IF mx5 > 18 THEN LET mx5 = 18
4740 LET my3 = my-u
4750 PRINT OVER u; INK mi; AT mx2, my; "  GRA C GRA
         ; AT mx, my3; "  GRA C GRA SHI 8 GRA SHI 8"
         ; AT mx, my6; "  GRA F"; AT mx4, my3;
          "  GRA E GRA SHI 8 GRA SHI 8"; AT mx4, my6;
          "  GRA 6"; AT mx5, my; "  GRA E GRA 6"
4760 LET s(8) = u
4770 RETURN
4800 IF s(9) = u THEN RETURN
4810 LET mx1 = mx-2 : IF mx1 < z THEN LET mx1 = z
4820 LET my2 = my-2 : IF my < z THEN LET my = z
4830 LET my7 = my+3 : IF my7 > 31 THEN LET my7 = 31
4840 LET mx6 = mx+3 : IF mx6 > 18 THEN LET mx6 = 18
4850 LET mx6 = mx+3 : IF mx6 > 18 THEN LET mx6 = 18
4860 PRINT OVER u; INK mi; AT mx1, my;
          "  GRA C GRA F"; AT mx2, my3;
          "  GRA H GRA SHI 8 GRA SHI 8"; AT mx2, my6;
          "  GRA I"; AT mx, my2; "  GRA C"; AT mx, my3;
          "  GRA SHI 8 GRA SHI 8 GRA SHI 8";
         AT mx, my6;
          "  GRA SHI 8"; AT mx, my7; "  GRA F";
         AT mx4, my2; "  GRA E"; AT mx4, my3;
          "  GRA SHI 8 GRA SHI 8 GRA SHI 8";
         AT mx4, my6;
          "  GRA SHI 8"; AT mx4, my7; "  GRA G";
         AT mx5, my3; "  GRA J GRA SHI 8 GRA SHI 8";
         AT mx5, my6; "  GRA K"; AT mx6, my;
          "  GRA E GRA 6"
4870 LET s(9) = u
4880 RETURN
5000 FOR i = z TO 16
5010 PRINT OVER u; FLASH u; AT i+u, u;
        b$(30*i+u TO 30*i+30)
5020 NEXT i
5030 PRINT FLASH u; OVER u; AT 20, 1;
         "▲▲▲▲▲▲▲▲▲▲▲▲▲▲▲▲▲▲";
         AT 21, 1; "▲▲▲▲▲▲▲▲▲▲▲▲▲▲▲▲▲▲"
5400 DIM s(10)
5500 FOR i = u TO 40 : BEEP RND /10, 10* RND -5
5510 IF i > 31 THEN GO SUB 8000-100*i
5520 NEXT i
5530 LET ov = 4 : LET v = 4
6000 FOR i = z TO 16
6010 PRINT OVER u; INK 2; FLASH z; AT i+1, 1;
        b$(30*i+1 TO 30*i+30)
6020 NEXT i
6030 PRINT FLASH z; INK 5; OVER 1; AT 20, 1;
         "▲ EXI SHI 0▲▲▲▲▲▲▲▲▲▲▲▲▲
         ▲▲▲ EXI SHI 5▲"; AT 21, 1; "▲ EXI SHI 0
```

```
            ▲▲▲▲▲▲▲▲▲▲▲▲▲▲▲▲
            EXI SHI 5. EXI SHI 0"
6035 PRINT OVER u; AT 20, 4; " GRA B"
6040 LET Li = Li-u
6050 PRINT OVER z; INK z; AT 21, 29; Li
6060 IF Li = z THEN STOP
6070 DIM s(10)
6200 GO TO 560
```

# Eliminator

Copyright (c) by Beam Software

You are the protector and defender of the humanoids on the surface of the planetoid. Your task is to ELIMINATE the invaders.

You must prevent at all costs their attempts to kidnap the humanoids under your care. Their survival and the survival of their planetoid depends on you.

The planetoid you are guarding is only a small one, and it is possible to fly right around it very quickly, but you can travel only in one direction.

The enemy kidnappers have released a heat-seeking missile against you, in order to distract your attention away from the real issue. Can you perform evasive action, shoot down the invaders and protect the humanoids?

Playing the game:
------------------

You are in control of the space craft in the centre of the screen. Your forward momentum does not allow you any flexibility in moving sideways.

Your only controls are therefore up and down, using the "W" and "X" keys.

You have at your disposal a laser blaster, controlled by pressing the "P" key, which will destroy the heat seeking missiles and kidnapping invaders, but it only brings temporary relief. As soon as you shoot one, the next one appears.

Your craft can sustain some damage, but after three hits, your craft is no longer operative.


Programming considerations:
---------------------------

There are no available commands in BASIC in order to simulate the movement of the spacecraft against the surface of the planet.
 Even if there were suitable commands (such as SCREEN$; note that this cannot be used as it does not recognise user defined graphics!!), horizontal scrolling of the screen would be painfully slow.

The only solution available, and the one that is used here, is to have the horizontal scrolling routine written in machine language. You will find this routine, 36 bytes long, in the DATA statement at line 3000.

What this routine does is to take each line of the screen, and wrap it around. ie. the character that was at 0,1 will go to 0,0, the character that was at 0,0 will go to 0,31, and so on.

The routine then does the same thing for the attributes, so that the colour associated with each shape moves with it.

This machine language routine is fully relocatable – in other words, you don't need to know anything about machine language to use it. Simply use a program similar to that in lines 140 and 150. Because this routine is fully relocatable, you can specify any address that will not be overwritten as the address it should be POKEd into.

You may be interested in trying to adapt this routine for other programs. You can be sure that Melbourne House is always keen to see any exciting programs you may develop.

The rest of the program is mainly taken up with keeping track of the variables relating to the spaceship (sx,sy), alien (ax,ay) and bomb (bx,by). Because of the continuous scrolling this is quite time consuming, but essential.


Structure of the program:
----------------------------

| 100 - 150 | Initialise variables, character set |
|---|---|
| 160 - 360 | Draw landscape, fit in men on towers |
| 1000 - 1020 | Draw ship, alien, bomb |
| 5000 - 5360 | Main loop<br>    Check for ship movement<br>    Make alien seek humanoids<br>    Make bomb head for ship<br>    Fire laser if key pressed<br>    Check for possible collisions |
| 7000 - 7330 | Kidnap loop<br>    Check if any humans left, etc |
| 8500 - 8760 | Damage to ship routine<br>    including end of program |

ELIMINATOR

```
 100 RESTORE 2000
 110 FOR i = USR "a" TO USR "k"-1
 120 READ x : POKE i, x
 130 NEXT i
 140 RESTORE 3000 : CLEAR 32500
 150 FOR i = 32500 TO 32535 : READ x : POKE i, x
       : NEXT i
 160 BORDER 1 : PAPER 1 : INK 0 : CLS
 170 PLOT 0, 8
 180 LET y = 8
 190 LET p = -1
 200 FOR j = 1 TO 3
 210 LET a = 3+ INT (7* RND )
 220 GO SUB 8100
 230 DRAW 4, 15-y : DRAW 8, 0
 240 LET y = 15
 250 LET p = p+a+1
 260 FOR k = 1 TO INT (4* RND )+1 : PRINT INK 5;
       OVER 1; AT 20-k, p; " GRA C" :
       NEXT k : PRINT INK 3; AT 20-k, p;
       " GRA B"; AT 19-k, p; " GRA A"
 270 NEXT j
 280 LET a = 30-p
 290 GO SUB 8100
 300 DRAW 11, 8-y
 310 LET sx = 3 : LET sy = 10
 320 LET ax = INT (15* RND ) : LET ay = 26
 330 LET bx = INT ( RND *15) : LET by = 30 :
       IF bx = ax THEN GO TO 330
 340 LET t = 0
 350 LET e = 0 : LET h = 3
 360 LET dm = 0 : LET sc = 0
1000 PRINT INK 1; AT sx, sy; " GRA F
       GRA G GRA H GRA I"
1010 PRINT INK 4; AT ax, ay; " GRA D GRA E"
1020 PRINT INK 2; AT bx, by; " GRA J"
2000 DATA 1, 57, 189, 187, 146, 254, 124, 124,
       56, 56, 56, 104, 76, 68, 68, 198
       : REM shape of humanoids
2010 DATA 126, 36, 60, 24, 60, 102, 195, 255
       : REM shape of platform
2020 DATA 63, 99, 193, 193, 127, 28, 7, 3, 252, 198,
       131, 131, 254, 56, 224, 192
       : REM shape of aliens
2030 DATA 255, 63, 15, 7, 3, 7, 255, 0, 192, 240,
       252, 255, 255, 255, 240, 3, 0, 0, 31, 249,
       224, 255, 252, 240, 0, 0, 0, 192, 248, 255,
       0, 0 : REM space ship shape
2040 DATA 28, 28, 244, 199, 227, 47, 56, 56
3000 DATA 33, 1, 64, 17, 0, 64, 26, 1, 31, 0, 237,
       176, 18, 35, 19, 62, 88, 188, 32, 242, 6,
       22, 197, 26, 1, 31, 0, 237, 176, 18, 35,
       19, 193, 16, 243, 201
5000 LET v = USR 32500
```

```
5010 LET x$ = INKEY$
5020 LET nx = sx+(x$ = "x")*(sx < 18) -
       (x$ = "w")*(sx > 0)
5030 IF nx = sx THEN GO TO 5060
5040 LET v$ = SCREEN$ (nx, sy+1) : LET w$ =
       SCREEN$ (nx, sy+2) : LET x$ =
       SCREEN$ (nx, sy+3) : LET v$ = v$+w$+x$
5050 IF v$ <> ".▲▲▲" THEN GO TO 8500
5060 IF SCREEN$ (nx, sy+4) <> "▲" THEN GO TO 8500
5070 PRINT OVER 1; AT sx, sy-1; "▲ GRA F
       GRA G GRA H GRA I"; AT nx, sy;
       " EXI SHI 6▲ GRA F GRA G
       GRA H GRA I" EXI SHI 0
5080 LET sx = nx
5090 LET by = by-1 : IF by < 0 THEN LET by = 31
5100 IF RND > .7 OR by = 31 THEN GO TO 5140
5110 LET nx = bx+(sx-1 > bx)-(sx-1 < bx)+(by = sy+2)
5120 PRINT OVER 1; AT bx, by; "▲ GRA J";
       AT nx, by; " EXI SHI 2▲ GRA J"
5130 LET bx = nx
5140 IF bx = sx AND ABS (by-sy-1) <= 1 THEN
       GO TO 8500
5200 IF x$ <> "p" THEN GO TO 5290
5210 BEEP .1, 4
5220 PLOT INK 3; OVER 1; 8*sy+43, 170-8*sx
5230 DRAW INK 3; OVER 1; 212-8*sy, 0
5240 BEEP .1, 8
5250 PLOT INK 0; OVER 1; 8*sy+43, 170-8*sx
5260 DRAW INK 0; OVER 1; 212-8*sy, 0
5270 IF ax = sx AND ay > sy+4 AND ay < 30 THEN
       FOR k = 1 TO 11 : BEEP .1, 5 :
       PRINT OVER 1; AT ax, ay-1;
       "▲ GRA D GRA E" : NEXT k :
       LET ax = INT (15* RND ) : LET ay = 29 :
       PRINT AT ax, ay-1; " EXI SHI 4▲ GRA D
        GRA E" EXI SHI 0 : LET sc = sc+100
5280 IF bx = sx AND by > sy+4 AND by < 30 THEN
       FOR k = 1 TO 5 : BEEP .1, 10 :
       PRINT OVER 1; AT bx, by; " EXI SHI 2
       ▲ GRA J" : NEXT k : LET bx =
       1+ INT ( RND *14) : LET by = 30 :
       PRINT AT bx, by; " EXI SHI 2
       ▲ GRA J" EXI SHI 0 : LET sc = sc+20
5290 LET ay = ay-1 : IF ay < 0 THEN LET ay = 31
5300 IF RND > .7 OR ay >= 29 THEN GO TO 5000
5310 LET nx = ax+(ax < 18)-t : IF ax = 18 THEN
       GO TO 5330
5320 LET v$ = SCREEN$ (nx, ay+1) :
       LET w$ = SCREEN$ (nx, ay+2) :
       IF v$+w$ <> "▲▲" THEN GO TO 7000
5330 LET ny = ay+(ax = 18)
5340 IF ny <> ay AND SCREEN$ (nx, ny+2) <> "▲"
       THEN GO TO 7000
5350 PRINT OVER 1; AT ax, ay; "▲ GRA D GRA E";
       AT nx, ny; " EXI SHI 4▲ GRA D
        GRA E" EXI SHI 0
```

```
5360 LET ay = ny : LET ax = nx
6000 GO TO 5000
7000 IF ABS (bx-ax) <= 1 AND ABS (by-ay) <= 1 THEN
     FOR k = 1 TO 11 : BEEP .1, 5 :
     PRINT OVER 1; AT ax, ay; "▲ GRA D ▮▮▮▮▮ D
      GRA E" : NEXT k :
     LET ax = INT (15* RND ) : LET ay = 29 :
     PRINT AT ax, ay; " EXI SHI 4▲ GRA D
      GRA E" EXI SHI O
7010 IF ABS (sx-ax) <= 2 AND ABS (by-sy) <= 2 THEN
     GO TO 8500
7020 PRINT OVER 1; AT ax, ay; "▲ GRA D GRA E";
     AT ax-1, ay; " EXI SHI 4▲
     GD GRA E" EXI SHI O
7030 LET ax = ax-1 : LET ay = ay-1 : LET by = by-1
7040 IF ay < 0 THEN LET ay = 31
7050 IF by < 0 THEN LET by = 31
7060 LET v = USR 32500
7070 PRINT OVER 1; AT sx, sy-1; "▲ GRA F GRA G
     GRA H GRA I"; AT sx, sy;
     " EXI SHI 6▲ GRA F GRA G
     GRA H GRA I" EXI SHI O
7080 LET f = 0
7090 FOR x = ax-3 TO ax+3
7095 IF x > 20 THEN GO TO 7125
7100 FOR y = ay+1 TO ay+3
7105 IF y < 0 OR y > 31 THEN GO TO 7120
7110 IF ATTR (x, y) = 11 THEN PRINT AT x, y;
     INK 1; "▲" : LET f = f+1
7120 NEXT y
7125 NEXT x
7130 IF f = 2 THEN GO TO 7200
7140 PRINT AT ax, ay+3; INK 1; "▲"; AT ax+1, ay+2;
     "▲▲▲"; AT ax+2, ay+2; "▲▲▲"
7145 LET ay = ay+1 : PRINT OVER 1; AT ax, ay-1;
     "▲ GRA D GRA E"; AT ax, ay;
     " EXI SHI 4▲ GRA D
     GRA E" EXI SHI O
7150 LET e = e+1 : IF e = 3 THEN GO TO 8550
7160 GO TO 5000
7200 PRINT OVER 1; AT ax, ay; "▲ GRA D GRA E";
     AT ax-1, ay; " EXI SHI 4
     ▲ GRA D GRA E" EXI SHI O
7210 LET ax = ax-1 : REM LET ay = ay-1 :
     IF ay < 0 THEN LET ay = 31
7220 LET by = by-1 : IF by < 0 THEN LET by = 31
7230 LET v = USR 32500
7240 PRINT INK 4; AT ax+1, ay; "▲ GRA A";
     AT ax+2, ay; "▲ GRA B"
7250 FOR k = ax-1 TO 0 STEP -1
7260 PRINT OVER 1; INK 4;
     AT k+1, ay; " GRA D GRA E";
     AT k+2, ay; "▲ GRA A";
     AT k+3, ay; "▲ GRA B";
     AT k, ay; " GRA D GRA E";
     AT k+1, ay; "▲ GRA A";
```

# Freeway Frog

You are a poor little frog desperately trying to get home across the highway. In your travels you must brave trucks, motor cycles, cars and worst of all high speed police cars that can appear at a moment's notice. To control your frog use the following keys

| | |
|---|---|
| 'Q' | to move up on the screen |
| 'A' | to move down |
| 'P' | to move right |
| 'O' | to move left |

You get points for moving up and down, so to get a higher score you can cross the highway as many times as you like. When a frog reaches the top of the screen he is home and you then move onto the next one to try and get him home.


How the program works

This program makes extensive use of the user defined graphic set of your SPECTRUM. If you don't know about these yet it might help to read chapter 14 of the manual. The SPECTRUM only allows you to have 21 user defined graphics at once. This program however requires 58 of them.

To allow the computer to access this many characters requires that the UDG area be moved back and forth between two or more sets of characters.

To do this we first need to make room for the number of characters required. For a 16 K system with only 21 user defined characters the UDG area is located at memory locations 32600 to 32767. This is 168 bytes of memory or given 8 bytes for each character this is 21 characters. Since we need 58 characters for our game we must have 464 bytes of memory for the UDG area. This corresponds to locations 32304 to 32767 so the first instruction in the program must be a

CLEAR 32303   (NOTE if a CLEAR is done after
                         any variables have been defined
                         in LET or DIM statements they
                         will be lost)

In this program we have three sets of specially defined characters :
The first two have 21 characters each and the third only 16. So to access any set all we need do is point the system variable UDG (locations 23675 and 23676) at the correct block. These are

| | | |
|---|---|---|
| 32600 | for the first set | (the normal set) |
| 32432 | for the second set | (32600 - 168) |
| 32304 | for the third set | (32432 - 128) |

Note the third set overlaps the second because it only has 16 characters.

To set the correct value for UDG requires a bit more calculation. The number to be POKEd into UDG is obtained by:

POKE 23675, 'value'-256* INT('value'/256)

and    POKE 23676, INT('value'/256)

Note we do not actually need to put these lines into the program since we can calculate the correct values ourselves and use them.

| E.G | TO GET | POKE 23675 | POKE 23676 |
|-----|--------|-----------|-----------|
|     | 32600  | 88        | 127       |
|     | 32432  | 176       | 126       |
|     | 32304  | 48        | 126       |

The values for the user defined graphics must somehow be input to the computer and since we have 58 characters or 464 bytes, we need to input 464 values. If these are put in data statements they take up a lot of space (so much in fact that there is not enough room for the game). And it would be silly to input them every time the game was loaded. So to overcome this problem the program has been split into two parts. The first builds the user defined graphics and when these are correct they are saved to tape as a block of bytes. When the game is run this block of bytes is loaded from the tape and the game can be played.

(Note you only need to load the block of bytes when the game is run the first time after being loaded from its tape. Once the characters are in the computer they will stay there until the power is turned off or another program overwrites them.)

Defining the Freeway Frog graphics

The following program will build the graphics for this game. It is important to take a lot of care when typing in the data statements, since any errors will be very hard to find later. When the program is run it will put all the data in the user defined graphics area, then print on the screen all the shapes used.

You should see on the screen,
     Four frogs in green at the top.
Each frog should look the same except that they should all point in different directions. (The first up, then right, down and the last left)
     Below these there should be
A white motor cylce, a red car, and a truck all facing left.
     And below these a white motor cycle

a yellow car and a truck all facing right

If all looks correct then the character set
may be saved to tape. Use the command
SAVE "frogshapes" CODE 32304,464
(the name does not matter anything will do)

Don't forget to save the program as well in
case you need it later.


The main program for Freeway Frog

The main program is fairly long so it might
be a good idea to type it in in stages being very
careful to check what is input carefully.
In particular the sections of the program
that draw the shapes contain many graphic characters
and color control codes. Since these will look very
different once the program is run (e.g a graphic A will
not be an 'A' once the characters have been loaded)
it is very important to type these in carefully. It
is almost impossible to find errors later on.

When the program is run it will wait to
load the graphic shapes from tape. You should
put the tape with the bytes you saved from above
in the recorder and start it playing. If you wish
to run the game and the bytes have already been
loaded use RUN 26.


The following is a breakdown of the game

| LINES | DESCRIPTION |
|-------|-------------|
| 20 - 25 | sets RAM TOP to allow room for the user defined grpahics and then proceeds to load them from tape. |
| 26 - 75 | initializes all the variables used sets the screen colors, the positions of the cars trucks and motor cycles and the variables used to change the UDG character set. (the program should be run from here if the user defined characters have already been loaded) |
| 80 - 100 | draws the highway |
| 105 | draws the frogs left on the screen |
| 106 | displays the score and high score |

| | |
|---|---|
| 110 - 150 | decides if a police car is to race across the highway. If one is to appear then the direction of its travel is determined and it is displayed. |
| 500 - 530 | checks to see if the frog has been squashed all over the highway If it has the program jumps to line 4000 |
| 600 - 700 | if the player is allowed to move (he can move only once every 2 cycles of the main loop) the keyboard is checked to see if he wants to move. If so the position of the frog is altered Its direction is changed if required and the score is increased if he has moved up or down. The old frog is then undrawn and the new one drawn. |
| 750 | moves all the motor cycles and redraws them |
| 800 - 820 | every second cycle this moves all the cars and redraws them |
| 900 - 950 | every fourth cycle this moves all the trucks and redraws them Then jumps back to 106 for another cycle |
| 990 - 999 | removes a frog from the screen The position of the frog is checked to see if the highway needs to be redrawn where the frog was |
| 1000 - 1070 | This consists of four subroutines used to draw the frogs facing in the four different directions |
| 1080 - 1117 | These 6 subroutines draw the cars trucks and motor cycles |
| 2000 - 2001 | draws all the cars on the screen |
| 2010 - 2012 | updates the positions of all the cars (i.e the cars moving right have there position increased and those moving left decreased) |
| 2100 - 2112 | draws all the motor cycles and updates their positions |
| 2200 - 2201 | draws all the trucks |

| 2210 - 2212 | updates the positions of all the trucks |
| --- | --- |
| 4000 - 4010 | indicates to the player that a frog has been run over, then decreases the number of frogs left. If there are any left the program jumps back to start with the next frog |
| 4020 - 4070 | prints a game over message, updates the high score if necessary and asks the player if he wants to play again. |
| 5000 - 5020 | A jump is made to here if a frog gets home, the number of frogs left is decreased and if any left the game continues otherwise the program goes to 4020 |

Score 0          HIGH SCORE 0

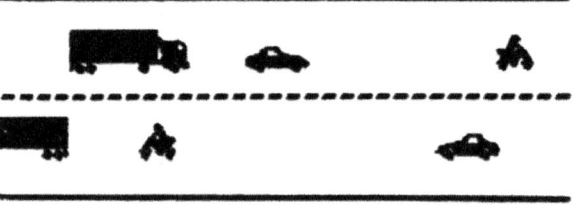

USER DEFINED GRAPHICS FOR FREEWAY FROG

```
 20 CLEAR 32303
 25 LET z = 0 : LET x = 255
 30 FOR i = 32304 TO 32767
 40 READ a : POKE i, a : NEXT i
 50 BORDER 0 : PAPER 0 : CLS
 60 POKE 23675, 48 : POKE 23676, 126
 70 PRINT AT 0, 9; " EXI SHI 4 GRA A GRA B
    ▲▲ GRA E GRA F▲▲ GRA I GRA J
    ▲▲ GRA M GRA N EXI SHI O"
 71 PRINT AT 1, 9; " EXI SHI 4 GRA C GRA D
    ▲▲ GRA G GRA H▲▲ GRA K GRA L
    ▲▲ GRA O GRA P EXI SHI O"
 80 POKE 23675, 176
 81 PRINT : PRINT : PRINT
    "▲▲▲▲▲▲▲▲▲▲▲▲▲▲▲▲▲▲▲▲
    ▲▲ EXI SHI 5 GRA D GRA D GRA D
    GRA D GRA C EXI SHI O"
 82 PRINT "▲▲ EXI SHI 7 GRA R GRA S
    EXI SHI O▲▲▲▲▲▲▲▲ EXI SHI 2
    ▲▲ GRA N GRA O EXI SHI O▲▲▲▲▲▲▲▲
    EXI SHI 3 GRA L GRA I EXI SHI 5 GRA
    SHI 8 GRA SHI 8 GRA SHI 8 GRA SHI 8
    GRA E EXI SHI O"
 83 PRINT "▲▲ EXI SHI 7 GRA T GRA U EXI SHI O
    ▲▲▲▲▲▲▲▲ EXI SHI 2 GRA A GRA B
    GRA P GRA Q EXI SHI O▲▲▲▲▲▲▲▲
    EXI SHI 3 GRA M GRA K EXI SHI 5 GRA J
    GRA G GRA G GRA H GRA F EXI SHI O"
 90 POKE 23675, 88 : POKE 23676, 127
 91 PRINT : PRINT : PRINT "▲▲▲▲▲▲▲▲▲▲▲▲▲
    ▲▲▲▲▲▲▲▲▲▲ EXI SHI 5 GRA C
    GRA D GRA D GRA D GRA D EXI SHI O"
 92 PRINT "▲▲ EXI SHI 7 GRA R GRA S
    EXI SHI O▲▲▲▲▲▲▲▲ EXI
    SHI 6 GRA N GRA O EXI SHI O▲▲▲▲▲▲▲▲▲▲
    EXI SHI 5 GRA F GRA SHI 8 GRA SHI 8 GRA
    SHI 8 GRA SHI 8 EXI SHI 3 GRA J GRA K
    EXI SHI O"
 93 PRINT "▲▲ EXI SHI 7 GRA T GRA U EXI SHI O
    ▲▲▲▲▲▲▲▲ EXI SHI 6
    GRA P GRA Q GRA A GRA B EXI SHI O
    ▲▲▲▲▲▲▲▲ EXI SHI 5
    GRA E GRA G GRA H GRA H GRA I EXI
    SHI 3 GRA L GRA M EXI SHI O"
100 IF INKEY$ = "" THEN GO TO 100
110 BORDER 7 : PAPER 7 : CLS
120 STOP
9000 DATA z, 1, 35, 37, 111, 79, 223, x
9001 DATA z, 128, 196, 164, 246, 242, 251, x
9002 DATA 111, 15, 31, 159, 220, 216, 120, 48
9003 DATA 246, 240, 248, 249, 59, 27, 30, 12
9004 DATA 56, 113, 193, 252, 127, 31, 31, 31
9005 DATA 192, 240, 156, 192, 240, 248, 244, 254
```

Chess

Adventure

Draughts

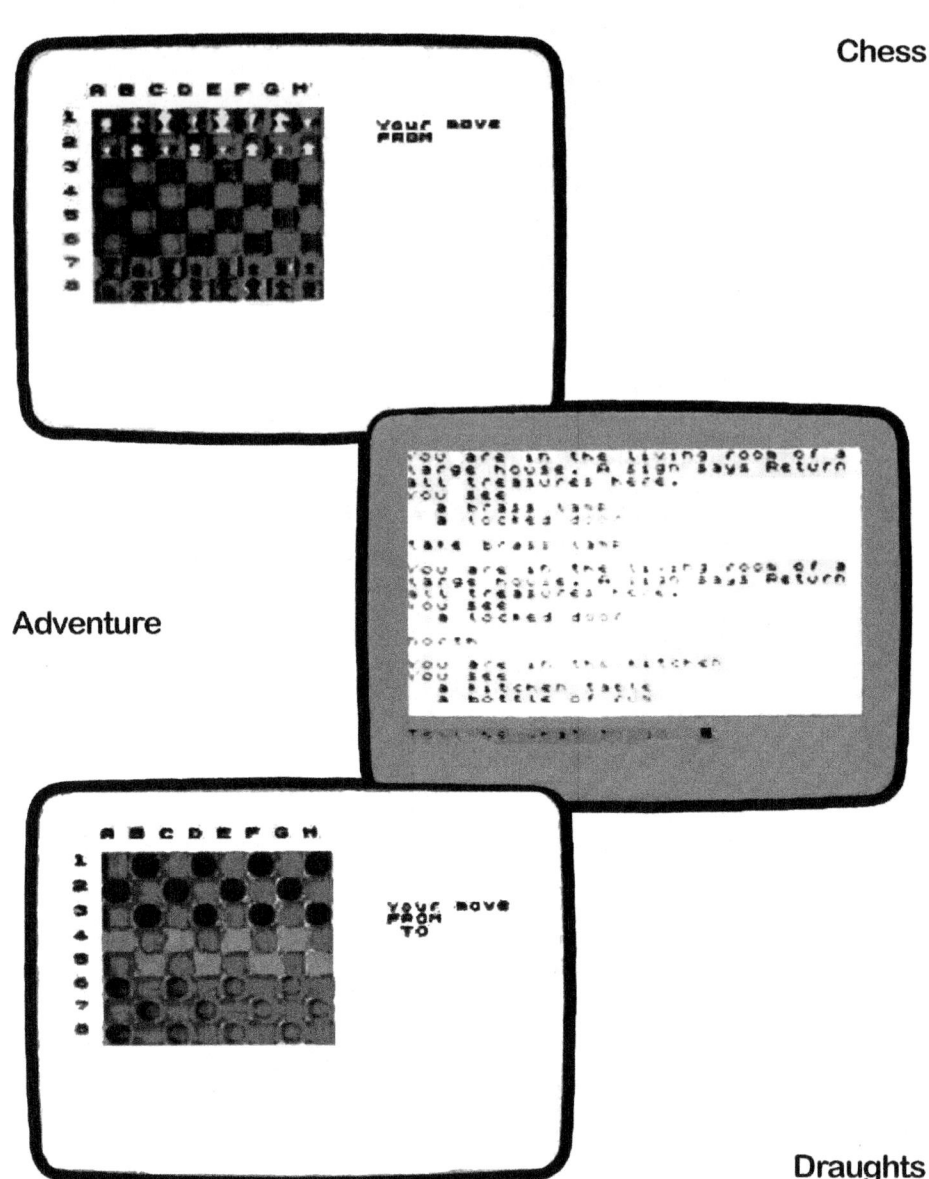

**Fruit Machine**

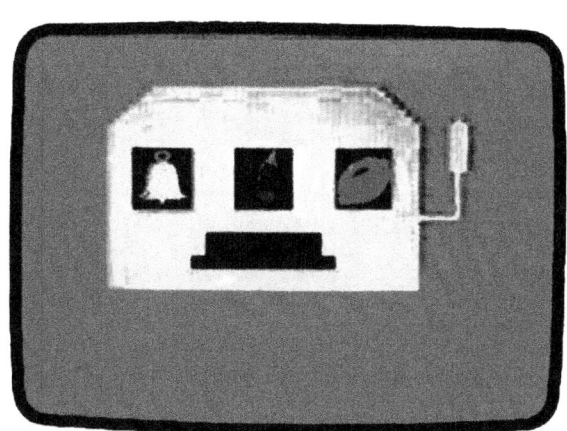

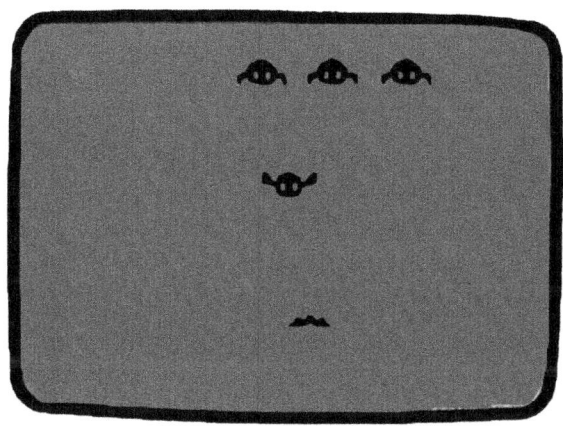

**Alien Blitz**

```
9006 DATA 31, 31, 31, 127, 252, 193, 113, 56
9007 DATA 254, 244, 248, 240, 192, 156, 240, 192
9008 DATA 48, 120, 216, 220, 159, 31, 15, 111
9009 DATA 12, 30, 27, 59, 249, 248, 240, 246
9010 DATA x, 223, 79, 111, 37, 35, 1, z
9011 DATA x, 251, 242, 246, 164, 196, 128, z
9012 DATA 3, 15, 57, 3, 15, 31, 47, 127
9013 DATA 28, 142, 131, 63, 254, 248, 240, 240
9014 DATA 127, 47, 31, 15, 3, 57, 15, 3
9015 DATA 240, 240, 248, 254, 63, 131, 142, 28
9016 DATA z, z, 3, 7, 15, 2, z, z
9017 DATA 7, x, x, 159, 111, 247, 240, 96
9018 DATA z, z, z, z, z, 254, 254, 254
9019 DATA z, z, z, z, z, x, x, x
9020 DATA 254, 254, 254, 254, 254, 254, 254, 254
9021 DATA 254, 254, 254, 4, 50, 122, 122, 48
9022 DATA x, x, x, z, z, z, z, z
9023 DATA x, x, x, z, 6, 15, 15, 6
9024 DATA 2, 2, 250, 250, 254, 252, 252, 248
9025 DATA x, x, x, x, 6, 15, 15, 6
9026 DATA 248, 252, 254, 127, 184, 216, 192, 128
9027 DATA z, z, 7, 9, 17, 17, 31, 31
9028 DATA 31, 31, 31, 62, 61, 59, 3, 1
9029 DATA z, z, z, z, z, 63, 97, 193
9030 DATA z, z, z, z, z, z, 128, 192
9031 DATA 128, x, x, x, x, 254, z, z
9032 DATA 240, 254, x, 159, 111, 246, 240, 96
9033 DATA 1, 3, 1, z, 3, 4, 14, 31
9034 DATA 128, 192, 192, 224, 224, 112, 119, 255
9035 DATA 31, 63, 115, 81, 169, 112, 112, 32
9036 DATA 254, 252, 252, 234, 213, 206, 14, 4
9037 DATA 224, x, x, 249, 246, 239, 15, 6
9038 DATA z, z, 192, 224, 240, 64, z, z
9039 DATA z, z, z, z, z, 127, 127, 127
9040 DATA z, z, z, z, z, x, x, x
9041 DATA 127, 127, 127, 32, 76, 94, 94, 12
9042 DATA 127, 127, 127, 127, 127, 127, 127, 127
9043 DATA x, x, x, z, 96, 240, 240, 96
9044 DATA x, x, x, z, z, z, z, z
9045 DATA x, x, x, x, 96, 240, 240, 96
9046 DATA 64, 64, 95, 95, 127, 63, 63, 31
9047 DATA z, z, 224, 144, 136, 136, 248, 248
9048 DATA 31, 63, 127, 254, 29, 27, 3, 1
9049 DATA 248, 248, 248, 124, 188, 220, 192, 128
9050 DATA z, z, z, z, z, z, 1, 3
9051 DATA z, z, z, z, z, 252, 134, 131
9052 DATA 15, 127, x, 249, 246, 111, 15, 6
9053 DATA 1, x, x, x, x, 127, z, z
9054 DATA 1, 3, 3, 7, 7, 14, 238, x
9055 DATA 128, 192, 128, z, 192, 32, 112, 248
9056 DATA 127, 63, 63, 87, 171, 115, 112, 32
9057 DATA 248, 252, 206, 138, 149, 14, 14, 4
```

FREEWAY FROG

```
 20 CLEAR 32303 : RANDOMIZE
 25 LOAD "" CODE
 26 LET hi = 0
 30 LET m1 = 2* INT RND *15 :
      LET m2 = 2* INT RND *15
 33 LET t1 = INT RND *30 : LET t2 = INT RND *30
 34 LET c1 = 2* INT RND *30 :
      LET c2 = 2* INT RND *30
 35 LET ce = 2 : LET cf = 6
 36 LET pz = 4 : LET tz = 4 : LET mz = 2
 40 BORDER 0 : PAPER 0 : INK 7 : CLS
 45 LET f = 4 : LET fc = 5
 50 LET uL = 23675 : LET uh = 23676
 55 LET sc = 0
 60 LET L1 = 88 : LET L2 = 176 : LET L3 = 48
 70 LET h1 = 127 : LET h2 = 126
 75 LET L10 = 8 : LET L11 = 9 : LET L12 = 7 :
      LET L20 = 13 : LET L21 = 14 : LET L22 = 12
 80 PLOT 0, 38 : DRAW 255, 0 : DRAW 0, 1 :
      DRAW -255, 0
 90 PLOT 0, 128 : DRAW 255, 0 : DRAW 0, 1 :
      DRAW -255, 0
100 FOR x = 2 TO 256 STEP 8 : PLOT x, 83 :
      DRAW 4, 0 : DRAW 0, 1 : DRAW -4, 0 : NEXT x
105 LET pa = 20 : LET py = 20 :
      FOR x = 0 TO (fc-1)*3 STEP 3 : LET px = x :
      GO SUB 1020 : NEXT x
106 PRINT AT 0, 0; " EXI SHI 6Score. EXI SHI 7"; sc;
      AT 0, 14; " EXI SHI 6HIGH.SCORE. EXI SHI 7"; hi
110 IF RND < .9 THEN GO TO 500
115 IF RND > .5 THEN GO TO 150
120 LET c = 5 : FOR j = 1 TO 6 : BEEP .2, 10 :
      BEEP .2, 20 : NEXT j : FOR x = -4 TO 30 STEP 2
      : GO SUB 1080 : NEXT x
130 GO TO 500
150 LET c = 5 : FOR j = 1 TO 6 : BEEP .2, 20 :
      BEEP .2, 10 : NEXT j : FOR x = 30 TO -4
      STEP -2 : GO SUB 1140 : NEXT x
500 IF py > 15 OR (py < 12 AND py > 9) OR py < 6
      THEN GO TO 600
510 LET i = 22528+py*32+px
520 IF PEEK i <> 4 OR PEEK (i+1) <> 4 THEN
      GO TO 4000
530 IF PEEK (i+32) <> 4 OR PEEK (i+33) <> 4 THEN
      GO TO 4000
600 IF pz THEN LET pz = pz-1 : GO TO 700
610 LET pz = 1 : LET z$ = INKEY$ : IF z$ = "" THEN
      GO TO 700
615 GO SUB 990
620 LET py = py-(z$ = "q")+(z$ = "a")
630 LET px = px+(z$ = "p")-(z$ = "o")
640 IF z$ = "q" THEN LET pa = 0
641 IF z$ = "p" THEN LET pa = 20
```

```
 642 IF z$ = "a" THEN LET pa = 40
 643 IF z$ = "o" THEN LET pa = 60
 650 IF py = 0 THEN GO SUB 5000
 660 LET sc = sc+10*(z$ = "q" OR z$ = "a")
 700 GO SUB 1000+pa
 750 GO SUB 2100
 800 IF mz THEN LET mz = mz-1
 810 GO SUB 2000
 820 IF NOT mz THEN LET mz = 2 : GO SUB 2010
 900 IF tz THEN LET tz = tz-1
 901 GO SUB 2200
 902 IF NOT tz THEN GO SUB 2210 : LET tz = 4
 950 GO TO 106
 990 PRINT AT py, px; "▲▲"; AT py+1, px; "▲▲" :
 991 IF py = 10 OR py = 11 THEN PLOT px*8+2, 83 :
     DRAW 4, 0 : DRAW 0, 1 : DRAW -4, 0 :
     PLOT px*8+10, 83 : DRAW 4, 0 : DRAW 0, 1 :
     DRAW -4, 0 : RETURN
 995 IF py = 17 OR py = 16 THEN PLOT px*8, 38 :
     GO TO 998
 996 IF py <> 5 AND py <> 4 THEN RETURN
 997 PLOT px*8, 128
 998 DRAW 16, 0 : DRAW 0, 1 : DRAW -16, 0
 999 RETURN
1000 POKE uL, L3 : POKE uh, h2
1010 PRINT INK f; AT py, px; " GRA A GRA B";
     AT py+1, px; " GRA C GRA D" : RETURN
1020 POKE uL, L3 : POKE uh, h2
1030 PRINT INK f; AT py, px; " GRA E GRA F";
     AT py+1, px; " GRA G GRA H" : RETURN
1040 POKE uL, L3 : POKE uh, h2
1050 PRINT INK f; AT py, px; " GRA I GRA J";
     AT py+1, px; " GRA K GRA L" : RETURN
1060 POKE uL, L3 : POKE uh, h2
1070 PRINT INK f; AT py, px; " GRA M GRA N";
     AT py+1, px; " GRA O GRA P" : RETURN
1080 POKE uL, L1 : POKE uh, h1
1085 IF x < 0 THEN PRINT AT L10, 0; INK c;
     "▲▲ GRA N GRA O▲▲"(1-x TO ); AT L11, 0;
     " GRA P GRA Q GRA P GRA Q GRA A GRA B"
     (1-x TO ) : RETURN
1090 IF x > 26 THEN PRINT AT L10, x; " EXI SHI O▲▲";
     INK c; " GRA N GRA O"( TO 30-x); AT L11, x;
     " EXI SHI O▲▲"; INK c; " GRA P GRA Q"
     ( TO 30-x) : RETURN
1095 PRINT AT L10, x; " EXI SHI O▲▲"; INK c;
     " GRA N GRA O▲▲"; AT L11, x; " EXI SHI O▲▲"
     ; INK c; " GRA P GRA Q GRA A GRA B" :
     RETURN
1100 POKE uL, L1 : POKE uh, h1
1104 IF x >= 0 AND x < 25 THEN PRINT AT L12, x;
     " EXI SHI O▲ EXI SHI 5 GRA C GRA D GRA D
     GRA D GRA D"; AT L10, x; " EXI SHI O
     ▲ EXI SHI 5 GRA F GRA SHI 8 GRA SHI 8
     GRA SHI 8 GRA SHI 8 EXI SHI 3 GRA J
     GRA K"; AT L11, x; " EXI SHI O▲ EXI SHI 5
```

```
          GRA E GRA G GRA H GRA H GRA I EXI SHI 3
          GRA L GRA M" : RETURN
1108 IF x < -5 THEN PRINT " EXI SHI 3"; AT L10, 0;
     " GRA J GRA K"(-5-x TO ); AT L11, 0;
     " GRA L GRA M"(-5-x TO ) : RETURN
1112 IF x < 0 THEN PRINT AT L12, 0; " EXI SHI 5";
     " GRA C GRA D GRA D GRA D GRA D"(-x TO );
     AT L10, 0; " GRA F GRA SHI 8 GRA SHI 8
     GRA SHI 8 GRA SHI 8"(-x TO ); " EXI SHI 3
     GRA J GRA K"; AT L11, 0; " EXI SHI 5";
     " GRA E GRA G GRA H GRA H GRA I"(-x TO );
     " EXI SHI 3 GRA L GRA M" : RETURN
1115 IF x = 25 THEN PRINT AT L12, x;
     " EXI SHI 0. EXI SHI 5 GRA C GRA D GRA D
     GRA D GRA D"; AT L10, x; " EXI SHI 0
     . EXI SHI 5 GRA F GRA SHI 8 GRA SHI 8
     GRA SHI 8 GRA SHI 8 EXI SHI 3 GRA J";
     AT L11, x; " EXI SHI 0. EXI SHI 5
     GRA E GRA G GRA H GRA H GRA I EXI SHI 3
     GRA L" : RETURN
1117 PRINT AT L12, x; " EXI SHI 0. EXI SHI 5";
     " GRA C GRA D GRA D GRA D GRA D"
     ( TO 31-x); AT L10, x; " EXI SHI 0
     . EXI SHI 5"; " GRA F GRA SHI 8
     GRA SHI 8 GRA SHI 8 GRA SHI 8"
     ( TO 31-x); AT L11, x; " EXI SHI 0
     . EXI SHI 5"; " GRA E GRA G GRA H
     GRA H GRA I"( TO 31-x) :
     RETURN
1120 POKE uL, L1 : POKE uh, h1
1125 IF x < 0 THEN PRINT AT L10, 0; INK 7;
     " GRA R GRA S"; AT L11, 0; INK 7;
     " GRA T GRA U" : RETURN
1130 IF x > 28 THEN PRINT AT L10, x; " EXI SHI 0.."
     ; AT L11, x; " EXI SHI 0.." : RETURN
1135 PRINT AT L10, x; " EXI SHI 0.. EXI SHI 7
     GRA R GRA S EXI SHI 0"; AT L11, x;
     " EXI SHI 0. EXI SHI 7 GRA T GRA U
     EXI SHI 0" : RETURN
1140 POKE uL, L2 : POKE uh, h2
1145 IF x > 26 THEN PRINT AT L20, x;
     INK c; ".. GRA N GRA 0"( TO 32-x);
     AT L21, x; INK c; " GRA A GRA B GRA P
     GRA Q"( TO 32-x) : RETURN
1150 IF x < 0 THEN PRINT AT L20, 0; INK c;
     ". GRA N GRA 0 EXI SHI 0.."
     (-x TO ); AT L21, 0; INK c; " GRA B GRA P
     GRA Q EXI SHI 0.."(-x TO ) : RETURN
1155 PRINT AT L20, x; INK c; ".. GRA N GRA 0
     EXI SHI 0.."; AT L21, x; INK c;
     " GRA A GRA B GRA P GRA Q EXI SHI 0.." :
     RETURN
1160 POKE uL, L2 : POKE uh, h2
1163 IF x >= 0 AND x < 25 THEN PRINT AT L22, x;
     " EXI SHI 0.. EXI SHI 5 GRA D GRA D
     GRA D GRA D GRA C EXI SHI 0."; AT L20, x;
```

```
              " EXI SHI 3 GRA L GRA I EXI SHI 5
         GRA SHI 8 GRA SHI 8 GRA SHI 8
         GRA SHI 8 GRA E EXI SHI 0."; AT L21, x;
         " EXI SHI 3 GRA M GRA K EXI SHI 5 GRA J
         GRA G GRA G GRA H GRA F EXI SHI 0." ÷
         RETURN
1165 IF x = -1 THEN PRINT AT L22, 0; " EXI SHI 0
     . EXI SHI 5 GRA D GRA D GRA D GRA D
     GRA C EXI SHI 0."; AT L20, 0;
         " EXI SHI 3 GRA I EXI SHI 5 GRA SHI 8
         GRA SHI 8 GRA SHI 8 GRA SHI 8 GRA E
         EXI SHI 0."; AT L21, 0;
         " EXI SHI 3 GRA K EXI SHI 5 GRA J
         GRA G GRA G GRA H GRA F EXI SHI 0." ÷
         RETURN
1170 IF x < -1 THEN PRINT AT L22, 0; " EXI SHI 5";
     ". GRA D GRA D GRA D GRA D GRA C
     EXI SHI 0."(-x TO ); AT L20, 0;
         " EXI SHI 5"; ". GRA SHI 8 GRA SHI 8
         GRA SHI 8 GRA SHI 8 GRA E EXI SHI 0."
         (-x TO ); AT L21, 0; " EXI SHI 5";
         ". GRA J GRA G GRA G GRA H GRA F
         EXI SHI 0."(-x TO ) ÷ RETURN
1173 IF x > 29 THEN PRINT AT L20, x; " EXI SHI 3";
         " GRA L GRA I"( TO 32-x); AT L21, x;
         " GRA M GRA K"( TO 32-x) ÷ RETURN
1175 PRINT AT L22, x; " EXI SHI 0.. EXI SHI 5";
     " GRA D GRA D GRA D GRA D GRA C"( TO 30-x);
     AT L20, x; " EXI SHI 3 GRA L GRA I
     EXI SHI 5"; " GRA SHI 8 GRA SHI 8
     GRA SHI 8 GRA SHI 8 GRA E"( TO 30-x);
     AT L21, x; " EXI SHI 3 GRA M GRA K
     EXI SHI 5"; " GRA J GRA G GRA G GRA H GRA F"
     ( TO 30-x) ÷ RETURN
1180 POKE uL, L2 ÷ POKE uh, h2
1185 IF x > 29 THEN PRINT AT L20, x; INK 7;
         " GRA R GRA S"; AT L21, x;
         " GRA T GRA U" ÷ RETURN
1190 IF x < 0 THEN PRINT AT L20, 0; INK 7;
     " GRA S EXI SHI 0.."(-x TO ); AT L21, 0;
     INK 7; " GRA U EXI SHI 0.."
     (-x TO ) ÷ RETURN
1195 PRINT AT L20, x; " EXI SHI 7 GRA R GRA S
     EXI SHI 0.."; AT L21, x;
         " EXI SHI 7 GRA T GRA U EXI SHI 0.." ÷
         RETURN
2000 LET c = ce ÷ LET x = c1 ÷ GO SUB 1080
2001 LET c = cf ÷ LET x = c2 ÷ GO TO 1140
2010 LET c1 = c1+2 ÷ IF c1 = 32 THEN LET c1 = -4
2011 LET c2 = c2-2 ÷ IF c2 = -6 THEN LET c2 = 30
2012 RETURN
2100 LET x = m1 ÷ GO SUB 1120
2101 LET m1 = m1+2 ÷ IF m1 = 32 THEN LET m1 = -2
2110 LET x = m2 ÷ GO SUB 1180
2111 LET m2 = m2-2 ÷ IF m2 = -4 THEN LET m2 = 30
2112 RETURN
```

```
2200 LET x = t1 : GO SUB 1100
2201 LET x = t2 : GO TO 1160
2210 LET t1 = t1+1 : IF t1 = 32 THEN LET t1 = -7
2211 LET t2 = t2-1 : IF t2 = -8 THEN LET t2 = 31
2212 RETURN
4000 LET f = 2 : FOR i = 50 TO 1 STEP -5 : GO SUB 990
        : GO SUB 1000+pa : BEEP .02, i : NEXT i
4005 GO SUB 990 : LET f = 4
4010 LET fc = fc-1 : IF fc <> 0 THEN GO TO 105
4020 PRINT AT 1, 10; "Game over"
4030 IF sc > hi THEN LET hi = sc : PRINT AT 2, 3;
        "But your score is the new
        HIGH SCORE"
4040 PRINT AT 4, 6; "HIT 'y' to play again"
4050 IF INKEY$ = "" THEN GO TO 4050
4060 IF INKEY$ = "y" THEN GO TO 30
4070 STOP
5000 FOR i = 1 TO 50 STEP 5 : GO SUB 990 :
        GO SUB 1000+pa : BEEP .02, i : NEXT i
5005 GO SUB 990
5010 LET fc = fc-1 : IF fc <> 0 THEN GO TO 105
5020 GO TO 4020
```

# High Resolution Graphics

Copyright (c) Beam Software


DESCRIPTION
------------

This program can be fun to just play around with, and
see greatly magnified the USER DEFINE GRAPHIC CHARACTER
SET.
But it is a MUST to COMPUTER programmers who want to
change the GRAPHIC CHARACTERS into HIGH RESOLUTION
graphicsfor their own use. eg GAMES.
An exceedingly powerful editor is implemented with
features like:

Dynamic display of graphic development
Instant blanking of characters
Instant filling  of characters
Large editing simulation display
Mirror image of existing characters
Four directional wrap around cursor
Option of one, two or four characters
Easily identifiable colours
Instant abort at any time without changes

More than these, at the end of editing, the memory
location of these characters are automatically updated
and all data corresponding to the characters are
displayed with the option of sending them to the printer.

You will be amazed at how handy this program can be.
When the computer is doing its processing, you will be
informed throughout.

To use the program :
    EDITING
        cursor control
            5          cursor left
            6          cursor down
            7          cursor up
            8          cursor right
            1          turn pixel under cursor ON.
            0          turn pixel under cursor OFF

        operation control
            b          Blank all pixels
            f          Fill all pixels
            m          Mirror image of the character blocks
            s          Save changed character blocks in memory
            E          Escape from editing with no changes to
                       character blocks (Note - you must use (shift) e)

PROGRAM STRUCTURE
-------------------

    The program uses an array to simulate the memory
bytes which defines the character block.
    The character set of first USER DEFINED GRAPHIC
character starts at memory location 65368 for 48K machine
and 32600 for 16K machine. Then follows 8 bytes of shape
definition for that character.

The structure of the  program is as follows:

INPUT:
    SET    VARIABLES OF DISPLAY FILE
    INPUT STARTING OF CHARACTER BLOCK
    INPUT NUMBER OF CHARACTERS (1 or 2 or 4)
    DEFINE DIMENSION OF simulation, memory address ptr,
                        mirror image working ARRAYS
MAIN LOOP:
    INITIALISE simulation, memory address ptr ARRAY
    READ MEMORY BYTES INTO simulation ARRAY
    DISPLAY ENLARGED and REGULAR SHAPE OF CHARACTER BLOCK
    PERFORM EDITING ROUTINE
            UNTIL    SAVE OR EXIT
    PROMPT   PRINTER OPTION
    IF MORE CHARACTER TO BE REDEFINE GO TO INPUT:


EDITING routine
    DETERMINE SIZE OF ENLARGED BLOCK TO BE EDITED
E1: FLASH CURSOR
    ACCEPT CONTROL KEY INPUT
    UNFLASH CURSOR
    CASE :   '5' or '8' calculates new cursor position
                        goto E1:
             '0'        set current simulation array
                        element to 0, update screen
                         display
                        goto E1:
             '1'        set current simulation array
                        element to 1, update screen
                        display
                        goto E1:
         'f' or 'b' fill whole simulation array to 1
                        if 'f', to 0 if 'b'
                        redisplay character block
                        goto E1:
             's'        prompt saving option
                        if save then store simulation
                         array into memory
                        if not save then goto E1:
             'm'        swap simulation array rows back to
                         front
                        goto E1:
             'E'        return

SPECIAL NOTES
--------------

The flashing and unflashing of the cursor is done by changing the attributes of character position in the display file. The memory location of the top left character position in display file is 22528, therefore

    3040 LET a = 22528 + 32 * x + y : POKE a, PEEK a + 128

will set line x column y to flash; in the same manner

    3060 POKE a, PEEK a - 128

will set that position to unflash.

To facilitate the COPY of screen onto the line printer, a blank pixel is displayed as PAPER yellow INK BLACK; a filled pixel is displayed as PAPER white INK BLUE.

Print instruction is used to display ENLARGED character size and Plot instruction to display REGULAR character size.

In order to reference the right USER DEFINED GRAPHIC character, any lower case character INPUT will be adjusted to UPPER case by

    8060 LET K$ = CHR$ ( CODE K$ - 32 )

A testing is also performed to check if the INPUT character is beyond the USER DEFINED CHARACTER set by

    8070 . . . OR ( CODE K$ + nc + 79 - 1 ) ) 164

ie the ASCII code of the first character in upper case plus the number of characters to be defined plus 79 minus 1 should not exceed 164, which is the ASCII value of the last USER DEFINED GRAPHIC character.

To obtain the start of the 8 memory bytes that define a particular USER DEFINED CHARACTER and put it into the array, refer to

    8150 LET S(1+1) = USR CHR$ ( CODE K$ + 1 )

The logic behind the setting of mirror image of the array is by dividing the array into two array and interchanging the two far-end elements and moving inward until the middle of the array is reached. In other words, an eight elements row will be divided into two halves of 4 elements each. The first element of the first half is swapped with last element of the second half. Then the second element of the first half will be swapped with the second last element of the second half. This will continue until the last element of the first half is swapped with the first element of the second half.  You can refer this logic to lines 3330 - 3400.

```
 100 REM USR
 110 REM User.define.GRAPHIC
 120 GO TO 8000
1000 REM Draw.character.set
1010 REM Input.r, c; starting.coordinates
1020 PRINT AT 8, 11; ".."
       : PRINT AT 9, 11; ".."
       : FOR H = 1 TO nc
1030 LET hr = 8*(H = 3 OR H = 4)
       : LET hc = 8*(H = 2 OR H = 4)
1040 FOR I = 1 TO 8
1050 FOR J = 1 TO 8
1060 PRINT AT (I+r+hr), (J+c+hc);
1070 IF B(I+hr, J+hc) = 0
       THEN PRINT PAPER 6; INK 0; "."
       : GO TO 1090
1080 PRINT PAPER 7; INK 1; " GRA SHI 8"
       : PLOT 87+J+hc, 112-I-hr
1090 NEXT J
1100 NEXT I
1110 NEXT H
1120 LET L$ = ".....................
       ................."
1130 RETURN
2000 REM
2010 REM char.into.array
2020 REM Input.K$, Output.B(I, J)
2030 REM
2040 FOR H = 1 TO nc
2050 LET hr = 8*(H > 2)
       : LET hc = 8*(H = 2 OR H = 4)
2060 FOR I = 1 TO 8
2070 LET m = PEEK (s(H)+I-1)
2080 FOR J = 8 TO 1 STEP -1
2090 LET B(I+hr, J+hc) = m-2* INT (m/2)
2100 LET m = INT (m/2)
2110 NEXT J
2120 NEXT I
2130 NEXT H
2140 RETURN
3000 REM Edit.CHAR, x = row, y = col
3010 REM Input.B(I, J)
3020 LET hr = 8*(nc > 2)
       : LET hc = 8*(nc = 2 OR nc = 4)
3030 LET x = r+1 : LET y = c+1
3040 LET a = 22528+32*x+y
       : POKE a, PEEK a+128 : PAUSE 200
3050 IF INKEY$ = "" THEN GO TO 3050
3060 LET M$ = INKEY$ : POKE a, PEEK a-128
       : REM unflash.old.pos
3070 IF M$ < "5" OR M$ > "8" THEN GO TO 3150
3080 LET y = y+(M$ = "8"
       AND (x <> 8+hr OR y <> 22+hc))-(M$ = "5"
       AND (x <> 1 OR y <> c+1))
```

```
3090 LET x = x+(M$ = "6")-(M$ = "7")
3100 IF x > 8+hr THEN LET x = 1
3110 IF x < 1 THEN LET x = 8+hr
3120 IF y > 22+hc THEN LET y = c+1 : LET x = x+1
3130 IF y < 15 THEN LET y = 22+hc : LET x = x-1
3140 GO TO 3040
3150 IF M$ <> "0" AND M$ <> "1" THEN GO TO 3190
3160 PRINT AT x, y;
3170 IF B(x-r, y-c) = 1 AND M$ = "0"
        THEN LET B(x-r, y-c) = 0
        : PRINT PAPER 6; INK 0; " ▲"
        : PLOT OVER 1; 87+y-c, 112-x+r
        : GO TO 3040
3180 IF B(x-r, y-c) = 0 AND M$ = "1"
        THEN LET B(x-r, y-c) = 1
        : PRINT PAPER 7; INK 1; " GBA SHI 8"
        : PLOT 87+y-c, 112-x+r : GO TO 3040
3190 IF  EXI SHI OM$ <> "f" AND M$ <> "F" AND M$ <> "b"
        AND M$ <> "B" THEN GO TO 3240
3200 LET b = (M$ = "f" OR M$ = "F")
3210 GO SUB 4000 : REM init▲ARRAY
3220 GO SUB 1000 : REM draw▲char
3230 GO TO 3030 : REM start▲again
3240 IF M$ <> "E" THEN GO TO 3260
3250 PRINT AT 19, 0; INK 2; "No▲change▲to▲this
        ▲character!" : RETURN
3260 IF M$ <> "s" AND M$ <> "S" THEN GO TO 3320
        : REM edit▲inkey
3270 PRINT AT 18, 0; "Store▲this?▲(y▲or▲n)▲";
3280 LET e$ = INKEY$ : IF e$ <> "y" AND e$ <> "n"
        THEN GO TO 3280
3290 PRINT INK 2; e$ : PAUSE 50
3300 IF e$ = "y" THEN GO SUB 5000 : RETURN
3310 FOR M = 1 TO 3 : PRINT AT 17+M, 0;
        : PRINT "▲▲▲▲▲▲▲▲▲▲▲▲▲▲▲▲▲▲▲▲
        ▲▲▲▲▲▲▲▲▲▲▲▲▲▲▲▲▲";
        : NEXT M : GO TO 3030
3320 IF M$ <> "m" AND M$ <> "M" THEN GO TO 3040
3330 PRINT AT 0, 26; FLASH 1; INVERSE 1; INK 3
        ; "MIRROR" : LET fc = INT (bc/2+.5)
3340 FOR I = 1 TO br
3350 FOR J = 1 TO fc
3360 LET M = B(I, J)
3370 LET B(I, J) = B(I, bc-J+1)
3380 LET B(I, bc-J+1) = M
3390 NEXT J
3400 NEXT I
3410 PRINT AT 0, 26; "▲▲▲▲▲▲"
3420 GO SUB 1000
3430 GO TO 3040
4000 REM Initialise▲simulation▲ARRAY
4010 FOR I = 1 TO br
4020 FOR J = 1 TO bc
4030 LET B(I, J) = b
4040 NEXT J
4050 NEXT I
```

```
4060 RETURN
4070 REM
5000 REM Transpose.array.to.mem
5010 PRINT AT  EXI SHI 00, 25; FLASH 1; PAPER 3; INK 7
     ; "SAVING"
5020 FOR H = 1 TO nc
5030 LET hr = 8*(H > 2)
     * LET hc = 8*(H = 2 OR H = 4)
5040 FOR I = 1 TO 8
5050 LET t = 0
5060 FOR J = 8 TO 1 STEP -1
5070 IF B(I+hr, J+hc) = 1 THEN LET t = t+2^(8-J)
5080 NEXT J
5090 POKE (s(H)+I-1), t
5100 NEXT I
5110 NEXT H
5120 PRINT AT 0, 25; "........"
5130 PRINT AT 0, 25; PAPER 3; INK 7; "SAVED!!"
5140 RETURN
6000 REM
6010 REM list.memory.value.of.char
6020 PRINT AT 0, 0; ".........."
6030 FOR H = 1 TO nc
6040 LET hc = (H = 2 OR H = 4)*5+1
     * LET hr = (H > 2)*9
6050 PRINT AT hr, hc-1; PAPER 1; INK 7; ".."
     ; CHR$ ( CODE K$+H-1); "."
6060 FOR I = 1 TO 8
6070 PRINT AT hr+I, hc; PEEK (S(H)+I-1)
6080 NEXT I
6090 NEXT H
6100 LET UG = CODE K$+79
     * PRINT AT 8, 11; OVER 0; CHR$ UG;
6110 IF nc >= 2 THEN PRINT CHR$ (UG+1)
6120 IF nc = 4 THEN PRINT  EXI SHI 0 AT 9, 11
     ; OVER 0; CHR$ (UG+2); CHR$ (UG+3)
6130 RETURN
8000 BORDER 5 * INK 0 * PAPER 7 * OVER 0 : FLASH 0
     * CLS
8010 REM key.repre.of.char * DIM K$(1)
8020 PRINT "Which.CHARACTER.to.be.redefined?"
     * PRINT "(A.to.U)"
8030 LET K$ = INKEY$ : IF K$ >= "A" AND K$ <= "U"
     THEN GO TO 8060
8040 IF K$ < "a" OR K$ > "u" THEN GO TO 8030
8050 LET K$ = CHR$ ( CODE K$-32)
8060 PRINT K$ * PRINT : PRINT
     "How.many.characters?.(1.-.4).";
8070 LET nc = (( CODE INKEY$ )-48)
     * IF nc < 1 OR nc > 4
         OR ( CODE K$+nc+79-1) > 164
       THEN GO TO 8070
8080 IF nc = 3 THEN LET nc = 4
8090 PRINT nc * FOR I = 1 TO 50 * NEXT I : CLS
8100 DIM S(nc)
     * REM memory.location.of.character.set
```

```
8110 LET br = 8*(1+(nc = 4))
       : LET bc = 8*(1+(nc > 1))
8120 DIM C(bc) : DIM B(br, bc)
       : REM simulation.array
8130 FOR I = 0 TO nc-1
8140 PRINT INK 2; CHR$ ( CODE K$+I); ".";
       : REM print.chars
8150 LET S(I+1) = USR CHR$ ( CODE K$+I)
       : REM mem.loc.of.char.set
8160 NEXT I
8170 PRINT AT 0, 25; FLASH 1; PAPER 1 EXI SHI 0; INK 7;
     "LOADING"
8180 LET b = 0 : GO SUB 4000
       : REM initialise.ARRAY
8190 GO SUB 2000 : REM char.to.array
8200 LET r = 0 : LET c = 14
8210 GO SUB 1000 : REM Restore.CHAR
8220 PRINT AT 0, 25; ".........."
8230 GO SUB 3000 : REM Edit.CHAR
8240 GO SUB 6000 : REM list.memory.value
8250 PRINT AT 20, 0;
       "Copy.onto.printer?.(y.or.n)";
8260 LET g$ = INKEY$
       : IF g$ <> "y" AND g$ <> "n" THEN GO TO 8260
8270 PRINT g$
8280 IF g$ = "n" THEN GO TO 8320
8290 PRINT AT 21, 0;
       "Press.any.key.when.ready." : PAUSE 2000
8300 IF INKEY$ = "" THEN GO TO 8300
8310 COPY
8320 PRINT AT 20, 0; L$ : PRINT AT 21, 0; L$
8330 PRINT AT 21, 0; L$
8340 PRINT AT 20, 0;
       "Change.any.other.chars?.(y.or.n)";
       : PAUSE 200
8350 LET g$ = INKEY$ : IF g$ <> "y" AND g$ <> "n"
       THEN GO TO 8350
8360 PRINT g$
8370 IF g$ = "n" THEN STOP
8380 CLS : RUN
```

# Line Renumbering

DESCRIPTION
-----------

These are a few programs that you may find useful if
you are in the habit of developing programs and find
youself at the end of the development with oddly numbered
lines and no room to fit in that last brilliantly
concieved routine in the middle.

Model 1 (RENUM1) is a short renumbering model
assuming automatic renumbering from line 100, the first
line, including all lines before 9990, where the model
1renumbering program starts. Line increment for model 1
is 10.

Model 2 (RENUM2) is a short renumbering model similar
in features to Model 1 except it displays on the screen
all GOTO and GOSUB within each line together with the new
line number .
GOTOs and GOSUBs are not renumbered because the ZX
SPECTRUM supports computed GOTO and GOSUB and these are
too difficult for the program to renumber . The best we
can do is to report where they are in the new renumbered
version and let you to work out what changes need to be
made.

Model 3 (RENUM3) is the long version of the
renumbering program . It allows you to renumber a block
of lines in any line increment value with GOTOs and
GOSUBs displayed . It also allows you to PRINT those
GOTOs and GOSUBs report onto the line printer. Not only
that, it is a complete screen driven program with high
emphasis on USER FRIENDLINESS.

To use any of these Models, you need to MERGE the
program instead of LOAD them because the later method
will result in a COMPLETE wipe out of your program from
the primary memory.

The following is the format of a BASIC program line:

2-byte: line number with a more siginificant byte in
front
2-byte: line length with a less significant  byte in
front
n-byte: line content includes last end of line character

The starting address of the BASIC program is 23755.

MODEL 1 RENUMBERING
====================
     Use RUN 9990 or GOTO 9990 to start the program.


PROGRAM STRUCTURE
-----------------

     INITIALISE NEW LINE # TO 100
     INITIALISE MEMORY POINTER TO 23755
L1: IF ENCODED LINE # )= 9990
          stop
     DECODE NEW LINE # INTO MEMORY
     GET INCREMENTED NEW LINE #
     MOVE MEMORY POINTER TO NEXT LINE
     GO TO   L1:


SPECIAL NOTES
-------------

     To delete the renumbering program after use, you may
need to load the LINE BLOCK DELETE program, another
exciting UTILITY program of this book.

     The program is from 9990 to 9995.


MODEL 2 RENUMBERING
===================
     Use RUN 9988 or GOTO 9988 to start the program .


PROGRAM STRUCTURE
-----------------

     INITIALISE NEW LINE #, INCREMENT, BEGINNING OF BLOCK,
               END OF BLOCK
     FIND MEMORY LOCATION OF THE BEGINNING OF BLOCK
L1: IF END OF BLOCK LINE REACHED THEN STOP
     POKE NEW LINE INTO MEMORY
     REPORT ANY GOTOs AND GOSUBs within the line
     UPDATE MEMORY LOCATION POINTER & LINE #
     GOTO    L1:


SPECIAL NOTES
-------------

     Since this MODEL has a built in code for finding the
memory location of the start of block, you can then
change the variables in line 9988 to suit your operation.
     Again, if you want to delete this short program, you
can either do it manuallly or you can use our LINE BLOCK
DELETE program in this book.
     No printer facilities are provided to copy the

108

displayed GOTOs and GOSUBs report; ie You have to do it manually.

The program is from 9988 to 9999.


## MODEL 3 RENUMBERING

Use RUN 9900 or GOTO 9900 to start the program.


## PROGRAM STRUCTURE

Screen handling technique is used to input the starting and ending line number block to be renumber, the increment of lines and the new starting line number of the block.

All the four input values will be round up to an integer .

The structure of the program is as follows:

```
INPUT STARTING and ENDING LINE NUMBER of the block
      INCREMENT and NEW STARTING NUMBER of the block
FIND  start of memory of starting line
CALL RENUMBERING MODULE (same as model 2)
OPTION AS TO CONTINUE RENUMBERING OTHER BLOCK
    OR    TO COPY REPORT OF GOTOs and GOSUBs
    OR    TO EXIT WITH OPTION OF DELETE MODEL 3
```


## SPECIAL NOTES

This model gives you the option of deleting the model itself at the end of the operation .

The renumbering of the block lines is inclusive.

The program is from 9900 to 9999.

If you choose the option of deleting the renumbering model itself. At the end of the deletion, you need to type 9900 (ENTER) to finalise the deletion. This is because all of the renumbering program have been turned into one very long REM statement.

If you do not choose the delete option and at the end you do want to delete the whole renumbering program, you can do so by GOTO 9945 followed by (ENTER).

One interesting use of this model is to define a REM statement containing the message which you want to display e.g. 10 REM Copyright (c) Beam Software

Then you can renumber this line to 0 by specifying the NEW LINE # as 0.

After the renumbering you can no longer access this line 0 again unless you use the renumbering program to change the line to any number greater than 0 .

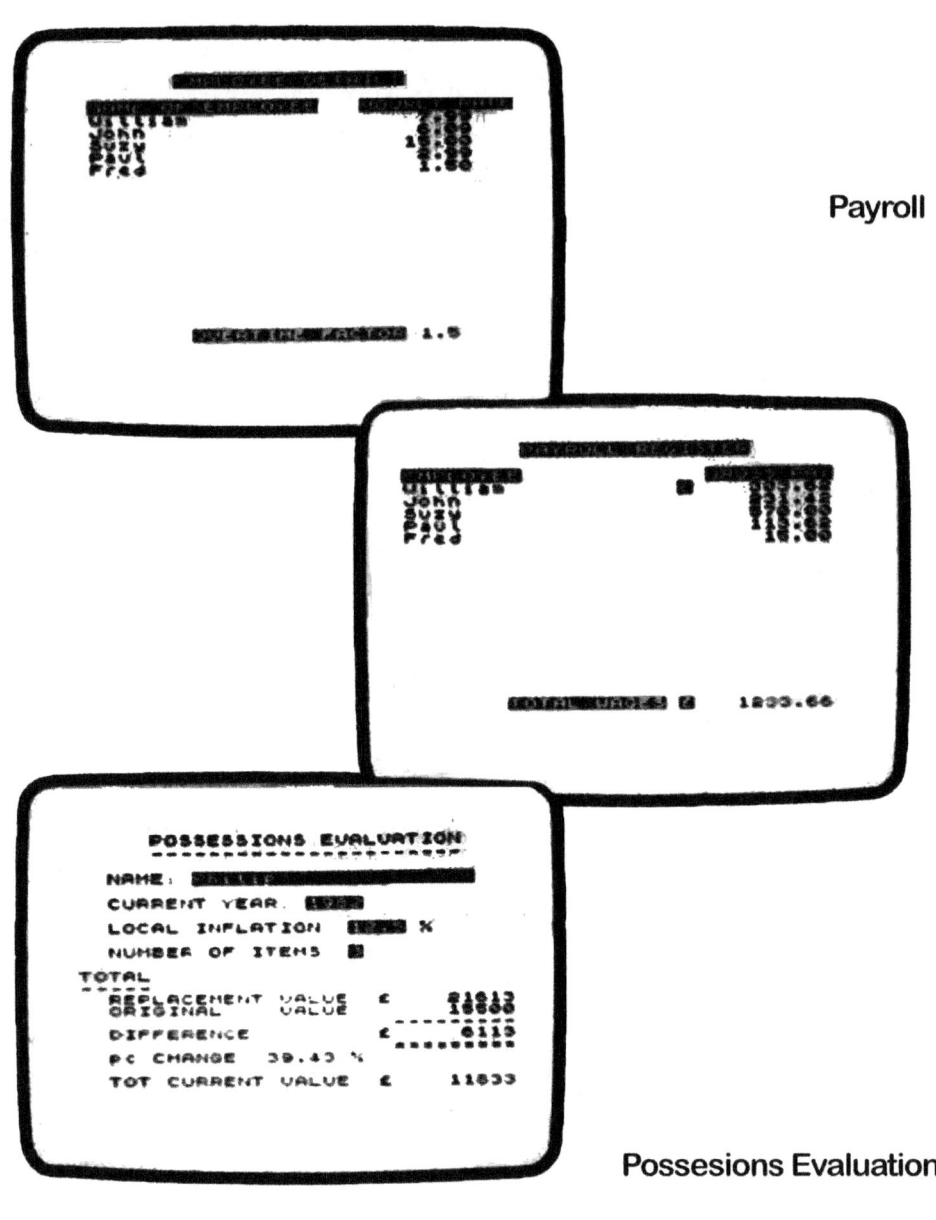

Payroll

Possesions Evaluation

**Space Escape**

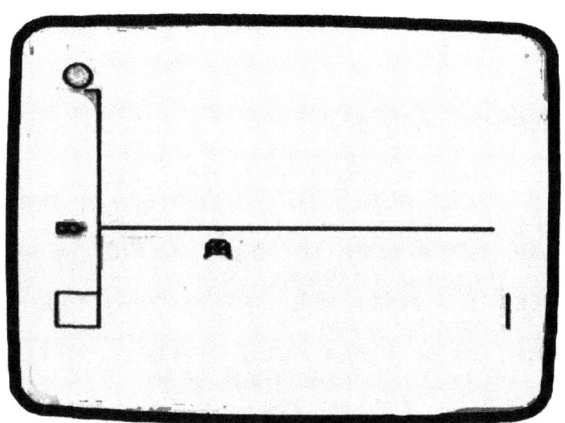

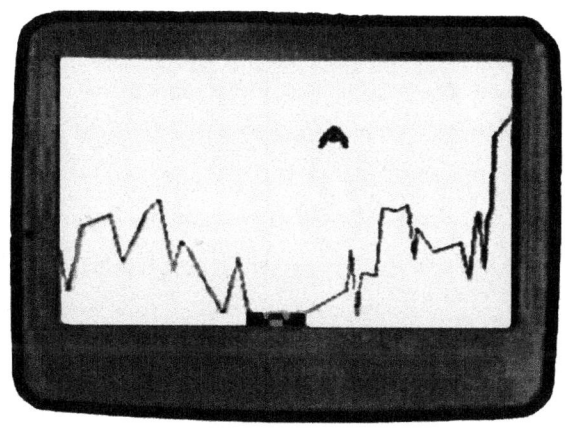

**Lunar Lander**

RENUMBERING MODEL 1

```
9990 REM
9991 LET L = 100 : LET N = 23755
9992 IF (256* PEEK N+ PEEK (N+1)) >= 9990
        THEN STOP
9993 POKE N, INT (L/256)
        : POKE (N+1), L- INT (L/256)*256
9994 LET L = L+10
        : LET N = N+3+ PEEK (N+2)+256* PEEK (N+3)+1
9995 GO TO 9992
```

RENUMBERING MODEL 2

```
9988 LET NEW = 100 : LET INC = 10
        : LET BOB = 100 : LET EOB = 9980
9989 LET L = NEW : LET N = 23755
9990 IF (256* PEEK N+ PEEK (N+1)) >= BOB
        THEN GO TO 9992
9991 LET N = N+3+ PEEK (N+2)+256* PEEK (N+3)+1
        : GO TO 9990
9992 LET n1 = (256* PEEK N+ PEEK (N+1))
        : IF n1 > EOB THEN STOP
9993 POKE N, INT (L/256)
9994 POKE N+1, L-256* INT (L/256)
9995 FOR I = N+4 TO N+3+ PEEK (N+2)+256* PEEK (N+3)
9996 IF PEEK I = 236 OR PEEK I = 237
        THEN PRINT L; "-"; CHR$ PEEK I
9997 NEXT I
9998 LET N = 1 : LET L = L+INC
9999 GO TO 9992
```

# RENUMBER MODEL 3

```
9900 REM
9901 REM Renumber.program
9902 LET BOB = 100 : LET EOB = 8999 :
       LET INC = 10 : LET NEW = 100
9903 BORDER 7 : PAPER 7 : INK 1 : CLS
9904 PRINT AT 0, 7; INVERSE 1; "LINE.RENUMBER.MENU"
9905 PRINT AT 2, 17; INVERSE 1; "CURRENT"; AT 2, 28;
       INVERSE 1; "NEW"
9906 PRINT AT 4, 0; "Starting.line.#"
9907 PRINT AT 4, 18+4- LEN ( STR$ BOB); BOB
9908 PRINT AT 6, 0; "Ending...line.#"
9909 PRINT AT 6, 18+4- LEN ( STR$ EOB); EOB
9910 PRINT AT 8, 0; "New......line.#"
9911 PRINT AT 8, 18+4- LEN ( STR$ NEW); NEW
9912 PRINT AT 10, 0; "Increment"
9913 PRINT AT 10, 18+4- LEN ( STR$ INC); INC
9914 PRINT AT 14, 4; INVERSE 1;
       "Press.ENTER.if .no.change"
9915 REM input.parameter
9916 PRINT AT 4, 26; FLASH 1; INVERSE 1; " > ";
       FLASH 0; INK 2; "...."
9917 INPUT S$ : IF S$ = "" THEN GO TO 9919
9918 LET BOB = INT ( VAL S$+.5)
9919 PRINT AT 4, 26; ".";
       AT 4, 27+4- LEN ( STR$ BOB); BOB
9920 PRINT AT 6, 26; FLASH 1; INVERSE 1; " > ";
       FLASH 0; INK 2; "...."
9921 INPUT S$ : IF S$ = "" THEN GO TO 9923
9922 LET EOB = INT ( VAL S$+.5)
9923 PRINT AT 6, 26; ".";
       AT 6, 27+4- LEN ( STR$ EOB); EOB
9924 PRINT AT 8, 26; FLASH 1; INVERSE 1; " > ";
       FLASH 0; INK 2; "...."
9925 INPUT S$ : IF S$ = "" THEN GO TO 9927
9926 LET NEW = INT ( VAL S$+.5)
9927 PRINT AT 8, 26; ".";
       AT 8, 27+4- LEN ( STR$ NEW); NEW
9928 PRINT AT 10, 26; FLASH 1; INVERSE 1; " > ";
       FLASH 0; INK 2; "...."
9929 INPUT S$ : IF S$ = "" THEN GO TO 9931
9930 LET INC = INT ( VAL S$+.5)
9931 PRINT AT 10, 26; ".";
       AT 10, 27+4- LEN ( STR$ INC); INC
9932 FOR I = 1 TO 50 : NEXT I
9933 REM find.first.number
9934 LET N = 23755
9935 IF 256* PEEK N+ PEEK (N+1) >= BOB THEN
       GO TO 9937
9936 LET N = (N+3+ PEEK (N+2)+256* PEEK (N+3)+1) :
       GO TO 9935
9937 CLS : PRINT AT 0, 11; FLASH 1; INK 2; INVERSE 1;
       "RENUMBERING"
9938 GO SUB 9991
```

```
9939 PRINT AT 0, 11; INK 2; INVERSE 1;
     "..FINISHED."
9940 INPUT """*""_to_exit, ""z""_to
     _copy_screen..Any_key_to_continue."; S$
9941 IF S$ = "z" THEN COPY : GO TO 9940
9942 IF S$ <> "*" THEN GO TO 9903
9943 INPUT """d""_to_delete_program
     ..........Any_key_to_exit.";
     k$
9944 IF k$ <> "d" THEN STOP
9945 LET N = 23755
9946 IF 256* PEEK N+ PEEK (N+1) >= 9900 THEN
     GO TO 9948
9947 LET N = (N+3+ PEEK (N+2)+256* PEEK (N+3)+1) :
     GO TO 9946
9948 LET DA = N+2 : LET DL = -4
9949 LET n1 = PEEK (N+2)+256* PEEK (N+3) :
     LET DL = DL+n1+4
9950 LET n2 = (256* PEEK N+ PEEK (N+1)) :
     IF n2 < 9999 THEN LET N = N+3+n1+1 :
     GO TO 9949
9951 LET n1 = INT (DL/256) : EXI SHI 0 POKE (DA+1), n1 :
     POKE DA, DL-n1*256 : POKE (DA+2), 234
9952 PRINT AT 21, 0; "Type_"; FLASH 1;
     "9900_ < ENTER > "; FLASH 0; "_to_delete"
9953 STOP
9991 LET L = NEW
9992 IF (256* PEEK N+ PEEK (N+1)) > EOB THEN RETURN
9993 POKE N, INT (L/256)
9994 POKE N+1, L-256* INT (L/256)
9995 FOR I = N+4 TO N+3+ PEEK (N+2)+256* PEEK (N+3)
9996 IF PEEK I = 236 OR PEEK I = 237 THEN PRINT L;
     "-"; CHR$ PEEK I
9997 NEXT I
9998 LET N = I : LET L = L+INC
9999 GO TO 9992
```

# Block Line Delete

DESCRIPTION
------------

    This is another UTILITY program which any SPECTRUM
BASIC programmer will find useful at program developement
stage.

    If you have read the RENUMBERING program in this
book, you will notice that this BLOCK LINE DELETE program
is particularly useful to delete the renumbering program
at the end of its operation.

    Besides that, this program will delete itself as
well.

    Again, screen handling techniques are used to input
starting line block and ending line block to be deleted;
the program is SMART enough to delete all lines with
numbers greater than or equal to the starting line block,
smaller than or equal to the ending line block. So, even
if your input line block number does not exist, it won't
CRASH the program.

    To use the program, first of all, you must enter the
starting and ending line number of the block you wanted
to delete. Notice that you can delete one line by having
the same starting and ending line number. After the
program finishes its house-keeping function, the program
will prompt an instruction to ask you delete the line
block by typing the starting line number followed by
(ENTER).

PROGRAM STRUCTURE
------------------

    The algorithm used in the program counts all bytes
from the memory after the line length location of the
starting line to the end of line character of the ending
line. This byte-length value will then be POKEd into the
starting line length location and the first byte content
of that line will be changed to 234 ( REM ); In effect,
the whole line block is converted into a single REM
statement. Therefore, re-entering the starting line
number with empty content will delete the whole line.

The structure of the program is as follows:

    INPUT LINE BLOCK NUMBER to be deleted
    DISPLAY REFORMATING message
    FIND STARTING LINE MEMORY LOCATION
    REMEMBER LINE LENGTH LOCATION and INITIALISE NEW
LENGTH
    COUNT byte-length UNTIL END OF BLOCK
    POKE  byte-length INTO  STARTING LINE LENGTH LOCATION
    DISPLAY FINISHED message
    DISPLAY FINAL message instruction

## SPECIAL NOTES

After the REFORMATING process has finished, if you
don't retype the starting line number with an empty
string, you can still reference any line within the block
except the starting line. Any future reference of the
starting line will delete the whole block.

It is then advisable to save your program before you
delete any part of it using this BLOCK LINE DELETE
program in case you delete the wrong block.

You have to MERGE this program with your own program;
don't use LOAD as this will destroy your program in the
LOADing process.

# BLOCK LINE DELETE

```
9973 REM
9974 REM BLOCK.LINE.DELETE
9975 OVER 0 : FLASH 0 : PAPER 7 : INK 1 : CLS
9976 PRINT AT 0, 8; INVERSE 1; "BLOCK.LINE.DELETE"
9977 PRINT AT 4, 0; "DELETE.INCLUSIVELY"
9978 PRINT AT 6, 9; "FROM.LINE"
9979 PRINT AT 8, 9; "TO...LINE";
9980 PRINT AT 6, 19; FLASH 1; " > "; FLASH 0; INK 2;
        INVERSE 1; "...."
9981 INPUT S$ : IF VAL S$ < 0 OR VAL S$ > 9972 THEN
        GO TO 9981
9982 LET SOD = INT ( VAL S$)
9983 PRINT AT 6, 19; "....."; AT 6,
        20+4- LEN ( STR$ SOD); SOD
9984 PRINT AT 8, 19; FLASH 1; " > "; FLASH 0;
        INK 2; INVERSE 1; "...."
9985 INPUT S$ : IF VAL S$ < 0 OR VAL S$ > 9972 THEN
        GO TO 9985
9986 LET EOD = INT ( VAL S$)
9987 PRINT AT 8, 19; "......"; AT 8,
        20+4- LEN ( STR$ EOD); EOD
9988 PRINT AT 11, 10; FLASH 1; INK 2; INVERSE 1;
        "REFORMATING"
9989 LET N = 23755
9990 IF 256* PEEK N+ PEEK (N+1) >= SOD THEN
        GO TO 9992
9991 LET N = (N+3+ PEEK (N+2)+256* PEEK (N+3)+1) :
        GO TO 9990
9992 LET DA = N+2 : LET DL = -4
9993 LET n1 = PEEK (N+2)+256* PEEK (N+3) : LET
        DL = DL+n1+4
9994 LET n2 = (256* PEEK N+ PEEK (N+1)) : IF
        n2 < EOD THEN LET N = N+3+n1+1 : GO TO 9993
9995 IF n2 > EOD THEN LET DL = DL-n1-4
9996 LET n1 = INT (DL/256) : POKE (DA+1), n1 : POKE
        DA, DL-n1*256 : POKE (DA+2), 234
9997 PRINT AT 11, 10; ".............";
        AT 11, 12; INK 2; INVERSE 1; "FINISHED"
9998 PRINT AT 15, 0; "TYPE."; FLASH 1; SOD;
        " < ENTER > "; FLASH 0; ".TO.DELETE.BLOCK"
9999 STOP
```

# Machine Code Monitor

In a few programs in this book we refer to machine language programs as being more efficient, and in some cases we show you examples of how writing programs in machine language can speed up execution time, and also save on memory.

You may therefore be asking yourselves what is the machine language these notes refer to? What is the difference between machine language and BASIC?

To set the scene correctly, you must accept first of all that the Spectrum does not really ever execute your BASIC program. In fact, the chip that does all the work, the Z80, doesn't even understand BASIC. All it can understand is its own set of instructions; and limited instructions at that.

The range of instructions the Z80 understands comprises of such simple things as add two numbers, subtract, compare, take a number from here and put it there, and so on. Admittedly most things can be achieved with these simple functions.

But even slightly more complex functions, simple by our standards, such as multiplication and division cannot be executed as such. You have to write a program to perform these tasks.

Your Spectrum computer comes inbuilt with a machine language program. This progam is stored in a chip inside the computer so that it does not have to be loaded from tape each time you want to use it. This program is in the ROM chip (ROM stands for Read Only Memory, which means you can't change it).

The function of this program is to take the information you give the computer via the keyboard and perform the instructions necessary to obtain the result you desire. A simple BASIC line may require hundreds of lines of machine language program to do its task.

You can understand that BASIC while being a much more efficient means of programming (one line instead of hundreds) probably results in slower execution of programs.

The program provided here does not pretend to teach you machine language. Whole books have been devoted to this subject, and we can certainly recommend two of our other titles if you are interested in this topic:
* Spectrum Machine Language For The Absolute Beginner
* Understanding Your Spectrum by Dr. Ian Logan

The structure of machine language programs:
----------------------------------------------

   Machine language programs are structured differently from
BASIC programs in several ways. Some of these are important
in this context:

   * There are no variables
         There is no direct equivalent to LET lives = 3
         All there is as far as the Z80 is concerned are
         memory locations.
         If you check your Spectrum manual you will find
         on pages 173 - 176 a list of memory locations used
         as variables by the program in the ROM.
         You can change the value held in those locations
         to achieve different effects, and to signify
         different things, but that is the limit of the
         analogy to variables.

   * There are no line numbers
         When executing instructions the Z80 will go from
         one instruction to the next, exactly as it finds
         them.
         Admittedly there are instructions that allows you
         to instruct the Z80 to GOTO another instruction or
         to GOSUB another set of instructions, but these
         GOTOs and GOSUBs are specified in terms of memory
         locations also - eg. one instruction might be "GOTO
         the instruction at memory location 16".
         This means that in general, programs are designed
         for very specific memory locations.
         Some programs however are relocatable, and we
         discuss these later.

   * All numbers used are either in the range 0 - 255 or
         0 - 65535, (depending on whether they occupy one
         memory location or two!)
         In other words the number occupying a single memory
         location can only be in the range 0 - 255. Because
         of this a special notation has been developed,
         that efficiently describes numbers in the range
         0 - 255.
         This is called Hex (or hexadecimal) notation.
         This book is not the place to explain this notation
         but you will find a conversion table from Hex to
         decimal in the Spectrum manual on pages 183 - 188.


What is PEEK and POKE?
----------------------

   Now that you have a slightly better understanding of way
the Spectrum functions, you understand that there can be no
simple equivalent to LET a = b.

   The closest equivalent is to think of a and b not as

variables, but as the contents of different locations. Given this equivalent, how can we find out what are the different memory locations?

The BASIC instruction PEEK lets us do exactly what its name suggests - we can PEEK into a memory location to find out what is there. Furthermore, a PEEK does not disturb what is there. We can PEEK to our hearts' content without doing any damage or disturbing anything.

So we can now at least find out what b is. Remember though that looking in a single memory location will give an answer in the range of 0 to 255 only.

How can we now change the contents of another location? We can POKE it. This instruction is again very much like what it sounds. You take what you want to fill the memory location with, and you POKE it in. As well, just as the name suggests, this is a rather rude and final instruction - you POKE a value in and it stays there. The potential damage you can wreak in programming terms is immense.

Do not be hesitant to use this instruction however, and to experiment with it. The worst you can do is to crash your program, or to have the Spectrum reset itself. There is no way you can damage the computer itself by POKEing anything anywhere.

Remember though that you can only POKE values in the range 0 - 255.


Hex notation:
--------------

You may have had a look at pages 183 - 188 of your Spectrum manual and seen the column of Hex numbers.

Certain things about this notation stand out:
        Each number is always 2 characters
        Only the numbers 0 - 9 and letters A - F
            are allowed.

These two points are in fact the major benefits of Hex notation.

Each of the letters A to F represents the numbers 10 through to 15.

To convert from Hex notation to decimal, take the number in the 'tens column', multiply it by 16 and add the number in the 'ones column'. Thus:
        0A Hex = 10 decimal
        11 Hex = 17 decimal, etc.

The Machine Code Monitor Program:
-------------------------------------

   This program enables you to examine the contents of any
memory location in the Spectrum, whether in the ROM or in the
RAM (that's the 'normal' memory, including the screen,
program area, variables, free memory and user defined
graphics area).

   It is not the most efficient program if you wish to POKE a
lot of data into a memory area, but it is very good if you
wish to examine any part of memory and modify it. To enter a
lot of data into memory see some of the other programs in
this book, such as in the Draughts program.

   Each line of the display shows the contents of 10 memory
locations, with the contents shown in Hex format. You can use
the arrows keys (Shift 6 to 8) to move the cursor around.

   Pressing any key other that the arrow keys will allow you
to change the contents of that memory location. The value you
enter must be in Hex format. Remember that only the numbers 0
- 9 and letters A - F are allowed and that a valid number is
made up of exactly two characters.


Some interesting exercises:
-------------------------------

* Try to modify the contents of memory locations in the ROM.
(Addresses below 16384). What happens?

* Try to modify the contents of memory locations in the range
22528 to 23295.
   This is the "attributes" area, which defines what colours
show up on the screen. You cannot damage the program or the
computer.

* Try to modify the contents of memory locations 16384 to
22527.
   This is the screen display memory area.
   Remember that each character space on the screen requires 8
memory locations in the screen display area to define it. The
eight memory locations are not consecutive. Can you find out
how these 8 memory locations are related to each other?
   You cannot damage the computer or the program doing this.


Relocatable Machine Language Programs:
-------------------------------------------

   There are some machine language programs which are said to
be relocatable. This means that it is not important where in
memory they start.

   Such programs are obviously very useful when used as
adjuncts to BASIC programs, because it means we can POKE them
anywhere there is free space.

One example is the screen movement routine in the Eliminator program contained in this book.

Here we give you another useful relocatable machine language program, this time a renumbering program. You will note that compared to the BASIC renumber programs listed elsewhere in this book, the machine language version is much shorter (only 27 bytes long!) and you will find it is also very much faster.

To "load" the program into memory, we need a short BASIC program as listed, or you could enter the bytes into memory through the machine code monitor program. (The Hex values are in the left column of the assembly listing given.)

Once the numbers have been POKEd into memory it is a good idea to save the program on tape, using the SAVE "" CODE command.

To "run" a machine code program, the USR function is used, such as PRINT USR 32500, or LET v = USR 32500. The number after the USR must be the address where the machine code program is.

Be sure to always place your machine code program in a area that cannot be overwritten - eg above CLEAR, or in the user defined graphics area, etc.

The machine code program given here renumbers all lines, starting with line 100 and incrementing in steps of 10. You can change the starting number by changing the 5th number (currently 90 = 100 - 10) and the step by changing the 13th number (currently 10). Note that it does NOT renumber GOTOs or GOSUBs.

Assembly listing for machine code renumber program:
------------------------------------------------------

```
11 CA 5C              LD DE, 5CCAH      ;start of BASIC
21 5A 00              LD HL, 90         ;start no. - step
13         nxtline    INC DE
1A                    LD A, (DE)        ;what's there?
FE 28                 CP 28H            ;end of line ?
DO                    RET NC            ;if not, finished!
01 0A 00              LD BC, 10         ;step size
09                    ADD HL,BC         ;new line no.
EB                    EX DE, HL         ;temporary swap
72                    LD (HL), D        ;put new line no in
23                    INC HL
73                    LD (HL), E
23                    INC HL            ;get length of line
4E                    LD C, (HL)        ;put it in BC
23                    INC HL
46                    LD B, HL
09                    ADD HL, BC        ;posn of end of line
EB                    EX DE, HL         ;end of swap
18 EB                 JR nxtlin         ;do next line
```

## MACHINE CODE MONITOR

```
100 PRINT INK 7; PAPER 2; AT 0, 0; "MACHINE.CODE
      .MONITOR........"
110 INPUT "Please.enter.starting.address
      ...(in.decimal)."; s
120 LET s = 10* INT (s/10)
130 LET x = 0 : LET y = 0
140 GO SUB 1000
150 PRINT INK 7; PAPER 2; AT 0, 0; "MACHINE.CODE
      .MONITOR........"
160 PRINT OVER 1; FLASH 1; AT 3+2*x, 3+3*y; ".."
170 LET a$ = INKEY$
180 IF CODE a$ < 12 AND CODE a$ > 7 THEN GO TO 600
190 IF CODE a$ = 0 THEN GO TO 170
200 INPUT "CHANGE.BYTE.VALUE.TO.(Hex)"; a$
210 IF LEN a$ <> 2 THEN GO TO 160
220 GO SUB 500
230 IF v < 0 OR v > 15 THEN GO TO 170
240 LET h = v
250 LET a$ = a$(2)
260 GO SUB 500
270 IF v < 0 OR v > 15 THEN GO TO 170
280 LET L = v
290 LET v = 16*h+L
300 POKE s+10*x+y, v
310 PRINT OVER 1; FLASH 0; AT 3+2*x, 3+3*y; ".."
320 IF y = 9 THEN GO SUB 1000
330 LET y = y+1
340 IF y > 9 THEN LET y = 0 : LET x = x+1
350 IF x < 10 THEN GO TO 140 : REM else.falls
      .through.to.next.page
360 GO TO 730
500 LET v = CODE a$-48-7*( CODE a$ > 64)
      -32*( CODE a$ > 96)
510 RETURN
600 PRINT OVER 1; FLASH 0; AT 3+2*x, 3+3*y; ".."
610 GO TO 540+10* CODE a$
620 LET y = y-1 : GO TO 660
630 LET y = y+1 : GO TO 700
640 LET x = x+1 : GO TO 730
650 LET x = x-1 : GO TO 680
660 IF y >= 0 THEN GO TO 160
670 LET y = 9 : LET x = x-1
680 IF x >= 0 THEN GO TO 140
690 LET s = s-10 : CLS : GO TO 130
700 IF y < 10 THEN GO TO 160
710 LET y = 0 : LET x = x+1
720 IF x < 10 THEN GO TO 140 : REM else.falls
      .through.to.next.page
730 IF x = 10 THEN CLS : LET s = s+10*x : GO TO 130
740 GO TO 140
1000 IF s < 0 OR s > 65530 THEN GO TO 110
1010 PRINT AT 2+2*x, 0; s+10*x : PRINT TAB 2;
1020 FOR i = s+10*x TO s+10*x+9
```

```
1030 IF i > 65535 THEN LET i = s+10*L+9 : GO TO 150
1040 LET v = PEEK i : LET h = INT (v/16) :
        LET L = v-16*h
1050 PRINT "▲"+ CHR$ (h+48+7*(h > 9))+
        CHR$ (L+48+7*(L > 9));
1060 NEXT i
1070 RETURN
```

Machine code Renumber

```
100 CLEAR 32500 : LET a = 32500
110 READ n : POKE a, n
120 LET a = a+1 : GO TO 110
130 DATA 17, 202, 92, 33, 90, 0, 19, 26, 254, 40,
        208, 1, 10, 0, 9, 235, 114, 35, 115, 35, 78,
        35, 70, 9, 235, 24, 235
140 FOR i = 0 TO 26
150 PRINT PEEK (32500+i); "▲";
160 NEXT i
```

# Payroll

Copyright (c) Beam software

DESCRIPTION
-----------

This payroll worksheet will calculate employee income
and produce a check register that may be used to produce
paychecks.
The register begins with the option of

EITHER      entering the NAME of the employee and his/her
            hourly rate, the overtime factor. An option is
            given if you want to save these EMPLOYEE
            DETAILS onto tape

OR          you can restore the stored EMPLOYEE DETAILS
            from previously saved tape


At the end of each pay period, you enter each
employee's hours ( regular and overtime ). The
MINI-PAYROLL model will calculate gross income for all
employee.

This PAYROLL model can only cater for a maximum of 18
employees. But for any small size business operation,
this will surely save either you or your secretary a lot
of time in calculating wages.

The whole model is screen driven, with appropriate
flashing cursor indicating which field the program is
expecting to receive. All numeric data input or output
will be right justified.
At the end of all input and calculation, any key
press will bring you to the next major three screens of
the model in the following order:
                    Employee details
                    Hourly payroll register
                    Wages payroll register

The wages calculation is correct to the nearest
pence.


PROGRAM STRUCTURE
------------------

This program is one of the three SPECTRUM financial
models in this book. One major difference of this type of
program from games or utilities is that INPUT/OUPUT must
be done in a USER FRIENDLY way. In term of processing,
you will find that it is mainly string manipulation and
calculation.

The structure of the program is as follows:


INITIALISATION
---------------
    INITIALISE ENTER MODE OF THE THREE SCREENS
    INITIALISE DISPLAY VARIABLES

EMPLOYEE DETAILS
----------------
    IF 'E' OR 'e' ( enter new information )
        input number of employee ( between 1 and 18 )
        define dimension of following ARRAYs
            E$  Employee details array
            R$  Regular  hours array
            O$  Overtime hours array
            G$  Gross income array
    IF 'R' OR 'r' ( retrieve information )
        input EMPLOYEE DETAIL from tape
        define dimension of above arrays except E$
I:  SET UP EMPLOYEE DETAIL SCREEN
    IF RM MODE IS ENTER (rm=0)
        set rm=1
        input employees name and hourly rate
        input overtime factor
        save EMPLOYEE DETAILS options
        return
    REDISPLAY EMPLOYEE DETAILS
        option of sending the display to printer
        return


PAYROLL hourly register
-----------------------
    SET UP PAYROLL HOURLY REGISTER SCREEN
    IF PM MODE IS INPUT (pm=0)
        set PM mode to display (pm=1)
        input regular and overtime hours
        return
    REDISPLAY PAYROLL HOUR REPORT
        option of sending the display to printer
        return


PAYROLL gross income register
-----------------------------
    IF PR MODE IS CALCULATE (pr=0)
        set display mode (pr=1)
        initialise TP (total gross wages)
        calculates and adds up all employee wages and
        enters into corresponding arrays
    SET UP PAYROLL INCOME REPORT
    REDISPLAY PAYROLL INCOME REPORT
        option of sending the display to printer
        return

```
MAIN LOOP
---------
     EMPLOYEE DETAILS
L1: PAYROLL hourly register
     PAYROLL income register
     GOSUB    I1:
     GOTO     L1:
```

SPECIAL NOTES
--------------

The EMPLOYEE DETAILS array is structured as follows:
* first record
     1 - 5    number of employee records in the
     array
     16- 21   overtime factor
* following records
     1 - 15   name of employee
     16- 21   hourly rate of the employee

You will notice that there are three major arrays
each having mainly two tasks to performed, namely,
display and input/calculation.

To choose which task to be performed, the program
first sets three mode variables to input/calculation (ie
0) at the beginning and these in turn will be set to
display (ie 1) mode after each routine gone through their
input/calculation task.

From this time onward, further re-entry to the array
will result in the performing of display task.

Routine 3000 performs the task of the conversion of
any string numeric input with number of digits before the
decimal point specified to a numeric string of that
specified number of digits before the decimal point and
two digits after the decimal point.

```
 100 REM PAYROLL
 110 REM mini▲payroll▲program
 120 LET rm = 0 : LET pm = rm : LET pr = rm :
     REM set▲enter▲mode
 130 OVER 0 : PAPER 7 : INK 1 : FLASH 0 : CLS :
     GO TO 9000
1000 REM
1010 REM initialise▲routine
1020 CLS : PRINT AT 0, 6; INVERSE 1; INK 1;
     "EMPLOYEE▲INFORMATION"
1030 PRINT AT 6, 1; INK 1; "ENTER▲new
     information▲----▲E"
1040 PRINT AT 8, 1; INK 1; "RETRIEVE▲▲information
     ----▲R"
1050 PRINT AT 15, 8; INK 1; "Press▲"""; FLASH 1;
     "E"; FLASH 0; """▲or▲"""; FLASH 1; "R";
     FLASH 0; """"
1060 LET  EXI SHI 0k$ = INKEY$ : IF k$ <> "E" AND
     k$ <> "R" AND k$ <> "e" AND k$ <> "r"
     THEN GO TO 1060
1070 IF k$ = "e" OR k$ = "r" THEN LET k$ = CHR$
     ( CODE k$-32)
1080 PRINT AT 15, 15; INK 1; INVERSE 1; "E";
     AT 15, 22; "R" : PRINT AT 18, 12;
1090 IF k$ <> "R" THEN GO TO 1150
1100 PRINT INVERSE 1; INK 2; "RESTORE";  : LET rm = 1
1110 INPUT "Press▲ < space >  < ENTER > ▲when▲ready
     "; k$
1120 IF k$ <> "▲" THEN GO TO 1110
1130 LOAD "minipay" DATA E$()
1140 LET NE = VAL E$(1, 1 TO 2) : LET F = VAL
     E$(1, 15 TO 21) : GO TO 1190
1150 PRINT INVERSE 1; INK 2; "▲ENTER▲" : PRINT
     AT 21, 2; INK 1; INVERSE 1; FLASH 1;
     " > "; FLASH 0; INVERSE 0;
     "no.▲of▲employee▲(1▲-▲18)▲ :▲";
     INVERSE 1; "▲▲"
1160 INPUT NE : IF NE > 18 OR NE < 1 THEN
     GO TO 1160
1170 PRINT AT 21, 30; "▲▲"; CHR$ 8; CHR$ 8; INK 1;
     INVERSE 1; NE
1180 DIM E$(NE+1, 21)
1190 DIM R$(NE, 6)
1200 DIM O$(NE, 6)
1210 DIM G$(NE, 8)
1220 FOR I = 1 TO 75 : NEXT I
1230 INK 1 : PAPER 7 : CLS : PRINT AT 0, 8;
     INVERSE 1 EXI SHI 0; "EMPLOYEE▲DETAILS"
1240 PRINT AT 2, 2; INVERSE 1; "NAME▲OF▲EMPLOYEE";
     AT 2, 21; "HOURLY▲RATE"
1250 IF rm = 1 THEN GO TO 1500
1260 REM enter▲employee▲details
1270 LET rm = 1
1280 FOR I = 2 TO NE+1
1290 LET E$(I, 1 TO 15) = "▲" : LET E$(I, 16 TO 21)
     = "000000"
```

128

```
1300 LET Ln = I+3-2
1310 PRINT AT Ln, 1;  : IF I > 10 THEN PRINT AT Ln, 0;
1320 PRINT I-1; FLASH 1; INVERSE 1; " > "; AT Ln, 3;
        FLASH 0; INK 2; "▲▲▲▲▲▲▲▲▲▲▲▲▲▲▲▲"
1330 INPUT S$ : IF S$ = "*" THEN RETURN
1340 LET E$(I, 1 TO 15) = S$ : PRINT AT Ln, 2;
        "▲"; E$(I, 1 TO 15)
1350 PRINT AT Ln, 20; INVERSE 1; FLASH 1; " > ";
        AT Ln, 23; FLASH 0; INK 2; "▲▲▲▲▲▲▲"
1360 INPUT S$ : IF VAL S$ < 0 THEN GO TO 1360
1370 LET ns = 3 : GO SUB 3000 : REM input▲numeric
string
1380 PRINT AT Ln, 20; "▲"; AT Ln, 23; "▲▲▲▲▲▲▲";
        AT Ln, 23; S$ : LET E$(I, 16 TO 21) = S$
1390 NEXT I
1400 PRINT AT 21, 9; INVERSE 1; "Overtime▲factor";
        AT 21, 25; FLASH 1; " > "; FLASH 0; INK 2;
        AT 21, 27; "▲▲▲▲▲▲"
1410 INPUT S$ : IF VAL S$ < 0 THEN GO TO 1410
1420 LET F = VAL S$ : PRINT AT 21, 25; "▲▲▲▲▲▲▲▲";
        AT 21, 25; F : LET E$(1, 16 TO 21) = S$
1430 LET E$(1, 1 TO 2) = STR$ NE
1440 FOR I = 1 TO 50 : NEXT I
1450 INPUT "Save▲EMPLOYEE▲DATA▲?▲(yes▲or▲no)"; k$
1460 IF k$ = "" THEN GO TO 1450
1470 IF k$(1) = "y" OR k$ = "Y" THEN SAVE "minipay"
        DATA E$() : RETURN
1480 IF k$(1) <> "n" AND k$(1) <> "N" THEN GO TO 1450
1490 RETURN
1500 REM redisplay▲employee▲record
1510 LET NE = VAL (E$(1, 1 TO 2)) : LET F =
        VAL (E$(1, 16 TO 21))
1520 FOR I = 2 TO NE+1
1530 LET Ln = I+3-2
1540 PRINT AT Ln, 2; E$(I, 1 TO 15); AT Ln, 23;
        E$(I, 16 TO 21)
1550 NEXT I
1560 PRINT AT 21, 9; INVERSE 1; "OVERTIME▲FACTOR"
1570 PRINT AT 21, 25; F
1580 LET k$ = INKEY$ : IF k$ = "" THEN GO TO 1580
1590 IF k$ = "z" THEN COPY : GO TO 1580
1600 RETURN
2000 REM
2010 REM enter/display▲payroll▲hour
2020 CLS : PRINT AT 0, 8; INVERSE 1; "PAYROLL▲REGISTER"
2030 PRINT AT 1, 17; INVERSE 1; "----▲HOURS▲----"
2040 PRINT AT 2, 0; INVERSE 1; "EMPLOYEE"; AT 2, 19;
        "REG"; AT 2, 27; "OT"
2050 IF pm = 1 THEN GO TO 2500
2060 LET pm = 1 : LET TR = 0 : LET TO = TR
2070 FOR I = 2 TO NE+1
2080 LET Ln = I+3-2
2090 PRINT AT Ln, 0; E$(I, 1 TO 15)
2100 PRINT AT Ln, 16; FLASH 1; " > "; FLASH 0; INVERSE 1;
        INK 2; "▲▲▲▲▲▲"
2110 INPUT n1 : IF n1 < 0 THEN GO TO 2110
2120 LET S$ = STR$ n1 : LET ns = 3 : GO SUB 3000
2130 PRINT AT Ln, 16; "▲"; S$ : LET TR =
        TR+n1 : LET R$(I-1) = S$
```

129

```
2140 PRINT AT Ln, 24; FLASH 1;   EXT SHT  0" > ";
        FLASH 0; INK 2; INVERSE 1; "▲▲▲▲▲▲▲"
2150 INPUT n1 ⁃ IF n1 < 0 THEN GO TO 2150
2160 LET S$ = STR$ n1 ⁃ LET ns = 3 ⁃ GO SUB 3000
2170 PRINT AT Ln, 24; "▲"; S$
2180 LET TO = TO+n1 ⁃ LET O$(I-1) = S$
2190 NEXT I
2200 LET S$ = STR$ TR ⁃ LET ns = 4 ⁃ GO SUB 3000
2210 PRINT AT 21, 8; INVERSE 1; "TOTALS"; AT 21, 16;
        INVERSE 0; S$
2220 LET S$ = STR$ TO ⁃ GO SUB 3000
2230 PRINT AT 21, 24; S$
2240 RETURN
2500 REM display▲hour▲report
2510 FOR I = 1 TO NE
2520 LET Ln = I+3-1
2530 PRINT AT Ln, 0; E$(I+1, 1 TO 15); AT Ln, 17;
        R$(I, 1 TO 6); AT Ln, 25; O$(I, 1 TO 6)
2540 NEXT I
2550 PRINT AT 21, 8; INVERSE 1; "TOTALS"
2560 LET S$ = STR$ TR ⁃ LET ns = 4 ⁃ GO SUB 3000
2570 PRINT AT 21, 16; S$
2580 LET S$ = STR$ TO ⁃ GO SUB 3000
2590 PRINT AT 21, 24; S$
2600 LET k$ = INKEY$ ⁃ IF k$ = "" THEN GO TO 2600
2610 IF k$ = "z" THEN COPY ⁃ GO TO 2600
2620 RETURN
3000 REM
3010 REM string▲input▲of▲value
3020 LET T$ = STR$ ( INT VAL S$)
3030 FOR J = 1 TO (ns- LEN T$) ⁃ LET T$ = "▲"+T$ ⁃ NEXT
J
3040 LET U$ = STR$ ( INT (( VAL S$- VAL T$)*100+.5)) ⁃
LET
        T$ = T$+"."
3050 IF VAL U$ = 0 THEN GO TO 3090
3060 FOR J = 1 TO LEN U$ ⁃ IF U$(J TO J) = "." THEN
        GO TO 3080
3070 NEXT J
3080 LET U$ = U$(1 TO (J-1))
3090 IF VAL U$ < 10 THEN LET U$ = "0"+U$
3100 LET S$ = T$+U$
3110 RETURN
4000 REM
4010 REM calculate/display▲pay
4020 IF pr = 1 THEN GO TO 4100
4030 LET pr = 1 ⁃ LET TP = 0
4040 FOR I = 1 TO NE
4050 LET n1 = ( VAL R$(I)+ VAL O$(I)*F)*( VAL
        E$(I+1, 16 TO 21))
4060 LET S$ = STR$ n1 ⁃ LET ns = 5 ⁃ GO SUB 3000
4070 LET G$(I, 1 TO 8) = S$
4080 LET TP = TP+n1
4090 NEXT I
4100 CLS ⁃ PRINT AT 0, 8; INVERSE 1;
        "PAYROLL▲REGISTER"
4110 PRINT AT 2, 0; INVERSE 1; "EMPLOYEE"; AT 2, 21;
        "GROSS▲PAY"; AT 3, 19; "<"
4120 FOR I = 1 TO NE
```

130

```
4130 LET Ln = I+3-1
4140 PRINT AT Ln, 0; E$(I+1, 1 TO 15); AT Ln, 22;
       G$(I, 1 TO 8)
4150 NEXT I
4160 PRINT AT 21, 7; INVERSE 1; "TOTAL▴WAGES";
        AT 21, 19; "'"; INVERSE 0;
4170 LET S$ = STR$ TP : LET ns = 6 : GO SUB 3000
4180 PRINT "▴"; S$
4190 LET k$ = INKEY$ : IF k$ = "" THEN GO TO 4190
4200 IF k$ = "z" THEN COPY : GO TO 4190
4210 RETURN
9000 REM
9010 REM main▴routine
9020 GO SUB 1000 : REM initialise
9030 GO SUB 2000 : REM payroll▴register
9040 GO SUB 4000 : REM display/calculate▴pay
9050 GO SUB 1230 : REM payroll▴record
9060 GO TO 9030
```

# Sales Analysis

This program uses a company's sales history over a number of years to determine what seasonal fluctuations occur in that business's sales, and what the overall trend has been for that number of years.

The results of this program would be useful to any company or sales manager of any company whose business is affected by seasonal fluctuations. For example, in book publishing, about 25% of annual sales occur in November and December.

The information required by the program is the sales value in each quarter for as many years as are available. As written, the program can only accept information for a maximum of 18 years.

After this information has been entered, the program will calculate seasonal ratios by dividing the actual sales by the average quarterly sales for all years.

The average of each quarter's ratios over the years produces the seasonal index.

The program will also chart in graph form the annual sales of the company, providing immediate visual information about the company's growth.


Programming notes:
--------------------

As with the other business programs presented in this book, a high emphasis has been placed on the interaction between the user and the computer. It is generally true that business programs must be able to be understood and be useful to people who have no knowledge of computing.

Screen-driven data entry is the name given to the input/output used in this program. The main benefit of this is that the user has immediate verification of what he has entered and the amount of information entered.

The results are displayed on two screens - one containing the actual sales, and the other the seasonal indeces. Pressing any key allows you to switch back and forth between the two screen. An additional option allows sending the screen display to the printer.

The graphical display makes use of the Spectrum's PLOT and DRAW facilities. The sales history screen is used, with the only the year and the average quarterly sales left on the screen. By using the minimum and maximum sales over the years to define the axis scales, the graph makes use of the entire display area available.

SALES ANALYSIS

```
 100 REM
 110 REM SEASONAL▲INDEX
 120 BORDER 7 : PAPER 7 : INK 1 : FLASH 0 : OVER
        0 : CLS 130 GO TO 8000
1000 REM
1010 REM input▲year▲range
1020 PRINT AT 0, 9; INVERSE 1; "SEASONAL▲INDEX"
1030 PRINT AT 4, 0; "SALES▲HISTORY(inclusive)"
1040 PRINT AT 7, 6; "FROM▲YEAR"
1050 PRINT AT 10, 6; "TO▲▲YEAR"
1060 PRINT AT 7, 17; FLASH 1; INVERSE 1; " > ";
        FLASH 0; INK 2; INVERSE 1; "▲▲▲▲"
1070 INPUT S$ : LET y1 = INT ( VAL S$) : IF
        y1 < 1900 OR LEN ( STR$ y1) > 4 THEN
        GO TO 1070
1080 PRINT AT 7, 17; "▲"; y1
1090 PRINT AT 10, 17; FLASH 1; INVERSE 1; " > ";
        FLASH 0; INK 2; INVERSE 1; "▲▲▲▲"
1100 INPUT S$ : LET y2 = INT ( VAL S$) :
        IF y2 < 1900 OR LEN ( STR$ y2) > 4 OR
        y2 < y1 OR y2 > y1+17 THEN GO TO 1100
1110 PRINT AT 10, 17; "▲"; y2
1120 LET NY = y2-y1+1
1130 DIM Y$(NY, 4) : REM year
1140 DIM H$(NY, 4, 4) : REM sales▲history
1150 DIM A$(NY, 7) : REM annual▲avr▲sales
1160 DIM R$(NY, 4, 6) : REM ratios
1170 DIM D$(4, 6) : REM seasonal▲index
1172 DIM Q(4) : REM sum▲of▲quarter▲ratios
1174 DIM C(NY) : REM draw▲curve▲dx
1180 DIM C(NY) : REM draw▲curve▲dx
1190 DIM C(NY) : REM draw▲curve▲dx
1200 FOR I = y1 TO y2 : LET Y$(I-y1+1) = STR$ I :
        NEXT I
1210 RETURN
2000 REM
2010 REM input▲sales▲history
2020 CLS : PRINT AT 0, 10; INVERSE 1; "SALES▲HISTORY"
2030 PRINT AT 1, 26; INVERSE 1; "AVR."; AT 2, 0;
        INVERSE 1; "YEAR"; AT 2, 5; INVERSE 1; "QTR1";
        AT 2, 10; "QTR2"; AT 2, 15; INVERSE 1; "QTR3";
        AT 2, 20; INVERSE 1; "QTR4"; AT 2, 26;
        INVERSE 1; "SALES"
2040 IF hm = 1 THEN GO TO 2500
2050 FOR I = 1 TO NY
2060 LET Ln = I+3-1 : PRINT AT Ln, 0; Y$(I)
2070 LET hp = 4 : LET ts = 0
2080 FOR J = 1 TO 4
2090 PRINT AT Ln, hp; FLASH 1; " > "; INVERSE 1;
        FLASH 0; INK 2; "▲▲▲▲"
2100 INPUT S$ : IF VAL S$ < 0 THEN GO TO 2100
2110 LET n1 = INT ( VAL S$+.5) : LET ts = ts+n1 :
        LET S$ = STR$ n1
2120 LET Z$ = "▲▲▲▲" : LET Z$(5- LEN S$ TO ) = S$
2130 PRINT AT Ln, hp; "▲"; Z$
2140 LET H$(I, J) = Z$ : LET hp = hp+5
2150 NEXT J
```

133

```
2160 LET S$ = STR$ (ts/4) ÷ LET ns = 4 ÷ LET nd = 2
2170 GO SUB 7000
2180 PRINT AT Ln, hp+1; S$
2190 LET A$(I) = S$
2200 NEXT I
2210 LET hm = 1 ÷ GO TO 2550
2500 REM
2510 REM display
2520 FOR I = 1 TO NY
2530 PRINT AT I+3-1, 0; Y$(I); "▲"; H$(I, 1); "▲";
        H$(I, 2); "▲"; H$(I, 3); "▲"; H$(I, 4);
        "▲"; A$(I)
2540 NEXT I
2550 INPUT "Copy▲this▲to▲printer(y▲or▲n)"; k$
2560 IF k$ = "y" OR k$ = "Y" THEN COPY ÷ GO TO 2550
2570 IF k$ = "N" OR  EXT SHI Ok$ = "n" THEN RETURN
2580 IF k$ = "E" THEN CLEAR ÷ STOP
2590 GO TO 2550
3000 REM
3010 REM calculate▲ratios
3020 CLS ÷ PRINT AT 0, 9; INVERSE 1; "COMPUTED▲RATIOS"
3030 PRINT AT 2, 0; INVERSE 1; "YEAR"; AT 2, 6; "QTR1";
        AT 2, 13; "QTR2"; AT 2, 20; "QTR3"; AT 2, 27;
        "QTR4"
3040 PRINT AT 21, 0; INVERSE 1; "INDEX"
3050 IF cm = 1 THEN GO TO 3500
3060 PRINT AT 1, 11; FLASH 1; INK 3; "CALCULATING"
3070 FOR I = 1 TO 4 ÷ LET Q(I) = 0 ÷ NEXT I
3080 FOR I = 1 TO NY
3090 LET n1 = VAL A$(I)
3100 FOR J = 1 TO 4
3110 LET n2 = VAL H$(I, J) ÷ LET n3 = n2/n1
3120 LET S$ = STR$ n3 ÷ LET ns = 1 ÷ LET nd = 4
3130 GO SUB 7000
3140 LET R$(I, J) = S$ ÷ LET Q(J) = Q(J)+ VAL S$
3150 BEEP .03, 12
3160 NEXT J
3170 NEXT I
3180 FOR I = 1 TO 4
3190 LET n1 = Q(I)/NY
3200 LET S$ = STR$ n1 ÷ LET ns = 1 ÷ LET nd = 4
3210 GO SUB 7000
3220 LET D$(I) = S$
3230 BEEP .05, 24
3240 NEXT I
3250 PRINT AT 1, 11; "▲"; INVERSE 1; INK 3;
        "FINISHED"; INVERSE 0; INK 1; "▲▲"
3260 LET cm = 1
3270 NEXT I
3280 PRINT AT 1, 11; "▲"; INVERSE 1; INK 3;
        "FINISHED"; INVERSE 0; INK 1; "▲▲"
3290 LET cm = 1
3500 REM
3510 REM redisplay▲ratios/index
3520 FOR I = 1 TO NY
3530 PRINT AT I+3-1, 0; Y$(I); "▲"; R$(I, 1); "▲";
        R$(I, 2); "▲"; R$(I, 3); "▲"; R$(I, 4)
3540 NEXT I
3560 PRINT AT 21, 5; D$(1); "▲"; D$(2); "▲"; D$(3);
```

```
                  "▲"; D$(4)
3570 INPUT "Copy▲this▲to▲printer(y▲or▲n)"; k$
3580 IF k$ = "y" OR k$ = "Y" THEN COPY ∶ GO TO 3570
3590 IF k$ = "n" OR k$ = "N" THEN RETURN
3600 IF k$ = "E" THEN CLEAR ∶ STOP
3610 GO TO 3570
4000 REM
4010 REM plot▲sales▲graph
4020 CLS ∶ PRINT AT 0, 10; INVERSE 1; "SALES▲GRAPH"
4030 PRINT AT 2, 0; INVERSE 1; "YEAR"; AT 1, 26;
        INVERSE 1; "AVE";   EXI SHI 0 AT 2, 26; INVERSE 1;
        "SALES"
4040 IF gm = 1 THEN GO TO 4500
4050 LET gm = 1
4060 PRINT AT 2, 12; INVERSE 1; INK 3;
        FLASH 1; "PLOTTING"
4080 LET max = INT ( VAL A$(1)) ∶ LET min = max
4090 FOR I = 2 TO NY
4100 LET n1 = INT ( VAL A$(I))
4110 IF n1 > max THEN LET max = n1
4120 IF n1 < min THEN LET min = n1
4130 BEEP .05, 0
4140 NEXT I
4150 LET ran = max-min
4160 LET rat = INT (ran/152+.5)
4170 LET ox = 40
4180 FOR I = 1 TO NY
4190 LET n1 = INT ( VAL A$(I)) ∶ LET nx = INT
                ((n1-min)/rat+.5)+40
4200 LET C(I) = nx-ox ∶ LET ox = nx
4210 BEEP .05, 24
4220 NEXT I
4230 PRINT AT 2, 12; "▲▲▲▲▲▲▲▲▲"
4500 REM
4510 REM redisplay▲sales▲curve
4520 FOR I = 1 TO NY
4530 LET Ln = I+3-1 ∶ PRINT AT Ln, 0; Y$(I); AT Ln, 25;
        A$(I)
4540 NEXT I
4550 PLOT 40, 155 ∶ DRAW 151, 0 ∶ PLOT 40, 155 ∶
        DRAW 0, -155
4560 PLOT 40+C(1), 147
4570 FOR I = 2 TO NY
4580 DRAW C(I), -8
4590 NEXT I
4600 INPUT "Copy▲to▲printer▲(y▲or▲n)▲"; k$
4610 IF k$ = "y" OR k$ = "Y" THEN COPY ∶ GO TO 4600
4620 IF k$ = "n" OR k$ = "N" THEN RETURN
4630 IF k$ = "E" THEN STOP
4640 GO TO 4600
7000 REM
7010 REM number▲trimming
7030 LET X$ = "▲▲▲▲▲▲▲▲▲▲" ∶ REM 10▲spaces
7040 LET W$ = "1000000" ∶ REM 6▲decimal▲places
7050 LET T$ = STR$ ( INT VAL S$)
7060 IF ns > 0 THEN LET T$ = X$(1 TO ns-
        LEN T$)+T$+"." ∶
        GO TO 7080
7070 LET T$ = ".0"
```

```
7080 LET n3 = VAL W$(1 TO nd+1) :
        REM nd.is.number.of.decimal.places
7090 LET U$ = STR$ ( INT (( VAL S$- VAL T$)*n3+.5))
7100 IF VAL U$ < VAL W$(1 TO nd) THEN LET
        U$ = W$(2 TO nd- LEN U$+1)+U$
7110 IF ns = 0 THEN LET T$ = "."
7120 LET S$ = T$+U$
7130 RETURN
8000 REM
8010 REM main.loop
8020 LET hm = 0 : LET cm = hm : LET gm = hm :
        REM init.display.mode
8030 GO SUB 1000 : REM input.year.range
8040 GO SUB 2000 : REM input.sales.history
8050 GO SUB 3000 : REM caculates
8060 GO SUB 4000 : REM plot.graph
8070 GO TO 8040
```

# Possessions Evaluation

DESCRIPTION
-----------

This is one of the three financial model programs in
this book. The model will assist individuals in
itemizing and evaluating their personal possessions. The
evaluation is useful for insurance coverage and claims
for fire or theft losses. It could also be used for
capital expenditure items in a small business, such as
office or manufacturing equipment.

Each possession is evaluated on its original cost,
resale value, and replacement cost.

The resale value is calculated according to
straight-line depreciation, and the replacement cost is
based on the local inflation rate.

Replacement value could also be evaluated using an
accepted price appreciation rate in place of the local
inflation rate.


HOW TO RUN THE PROGRAM
-----------------------

The whole model is again screen driven. You have to
enter BASIC INFORMATION first before you can enter any
information about items that you own.

```
    BASIC INFORMATION -:
        NAME              : 20 chars
        CURRENT YEAR      : 4 chars, has to be at least
                            1982
        LOCAL INFLATION   : less than 100 percent
        NUMBER OF ITEMS   : less than 100

    ITEM INFORMATION -:
        DESCRIPTION       : 18 chars
        LOCATION          : 10 chars
        DATE ACQUIRED     : 4 chars before this year
        LIFE              : within 100 years
        ORIGINAL COST     : numeric
```


PROGRAM STRUCTURE
------------------

The structure of the program is as follows:

INITIALISATION
----------------
    INITIALISE  STRING VARIABLES ( NAME AND YEAR )
    INPUT BASIC INFORMATION
    INITIALISE  ARRAYS OF description
                        location
                        date acquired
                        life


    INITIALISE  ARRAYS

INPUT ITEM INFORMATION
------------------------
    SET UP ITEM SCREEN
    INPUT ITEM DATA FIELDS
    CALCULATES RESALE VALUE
    CALCULATES REPLACEMENT COST

MAIN LOOP
---------
    PERFORM INPUT ITEM INFORMATION
            UNTIL all items finished OR inkey$ = '*'
    LOAD HEADER SCREEN
    DISPLAY FINAL HEADER INFORMATION
    STOP


SPECIAL NOTES
--------------

    You will notice that all values in this model are
displayed as integer only. This is justifiable as all
long term possessions need only to be valued to the
nearest dollar.

    The author has decided to leave you the challenge of
further developing this program to make it capable of :
    *    redisplaying each item information sequence
    *    finding items in the same location and grouping
            them together

POSSESSIONS EVALUATION

```
 100 REM EVALUATE
 110 REM possessions.evaluation.program
 120 GO TO 9000
1000 REM
1010 REM Header.display.routine
1020 REM
1030 REM Display.screen
1040 CLS : PRINT AT 1, 6; "POSSESSIONS.EVALUATION" :
        PRINT AT 2, 6; "----------------------"
1050 PRINT AT 4, 3; "NAME :."
1060 PRINT AT 6, 3; "CURRENT.YEAR :."
1070 PRINT AT 8, 3; "LOCAL.INFLATION :...·..%"
1080 PRINT AT 10, 3; "NUMBER.OF.ITEMS :."
1090 PRINT AT 12, 1; "TOTAL" : PRINT AT 13, 1; "-----"
1100 PRINT AT 14, 3; "REPLACEMENT.VALUE.."'"
1110 PRINT AT 15, 3; "ORIGINAL....VALUE"
1120 PRINT AT 16, 23; "--------"
1130 PRINT AT 17, 3; "DIFFERENCE"; AT 17, 22; "'"
1140 PRINT AT 18, 23; " = = = = = = = = ="
1150 PRINT AT 19, 3; "pc.CHANGE"; AT 19, 14;
        "..·..%"
1160 PRINT AT 21, 3; "TOT.CURRENT.VALUE..'"
1170 RETURN
5000 REM
5010 REM Record.routine
5020 REM Display.record.screen
5030 FOR I = 1 TO NI
5040 CLS : PRINT AT 1, 8; "ITEM.DESCRIPTION" :
        PRINT AT 2, 8; "----------------"
5050 PRINT AT 4, 1; "DESCRIPTION :"
5060 PRINT AT 6, 1; "LOCATION :"
5070 PRINT AT 8, 1; "DATE.ACQUIRED :"; AT 8, 22;
        "LIFE :..yrs"
5080 PRINT AT 10, 1; "ORIGINAL.COST :'"
5090 PRINT AT 13, 1; "CURRENT" : PRINT AT 14, 1;
        "--------"
5100 PRINT AT 16, 3; "RESALE.VALUE"; AT 16, 21; "'"
5110 PRINT AT 18, 3; "REPLACEMENT.COST"
5120 PRINT AT 4, 14; INVERSE 1;
        "................."
5130 PRINT AT 6, 11; INVERSE 1; "..........."
5140 PRINT AT 8, 16; INVERSE 1; "....."
5150 PRINT AT 8, 27; INVERSE 1; ".."
5160 PRINT AT 10, 16; INVERSE 1; "......"
5170 REM input.item.data
5180 PRINT AT 4, 0; FLASH 1; " > "
5190 INPUT D$(I) : IF D$(I, 1) = "*" THEN GO TO 5410
5200 PRINT AT 4, 14; INVERSE 1; D$(I)
5210 PRINT AT 4, 0; "." : PRINT AT 6, 0; FLASH 1; " >
"
5220 INPUT L$(I) : IF L$(I) = "*" THEN GO TO 5410
5230 PRINT AT 6, 11; EXT SHI 0 INVERSE 1; L$(I)
5240 PRINT AT 6, 0; "." : PRINT AT 8, 0; FLASH 1; " >
"
```

139

```
5250 INPUT T$(I) : IF VAL T$(I, 1 TO 4) > VAL
        C$(1 TO 4) THEN GO TO 5250
5260 PRINT AT 8, 16; INVERSE 1; T$(I)
5270 PRINT AT 8, 0; ".▲" : PRINT AT 8, 21; FLASH 1;
        " > "
5280 INPUT L : IF L < 0 THEN GO TO 5280
5290 LET L = INT L : PRINT AT 8, 27; INVERSE 1; L
5300 PRINT AT 8, 21; "▲" : PRINT AT 10, 0; FLASH 1;
        " > "
5310 INPUT O : IF O < 0 THEN GO TO 5310
5320 LET O = INT O : PRINT AT 10, 16; INVERSE 1; O
5330 PRINT AT 10, 0; "▲"
5340 REM calculate▲resale▲value
5350 LET yu = VAL C$- VAL T$(I)
        :LET yu =(yu < L)*yu + (yu >= L)*L
        : LET rv = INT ((L-yu)*O/L)
5360 LET TC = TC+rv : PRINT AT 16, 23+7-
        LEN ( STR$ rv); rv
5370 LET rc = INT (O*(1+LI/100)^yu)
        : LET TR = TR+rc
        : PRINT AT 18,23+7- LEN ( STR$ rc); rc
5380 LET TO = TO+O
5390 IF INKEY$ = ""▲ THEN GO TO 5390
5400 NEXT I
5410 RETURN
6000 REM
6010 REM display▲final▲header
6020 PRINT AT 4, 9; INVERSE 1; N$
6030 PRINT AT 6, 17; INVERSE 1; C$
6040 PRINT AT 8, 20; INVERSE 1; INT (LI*100)/100
6050 PRINT AT 10, 20; INVERSE 1; NI
6060 PRINT AT 14, 24+8- LEN ( STR$ TR); TR
6070 PRINT AT 15, 24+8- LEN ( STR$ TO); TO
6080 LET di = ABS (TR-TO) : PRINT AT 17,
        24+8- LEN ( STR$ di); di
6090 IF TR < TO THEN PRINT AT 17, 21; "-" : PRINT
        AT 19, 12; "-"
6100 PRINT AT 19, 14; INT ((di/TO)*10000)/100; "▲%"
6110 PRINT AT 21, 24+8- LEN ( STR$ TC); TC
6120 IF INKEY$ <> "*" THEN GO TO 6120
6130 RETURN
8000 REM
8010 REM initialise▲data
8020 DIM C$(4) : DIM N$(20) : LET N$ = "▲" : LET
        CY = 0 : LET LI = 0 : LET NI = 0 : LET
        TR = 0 : LET TO = 0 : LET TC = 0
8030 GO SUB 1000 : REM display▲header
8040 PRINT AT 4, 9; INVERSE 1;
        "▲▲▲▲▲▲▲▲▲▲▲▲▲▲▲▲▲▲▲▲▲▲▲▲"
8050 PRINT AT 6, 17; INVERSE 1; "▲▲▲▲▲"
8060 PRINT AT 8, 20; INVERSE 1; "▲▲"; AT 8, 23;
        "▲▲"
8070 PRINT AT 10, 20; INVERSE 1; "▲▲"
8080 REM input▲fields
8090 PRINT AT 4, 2; FLASH 1; " > "
8100 INPUT N$ : IF N$ = "▲" THEN GO TO 8100
```

```
8110 PRINT AT 4, 9; INVERSE 1; N$(1 TO 20)
8120 PRINT AT 4, 2; "▲" : PRINT AT 6, 2; FLASH 1; " >
"
8130 INPUT C$ : IF VAL C$ < 1982 THEN GO TO 8130
8140 PRINT AT 6, 17; INVERSE 1; C$
8150 PRINT AT 6, 2; "▲"
8160 PRINT AT 8, 2; FLASH 1; " > "
8180 INPUT LI : IF LI > 100 OR LI < 0 THEN GO TO 8180
8190 PRINT AT 8, 20; " EXI O EXI SHI 7"+ STR$ ( INT
(LI*100)/100)+" EXI 7 EXI SHI O"
8210 PRINT AT 8, 2; "▲" : PRINT AT 10, 2; FLASH 1;
        " > "
8220 INPUT NI : PRINT AT 10, 20;
        " EXI O EXI SHI 7"+ STR$ NI+" EXI 7 EXI SHI O"
8230 PRINT AT 10, 2; "▲"
8240 PRINT AT 12, 9; FLASH 1; INK 3; "INITIALISING"
8250 DIM D$(NI, 18)
8260 DIM L$(NI, 10)
8270 DIM T$(NI, 4)
8280 DIM L(NI)
8290 DIM O(NI)
8300 FOR I = 1 TO NI
8310 LET D$(I) = "▲" : LET L$(I) = "▲" : LET
        T$(I) = "▲"
8320 LET L(I) = 0 : LET O(I) = 0
8330 NEXT I
8340 PRINT AT 12, 9; INK 3; "FINISHED▲▲▲▲" : FOR
        I = 1 TO 50 : NEXT I
8350 LET TR = 0 : LET TO = TR : LET TC = TR
8360 RETURN
9000 REM
9010 REM main▲loop
9020 GO SUB 8000 : REM input▲header▲data
9030 GO SUB 5000 : REM input▲item
9040 REM display▲final▲header▲info
9050 GO SUB 1000
9060 GO SUB 6000
9070 PRINT AT 12, 9; FLASH 1; INK 1; "PROGRAM▲ENDED"
9080 STOP
```

# Chess

Copyright (c)  Clifford Ramshaw and Beam Software

    This program will allow you to challenge the computer to a game of chess. But be warned the computer is a terrible player and it is very very slow.

    Hovever this program does have some nice graphics and for anyone who is a keen chess player it should not be too hard to turn the computer into a better player. Alternatively the program could be changed to allow two human players to have a game. The choice is yours.
    This program is an excellent example of what is possible on the SPECTRUM. Chess is generally considered a game that is difficult for computers to play. While this program in no way pretends to play well it does show just what can be done in SPECTRUM basic with a little effort.

    When the program is run the computer will set up the variables used, draw the board and pieces and then ask you for a move. You are white (at the top) and your move is entered as letter from 'a' to 'h' followed by a number from '1' to '8'.
    The computer does not check to see if your move is a legal one so be careful, (unless you are unscrupulous and want to cheat).

How the program works

    The following is a breakdown of the program

| lines | description |
| --- | --- |
| 1 - 4 | initialization of the screen and some variables that are used to save space in the data statements used to build the graphic chess pieces |
| 10 - 270 | builds the chess pieces in the user defined graphics set from the data statments in lines 30 - 220 |
| 280 - 315 | draws the empty board on the screen |
| 318 - 360 | dimensions the board array and the arrays used to define the allowed moves of the pieces, then fills the board array |
| 370 | calls the subroutine to put the pieces |

on the screen

```
  1 PAPER 7 : BORDER 7 : CLS
  2 LET p = 248 : LET t = 31 : LET a = 128 :
    LET g = 13 : LET h = 160
  3 LET b = 192 : LET d = 224 : LET e = 240 :
    LET f = 15
  4 LET x = 0 : LET y = 1 : LET z = 3 : LET c = 7 :
    LET i = 160
  5 LET f$ = "" : DIM A$(1, 1)
  6 LET kx = 5 : LET ky = 8 : LET q = 0
 10 FOR m = USR "a" TO USR "t"+7
 20 READ n : POKE m, n : NEXT m
 30 DATA x, x, x, x, x, x, y, z
 40 DATA x, x, x, x, x, x, a, b
 50 DATA c, c, z, y, z, c, x, x
 60 DATA d, d, b, a, b, d, x, x
 70 DATA y, c, c, y, g, f, f, c
 80 DATA a, d, d, a, 176, e, e, d
 90 DATA z, z, z, y, c, f, 31, x
100 DATA b, b, b, a, d, e, p, x
110 DATA 4, 5, 2, y, z, c, c, c
120 DATA 32, h, 64, a, b, d, d, d
130 DATA z, y, y, y, z, c, f, x
140 DATA b, a, a, a, b, d, e, x
150 DATA y, z, c, c, 14, g, c, z
160 DATA a, b, h, 112, e, d, d, b
170 DATA x, x, x, x, x, 5, 5, c
180 DATA x, x, x, x, x, h, h, d
190 DATA x, x, x, y, z, c, c, z
200 DATA x, x, a, b, d, e, p, 152
210 DATA y, y, y, z, c, c, f, x
220 DATA a, a, a, b, d, d, e, x
230 DIM t$(7, 2) : DIM b$(7, 2)
240 FOR x = 1 TO 7 : READ t$(x), b$(x) : NEXT x
250 DATA " GRA A GRA B", " GRA C GRA D",
    " GRA Q GRA R", " GRA S GRA T"
260 DATA " GRA M GRA N", " GRA K GRA L",
    " GRA O GRA P", " GRA C GRA D"
270 DATA " GRA I GRA J", " GRA K GRA L",
    " GRA E GRA F", " GRA G GRA H",
    " ▲▲", " ▲▲"
280 LET i = 2 : LET p = 4 : PRINT
    "▲▲A▲B▲C▲D▲E▲F▲G▲H"
290 PRINT : FOR x = 0 TO 7 : FOR y = 0 TO 1 :
    PRINT "▲▲";
300 FOR z = 0 TO 3 : PRINT PAPER p; "▲▲"; PAPER i;
    "▲▲";
310 NEXT z : PRINT : NEXT y : LET t = i : LET i = p
    : LET p = t : NEXT x
315 FOR y = 1 TO 8 : PRINT AT y+y, 0; y : NEXT y
320 DIM b(8, 8) : FOR y = 1 TO 8 : FOR x = 1 TO 8
330 LET z = (y = 8)*-b(x, 1)+(y = 2)*-1+(y = 7)
340 IF y = 1 THEN READ z
350 LET b(x, y) = z : NEXT x : NEXT y
```

```
360 DATA -4, -2, -3, -5, -6, -3, -2, -4
370 GO SUB 2000
380 DIM d(6, 8, 2) : DIM p(6)
390 FOR x = 1 TO 6 : LET p(x) = 2 : FOR y = 1 TO 8
400 LET d(x, y, 7) = ((y < 3) OR (y = 8))+((y > 3)
        AND (y < 7))*-1
410 LET d(x, y, 1) = ((y > 1) AND
        (y < 5))+(y > 5)*-1
420 NEXT y : IF x <> 2 THEN GO TO 460
430 FOR y = 1 TO 4 : READ d(x, y, 1), d(x, y, 2) :
        LET d(x, y+4, 1) = -d(x, y, 1) :
        LET d(x, y+4, 2) = -d(x, y, 2)
440 NEXT y
450 DATA -2, 1, -1, 2, 1, 2, 2, 1
460 IF x = 1 THEN LET p(x) = 8
470 IF x > 4 THEN LET p(x) = 1
480 NEXT x
490 DIM c$(5) : FOR x = 1 TO 5 : READ c$(x) : NEXT x
500 DATA "p", "n", "b", "r", "q"
600 GO SUB 3000
610 PRINT AT 8, 22; FLASH 1; "THINKING";
620 GO SUB 4000
630 GO TO 600
800 LET A$(1) = INKEY$ : IF A$(1) = "p" THEN
        GO TO 900
805 IF (A$(1) = "") OR (A$(1) < "a") OR
        (A$(1) > "h") THEN GO TO 800
810 PRINT A$(1); ".";
820 LET X1 = CODE A$(1)-96
830 LET A$(1) = INKEY$ : IF (A$(1) = "") OR
        (A$(1) < "1") OR (A$(1) > "8") THEN GO TO 830
840 PRINT A$(1);
850 LET Y1 = CODE A$(1)-48
860 RETURN
900 LET X1 = 999 : LET Y1 = 0 : RETURN
1000 LET z1 = INT (( ATTR (y+y, x+x))/8) : IF z1 >= 8
        THEN LET z1 = z1-8
1010 PRINT BRIGHT 1; PAPER z1; INK i; AT y+y, x+x;
        t$(c); AT y+y+1, x+x; b$(c);
1020 RETURN
2000 FOR y = 1 TO 8 : FOR x = 1 TO 8
2010 LET z = b(x, y) : IF z = 0 THEN GO TO 2040
2020 LET i = 7 : IF z > 0 THEN LET i = 0
2030 LET c = ABS z : GO SUB 1000
2040 NEXT x : NEXT y
2050 RETURN
3000 IF f$ = "1" THEN PRINT AT 20, 22; "CHECKMATE" :
        STOP
3010 PRINT AT 3, 22; "Your.move" : PRINT AT 4, 22;
        "FROM."; : GO SUB 800 : IF X1 = 999 THEN
        STOP
3020 LET X = X1 : LET Y = Y1
3030 PRINT AT 5, 24; "TO."; : GO SUB 800 :
        LET XB = X1 : LET YB = Y1
3040 IF b(XB, YB) > 0 THEN
        LET p(b(XB, YB)) = p(b(XB, YB))-1
```

```
3050 LET b(XB, YB) = b(X, Y)
3060 LET b(X, Y) = 0 : LET i = 7
3070 IF b(XB, YB) < -1 OR YB < 8 THEN GO TO 3120
3080 PRINT AT 6, 21; "Piece.";
3090 LET A$(1) = INKEY$ :
3100 LET a = 0 : FOR z = 1 TO 5 : IF c$(z) = A$(1)
     THEN LET a = -z
3110 NEXT z : IF a = 0 THEN GO TO 3090
3115 PRINT A$(1); : LET b(XB, YB) = a
3120 LET c = 7 : GO SUB 1000
3130 LET c = -b(XB, YB) : LET x = XB : LET y = YB :
     GO SUB 1000
3140 PRINT AT 3, 22; ".........."; AT 4, 22;
     ".........."; AT 5, 24; "......";
     AT 6, 21; "........";
3150 RETURN
4000 LET xb = 0 : LET yb = xb : LET db = xb :
     LET cL = 1 : LET bp = xb : LET x = 9
4010 LET ax = kx : LET ay = ky : LET g$ = "" :
     GO SUB 5010 : LET g$ = f$
4020 FOR y = 1 TO 8 : FOR x = 1 TO 8 : LET tb = 0 :
     LET cz = 1 : LET ty = 0 : LET tx = 0 :
     LET d = 0
4030 IF b(x, y) < 1 THEN GO TO 4370
4040 LET p = b(x, y) : FOR i = 1 TO 8 :
     LET dy = d(p, i, 2) : LET dx = d(p, i, 1) :
     LET ax = kx : LET ay = ky : LET c1 = 1 :
     LET po = 0
4050 IF x+dx < 1 OR x+dx > 8 OR y+dy < 1 OR y+dy > 8
     THEN GO TO 4300
4060 IF p > 2 AND p < 6 THEN GO TO 4210
4070 IF dy > -1 AND p = 1 THEN GO TO 4300
4080 IF y > 1 OR p > 1 THEN GO TO 4130
4090 LET p(5) = p(5)+1
4100 LET b(x, y) = 5
4120 GO TO 4300
4130 IF dx <> 0 AND b(x+dx, y+dy) > -1 THEN
     GO TO 4300
4140 IF p = 6 THEN LET kx = x : LET ky = y :
     LET ax = x+dx : LET ay = y+dy : GO SUB 5000 :
     IF f$ = "1" THEN GO TO 4300
4150 IF dx = 0 AND b(x, y+dy) <> 0 THEN GO TO 4300
4160 LET po = 8-p-b(x+dx, y+dy)*3
4170 IF y <> 7 OR dx <> 0 OR b(x, 5) <> 0 OR p > 1
     THEN GO TO 4300
4180 IF g$ = "1" THEN GO SUB 5000 : IF f$ = "" THEN
     GO TO 4300
4190 IF g$ = "1" OR RND > .3 THEN LET c1 = 2
4200 GO TO 4300
4210 LET x1 = x : LET y1 = y
4220 IF p = 3 AND INT (i/2)*2 < i THEN GO TO 4300
4230 IF p = 4 AND INT (i/2)*2 = i THEN GO TO 4300
4240 IF x1+dx < 1 OR x1+dx > 8 OR y1+dy < 1 OR
     y1+dy > 8 THEN LET c1 = c1-1 : GO TO 4300
4250 IF b(x1+dx, y1+dy) > 0 THEN LET c1 = c1-1 :
     GO TO 4300
```

146

```
4260 LET po = 8-p+ INT ( RND *3)-b(x1+dx, y1+dy)*3
4270 IF g$ = "1" THEN GO SUB 5000 : IF f$ = "" THEN
     LET po = po+50 : GO TO 4340
4280 IF b(x1+dx, y1+dy) <> 0 THEN GO TO 4300
4290 LET c1 = c1+1 : LET x1 = x1+dx : LET y1 = y1+dy
     : GO TO 4240
4300 IF po = 0 THEN GO TO 4340
4310 IF g$ = "1" THEN GO SUB 5000 : IF f$ = "" THEN
     LET po = po+50 : GO TO 4340
4320 IF g$ = "" THEN GO SUB 5000 : IF f$ = "1" THEN
     LET po = 0 : GO TO 4340
4330 IF po >= tb THEN LET ax = x+dx*c1 :
     LET ay = y+dy*c1 : GO SUB 5000 : IF f$ = "1"
     THEN LET po = po-p*2
4340 IF po > tb THEN LET tb = po : LET tx = x :
     LET ty = y : LET d = i : LET cz = c1
4350 NEXT i
4360 IF tb > bp OR (tb = bp AND ( RND > .9 OR
     (ty < yb AND RND > .5))) THEN LET bp = tb :
     LET xb = tx : LET yb = ty : LET cL = cz :
     LET db = d
4370 NEXT x : NEXT y : LET p = b(xb, yb) :
     LET x1 = xb+d(p, db, 1)*cL :
     LET y1 = yb+d(p, db, 2)*cL : IF p = 6 THEN
     LET kx = x1 : LET ky = y1
4380 LET ax = kx : LET ay = ky :
     LET b(x1, y1) = b(xb, yb) : LET b(xb, yb) = 0
     : LET q = 1 : GO SUB 5010 : LET q = 0
4385 PRINT AT 8, 22; "▲▲▲▲▲▲▲▲▲"; AT 9, 22;
     "My▲move"; AT 10, 22; "FROM▲"; CHR$ (xb+95);
     "-"; CHR$ (yb+48);
4386 PRINT AT 11, 24; "TO▲"; CHR$ (x1+95); "-";
     CHR$ (y1+48);
4390 LET i = 0 : LET c = 7 : LET x = xb : LET y = yb
     : GO SUB 1000
4400 LET c = b(x1, y1) : LET x = x1 : LET y = y1 :
     GO SUB 1000
4410 RETURN
5000 LET pc = b(x+dx*c1, y+dy*c1) :
     LET b(x+dx*c1, y+dy*c1) = b(x, y) :
     LET b(x, y) = 0
5010 LET f$ = "" : FOR r = 1 TO 6 : FOR j = 1 TO 8 :
     LET d1 = d(r, j, 1) : LET d2 = d(r, j, 2) :
     LET L = 1
5020 IF ax+d1*L < 1 OR ax+d1*L > 8 OR ay+d2*L < 1 OR
     ay+d2*L > 8 THEN GO TO 5060
5030 IF r = 1 AND d2 < 1 AND q = 0 THEN GO TO 5060
5040 IF b(ax+d1*L, ay+d2*L) = -r THEN LET f$ = "1" :
     GO TO 5070
5050 IF r > 2 AND r < 6 AND b(ax+d1*L, ay+d2*L) = 0
     THEN LET L = L+1 : GO TO 5020
5060 NEXT j : NEXT r
5070 IF x > 8 THEN GO TO 5090
5080 LET b(x, y) = b(x+dx*c1, y+dy*c1) :
     LET b(x+dx*c1, y+dy*c1) = pc
5090 RETURN
```

# Draughts

This program is a combination of basic and machine language that plays a pretty fair game of draughts.

The computer displays a graphic draughts board, with your pieces (red) at the bottom and its pieces (black) at the top. You always move first and your move is input as a "from value" that tells the computer which piece to move and a "to value" which tells the computer where to move it.

The squares are identified by a letter and a number. The letters range from 'a' to 'h' and are the columns of the board. The numbers go from '1' to '8' and are the rows. For example an opening move could be 'FROM a6, TO b5' (you type 'a6' and 'b5').

If you should happen to lose the game or wish to quit just hit '0' as the first key when the computer asks you for your move.

All your moves are checked for legality so you can't cheat; but captures are not compulsory (for you), and multiple jumps are not allowed. The computer always captures if it can.

You make a king by getting a piece to the last line. Kings move only one square and can only make single captures but may move forwards or backwards

How it works:

The BASIC part of the program performs the housekeeping functions. It sets up the board, accepts and executes the player's moves and graphically displays all moves on the screen. A short machine language program is used to make the computer's move. This was done to allow the game to be played without having to wait forever for the computer to make its move. For those with an understanding of machine language, a listing of this part of the program is included.

If you do not understand machine language do not worry as this part of the program is typed in as data statements at lines 9000 - 9450. Just be careful when typing them in.

As part of the machine language section the computer has a representation of the board in memory as a series of bytes. This is why PEEKs and POKEs are used to make changes rather than using an array. It is easier for the machine language program to access this board in memory than in an array.

The program

```
   LINES                DESCRIPTION
   -----                -----------
   10 - 20                  These two lines set the top of
                        memory so that the machine language
                        program will be protected. The subroutine
                        at 9000 is then called to put the machine
                        language in memory.

   30 - 79                  This section sets the screen
                        attributes, and builds the board
                        representation in memory

   80 - 160                 Sets up the user defined graphics
                        for the pieces then displays the empty
                        board.

   170 - 230                Puts the pieces on the screen in
                        initial configuration.

   300 - 320                Main loop
                     1   get players move
                         get computers move
                         goto 1

   1000 - 1060              Draws a piece on the board at position
                        x,y with color c. The piece is determined
                        by p : 0 = blank
                               1 = normal man
                               2 = king

   2000 - 2540              Inputs the player's move
                        It can be broken down as follows:
               2000 - 2020  displays message
               2030 - 2050  gets from value and checks if
                            it is legal
               2060 - 2110  gets to value and checks if
                            it is a valid direction to move
               2120 - 2200  makes the player's move if it was
                            a capture
               2500 - 2540  makes a normal move for the player

   3000 - 3110              Calls the machine language program
                        for the computer's move and does that
                        move on the board

   3500                     Displays the x,y values of the
                        computer's move

   3900 - 3904              The program jumps to here if the
                        computer has lost

   4000 - 5010              Inputs an x,y value to be used in
                        the player's move
                        If the player hits '0' as the first key
```

the game ends and he is asked if he wishes
to play again

9000 - 9020            Reads the machine language program

from the data statements and stores
it into memory.

9100 - 9450            Comprises the data statements that
make up the machine language program.

DRAUGHTS

```
 10 CLEAR 32019
 20 GO SUB 9000
 30 RESTORE 70
 40 BORDER 7 : PAPER 7 : INK 0 : CLS
 50 FOR x = 32420 TO 32420+89
 60 READ a : POKE x, a : NEXT x
 70 DATA 255, 255, 255, 255, 255, 255, 255, 255, 255
 71 DATA 0, 1, 0, 1, 0, 1, 0, 1, 255
 72 DATA 1, 0, 1, 0, 1, 0, 1, 0, 255
 73 DATA 0, 1, 0, 1, 0, 1, 0, 1, 255
 74 DATA 0, 0, 0, 0, 0, 0, 0, 0, 255
 75 DATA 0, 0, 0, 0, 0, 0, 0, 0, 255
 76 DATA 2, 0, 2, 0, 2, 0, 2, 0, 255
 77 DATA 0, 2, 0, 2, 0, 2, 0, 2, 255
 78 DATA 2, 0, 2, 0, 2, 0, 2, 0, 255
 79 DATA 255, 255, 255, 255, 255, 255, 255, 255, 255
 80 FOR x = USR "a" TO 63+ USR "a"
 90 READ a : POKE x, a : NEXT x
100 DATA 0, 7, 31, 63, 63, 127, 127, 127
101 DATA 0, 224, 248, 252, 252, 254, 254, 254
102 DATA 127, 127, 127, 63, 63, 31, 7, 0
103 DATA 254, 254, 254, 252, 252, 248, 224, 0
104 DATA 0, 7, 31, 60, 56, 116, 98, 97
105 DATA 0, 224, 248, 60, 28, 46, 70, 134
106 DATA 97, 98, 116, 56, 60, 31, 7, 0
107 DATA 134, 70, 46, 28, 60, 248, 224, 0
110 PRINT "▴▴A▴B▴C▴D▴E▴F▴G▴H" : PRINT
115 LET d = 3 : LET L = 5
120 FOR y = 1 TO 8 : PRINT AT y+y, 0; y; "▴";
130 FOR z = 1 TO 2 : FOR x = 1 TO 4
140 PRINT PAPER d; "▴▴"; PAPER L; "▴▴"; :
       NEXT x : PRINT : PRINT "▴▴"; : NEXT z
150 LET t = d : LET d = L : LET L = t
160 NEXT y
170 LET p = 1
180 FOR x = 2 TO 8 STEP 2
190 LET c = 0 : LET y = 1 : GO SUB 1000 : LET y = 3
     : GO SUB 1000
200 LET c = 2 : LET y = 7 : GO SUB 1000 : NEXT x
210 FOR x = 1 TO 7 STEP 2
220 LET c = 0 : LET y = 2 : GO SUB 1000
230 LET c = 2 : LET y = 6 : GO SUB 1000 : LET y = 8
       : GO SUB 1000 : NEXT x
300 GO SUB 2000
310 GO SUB 3000
320 GO TO 300
1000 PAPER L : INK c : PRINT AT y+y, x+x;
1005 IF p = 0 THEN PRINT "▴▴";
1010 IF p = 1 THEN PRINT " GRA A GRA B";
1020 IF p = 2 THEN PRINT " GRA E GRA F";
1030 PRINT AT y+y+1, x+x;
1035 IF p = 0 THEN PRINT "▴▴";
1040 IF p = 1 THEN PRINT " GRA C GRA D";
```

```
1050 IF p = 2 THEN PRINT " ▓▓▓ G ▓▓▓ H";
1060 RETURN
2000 PAPER 7 : INK O : PRINT AT 6, 22; "Your▪move"
2010 BEEP .5, 10 : PRINT AT 7, 22; "FROM▪ :▪▪▪";
2020 PRINT AT B, 22; "▪TO▪▪ :▪▪▪";
2030 LET L = 7 : GO SUB 4000 : LET fx = x :
        LET fy = y
2040 LET fp = 32419+9*fy+fx : LET f = PEEK fp
2050 IF f <> 2 AND f <> 130 THEN GO TO 2010
2060 LET L = B : GO SUB 4000 : LET tx = x :
        LET ty = y
2070 LET tp = 32419+9*ty+tx : LET t = PEEK tp
2080 LET dx = tx-fx : LET dy = ty-fy
2090 IF ( ABS dx <> 1 AND ABS dx <> 2) OR
        ABS dx <> ABS dy THEN GO TO 2010
2100 IF (dy = 1 OR dy = 2) AND f = 2 THEN GO TO 2010
2110 IF ABS dx = 1 THEN GO TO 2500
2120 IF t <> 0 THEN GO TO 2010
2130 LET jx = fx+dx/2 : LET jy = fy+dy/2
2140 LET jp = 32419+9*jy+jx : LET j = PEEK jp
2150 IF j <> 1 AND j <> 129 THEN GO TO 2010
2160 LET c = 2 : LET p = 0 : LET x = fx : LET y = fy
        : GO SUB 1000 : POKE fp, 0
2170 LET p = 1 : IF f = 130 OR ty = 1 THEN LET p = 2
2180 LET x = tx : LET y = ty : GO SUB 1000 :
        POKE tp, f : IF ty = 1 THEN POKE tp, 130
2190 LET p = 0 : LET x = jx : LET y = jy :
        GO SUB 1000 : POKE jp, 0
2200 RETURN
2500 IF t <> 0 THEN GO TO 2010
2510 LET p = 0 : LET c = 2 : LET x = fx :
        LET y = fy : GO SUB 1000 : POKE fp, 0
2520 LET p = 1 : IF f = 130 OR ty = 1 THEN LET p = 2
2530 LET x = tx : LET y = ty : GO SUB 1000 :
        POKE tp, f : IF y = 1 THEN POKE tp, 130
2540 RETURN
3000 LET mp = USR 32020
3002 PAPER 7 : INK O : PRINT AT 10, 22; "MY▪move"
3003 PRINT AT 11, 22; "FROM▪ :▪▪▪";
3004 PRINT AT 12, 22; "▪TO▪▪ :▪▪▪";
3005 FOR i = 1 TO 50 : NEXT i
3010 IF mp = 0 THEN GO TO 3900
3020 LET fy = INT (mp/256) : LET ty = mp-256*fy
3030 LET fx = INT (fy/16) : LET fy = fy-16*fx
3040 LET tx = INT (ty/16) : LET ty = ty-16*tx
3045 LET x = fx : LET y = fy : LET z = 11 :
        GO SUB 3500 : LET x = tx : LET y = ty :
        LET z = 12 : GO SUB 3500
3050 LET p = 0 : LET x = fx : LET y = fy :
        GO SUB 1000
3060 LET tp = 32419+9*ty+tx : LET t = PEEK tp
3070 LET p = 1 : IF t = 129 THEN LET p = 2
3080 LET c = 0 : LET x = tx : LET y = ty :
        GO SUB 1000
3090 IF ABS (tx-fx) <> 2 THEN RETURN
3100 LET x = fx+(tx-fx)/2 : LET y = fy+(ty-fy)/2
```

```
3110 LET p = 0 : GO SUB 1000 : RETURN
3500 PRINT AT z, 28; CHR$ (x+64); CHR$ (y+48) :
     RETURN
3900 PRINT INK 0; AT 20, 0; "I have no move --
     YOU WIN"
3901 PRINT AT 21, 0; "Another game ? "
3902 IF INKEY$ = "" THEN GO TO 3902
3903 IF INKEY$ = "y" THEN GO TO 50
3904 STOP
4000 PRINT AT L, 28; FLASH 1; " "; CHR$ 8;
4010 LET a$ = INKEY$
4015 IF a$ = "0" THEN GO TO 5000
4020 IF a$ < "a" OR a$ > "h" THEN GO TO 4010
4030 PRINT a$ : LET x = CODE a$-96
4040 PRINT AT L, 29; FLASH 1; " "; CHR$ 8;
4050 LET a$ = INKEY$
4060 IF a$ < "1" OR a$ > "8" THEN GO TO 4050
4070 PRINT a$ : LET y = CODE a$-48
4080 RETURN
5000 PRINT INK 0; AT 20, 0; "Bad luck -- I WON"
5010 GO TO 3901
9000 RESTORE 9100 : FOR x = 32020 TO 32301
9010 READ a : POKE x, a : NEXT x
9020 RETURN
9100 DATA 175, 33, 177, 125, 6, 10, 119, 35
9110 DATA 16, 252, 6, 35, 33, 174, 126, 126
9120 DATA 254, 1, 40, 16, 254, 129, 32, 24
9130 DATA 17, 246, 255, 205, 187, 125, 17, 248
9140 DATA 255, 205, 187, 125, 17, 8, 0, 205
9150 DATA 187, 125, 17, 10, 0, 205, 187, 125
9160 DATA 35, 35, 16, 219, 58, 182, 125, 167
9170 DATA 40, 18, 42, 183, 125, 237, 91, 185
9180 DATA 125, 229, 126, 54, 0, 25, 54, 0
9190 DATA 25, 119, 24, 19, 58, 177, 125, 167
9200 DATA 40, 29, 42, 178, 125, 237, 91, 180
9210 DATA 125, 126, 54, 0, 229, 25, 119, 235
9220 DATA 225, 205, 135, 125, 121, 230, 15, 254
9230 DATA 8, 192, 26, 246, 128, 18, 201, 1
9240 DATA 0, 0, 201, 235, 205, 146, 125, 79
9250 DATA 235, 205, 146, 125, 71, 201, 229, 213
9260 DATA 197, 17, 164, 126, 175, 237, 82, 61
9270 DATA 17, 9, 0, 60, 237, 82, 48, 251
9280 DATA 71, 25, 125, 60, 7, 7, 7, 7
9290 DATA 128, 193, 209, 225, 201, 0, 0, 0
9300 DATA 0, 0, 0, 0, 0, 0, 0, 205
9310 DATA 19, 126, 254, 255, 200, 230, 127, 254
9320 DATA 1, 200, 254, 2, 40, 78, 229, 25
9330 DATA 213, 17, 246, 255, 205, 13, 126, 40
9340 DATA 39, 17, 248, 255, 205, 13, 126, 40
9350 DATA 31, 17, 8, 0, 205, 5, 126, 40
9360 DATA 23, 17, 10, 0, 205, 5, 126, 40
9370 DATA 15, 209, 225, 34, 178, 125, 237, 83
9380 DATA 180, 125, 62, 1, 50, 177, 125, 201
9390 DATA 58, 177, 125, 167, 40, 235, 209, 225
9400 DATA 201, 205, 19, 126, 230, 127, 254, 2
9410 DATA 201, 205, 19, 126, 254, 130, 201, 229
```

```
9420 DATA 25, 126, 225, 201, 229, 25, 205, 19
9430 DATA 126, 225, 254, 0, 192, 62, 1, 50
9440 DATA 182, 125, 34, 183, 125, 237, 83, 185
9450 DATA 125, 201
```

# ASSEMBLY LISTING FOR DRAUGHTS

Note: The formatting of the following text has been altered for ease of use. The contents remain unaltered.

```
                00110 ;
7D14            00120          ORG
                00130 ;
0000            00140 BLANK    EQU
FFFF            00150 NULL     EQU
0001            00160 BLACK    EQU
0002            00170 WHITE    EQU
0080            00180 KING     EQU
                00190 ;
7EA4            00200 BOARD    EQU
                00210 ;
7D14            00220 START    EQU
7D14 AF         00230          XOR
7D15 21B17D     00240          LD
7D18 060A       00250          LD
7D1A 77         00260 CLEAR    LD
7D1B 23         00270          INC
7D1C 10FC       00280          DJNZ
                00290 ;
7D1E 0623       00300          LD
7D20 21AE7E     00310          LD
                00320 ;
7D23 7E         00330 NEXT     LD
7D24 FE01       00340          CP
7D26 2810       00350          JR
7D28 FE81       00360          CP
7D2A 2018       00370          JR
7D2C 11F6FF     00380          LD
7D2F CD887D     00390          CALL
7D32 11F8FF     00400          LD
7D35 CD887D     00410          CALL
7D38 110800     00420 MANFND   LD
7D3B CD887D     00430          CALL
7D3E 110A00     00440          LD
7D41 CD887D     00450          CALL
7D44 23         00460 ENDSCH   INC
7D45 23         00470          INC
7D46 10DB       00480          DJNZ
                00490 ;
7D48 3A867D     00500          LD
7D4B A7         00510          AND
7D4C 2812       00520          JR
7D4E 2A877D     00530          LD
7D51 ED5B897D   00540          LD
7D55 E5         00550          PUSH
7D56 7E         00560          LD
7D57 3600       00570          LD
7D59 19         00580          ADD
7D5A 3600       00590          LD
7D5C 19         00600          ADD
7D5D 77         00610          LD
7D5E 1813       00620          JR
7D60            00630 NORMOV   EQU
7D60 3A817D     00640          LD
7D63 A7         00650          AND
7D64 281D       00660          JR
7D66 2A827D     00670          LD
7D69 ED5B847D   00680          LD
```

156

```
32020

0           ; CODE FOR EMPTY SQUARE
-1          ; CODE FOR EDGE OF BOARD
1           ; CODE FOR A BLACK PIECE
2           ; CODE FOR A WHITE PIECE
128         ; ADD THIS FOR A KING

32420       ; ADDRESS OF BOARD


A
HL,MOVE     ; CANCEL OLD MOVES FROM MEMORY
B,10
(HL),A
HL
CLEAR

B,35        ; B = COUNT OF POSITIONS TO CHECK
HL,BOARD+10 ; HL = POSITION ON BOARD

A,(HL)      ; GET PIECE
BLACK       ; IS IT THE COMPUTERS MAN
Z,MANFND    ; YES => NORMAL PIECE
BLACK+KING  ; IS IT THE COMPUTERS KING
NZ,ENDSCH   ; NO => TRY NEXT PIECE
DE,-10      ; TEST BACKWARD JUMPS
TEST
DE,-8       ; FOR A KING
TEST
DE,8        ; TEST FORWARD JUMPS FOR
TEST
DE,10       ; EITHER KING OR NORMAL MAN
TEST
HL          ; NEXT PIECE (ONLY NEED TO CHECK
HL          ; EVERY SECOND POSITION)
NEXT

A,(CAPT)    ; CHECK TO SEE IF A CAPT WAS
A                   ; WAS FOUND
Z,NORMOV    ; NO => TRY A NORMAL MOVE
HL,(CAPTF)  ; WAS A CAPTURE SO MAKE
DE,(CAPTO)  ; MOVE ON BOARD
HL
A,(HL)      ; PIECE MOVING
(HL),BLANK  ; NOW AN EMPTY SQUARE
HL,DE
(HL),BLANK  ; REMOVE PIECE JUMPED
HL,DE
(HL),A      ; PUT PIECE BACK IN NEW SQUARE
GOTMOV      ; RETURN MOVE TO BASIC PROGRAM

A,(MOVE)    ; CHECK FOR A MOVE FOUND
A
Z,NOMOVE    ; NO => COMPUTER LOSES
HL,(FROM)   ; WAS A MOVE SO DO IT ON
DE,(DIR)    ; BOARD
```

```
7D6D  7E         00690
7D6E  3600       00700
7D70  E5         00710
7D71  19         00720
7D72  77         00730
7D73  EB         00740
7D74  E1         00750
7D75  CD0770     00760
7D78  79         00770
7D79  E60F       00780
7D7B  FE0B       00790
7D7D  C0         00800
7D7E  1A         00810
7D7F  F680       00820
7D81  12         00830
7D82  C9         00840
                 00850
7D83  010000     00860
7D86  C9         00870
                 00880
                 00890
                 00900
                 00910
                 00920
                 00930
                 00940
                 00950
                 00960
                 00970
                 00980
7D87             00990
7D87  EB         01000
7D88  CD927D     01010
7D8B  4F         01020
7D8C  EB         01030
7D8D  CD927D     01040
7D90  47         01050
7D91  C9         01060
                 01070
                 01080
                 01090
                 01100
                 01110
                 01120
                 01130
                 01140
7D92  E5         01150
7D93  D5         01160
7D94  C5         01170
7D95  11A47E     01180
7D98  AF         01190
7D99  ED52       01200
7D9B  3D         01210
7D9C  110900     01220
7D9F             01230
7D9F  3C         01240
7DA0  ED52       01250
7DA2  30FB       01260
```

```
        LD      A,(HL)          ; SAVE PIECE
        LD      (HL),BLANK      ; EMPTY SQUARE
        PUSH    HL
        ADD     HL,DE
        LD      (HL),A          ; PUT PIECE IN NEW SQUARE
GOTMOV  EX      DE,HL           ; DE = NEW BOARD POSITION
        POP     HL              ; RESTORE OLD BOARD POSITION
        CALL    CONV            ; CONVERT IT FOR BASIC PROGRAM
        LD      A,C
        AND     15              ; CHECK FOR PROMOTION
        CP      8               ; TO KING
        RET     NZ              ; NO => RETURN TO BASIC
        LD      A,(DE)          ; GET PIECE
        OR      KING            ; MAKE IT A KING
        LD      (DE),A
        RET
;
NOMOVE  LD      BC,0            ; RETURN FAILURE TO
        RET                     ; BASIC
;
; THIS SUBROUTINE TAKES HL AND DE AS BOARD
; POSITIONS AND CONVERTS THEM TO X,Y CO-ORDINATES
; FOR THE BASIC PROGRAM
;       HL => B    ( THIS WILL BE THE X,Y VALUE OF THE
;                    'FROM' POSITION FOR THE COMPUTERS
;                    MOVE )
;       DE => C    ( X,Y VALUE OF THE 'TO' POSITION )
; THE X VALUE IS IN THE TOP HALF OF THE REGISTER
; (B OR C) AND THE Y VALUE IS IN THE BOTTOM HALF
;
CONV    EQU     $
        EX      DE,HL
        CALL    CONVIT          ; CONVERT DE
        LD      C,A             ; INTO C
        EX      DE,HL
        CALL    CONVIT          ; CONVERT HL
        LD      B,A             ; INTO B
        RET
;
; CONVERT HL INTO X,Y CO-ORDINATES AND RETURNS
; THE RESULT IN A
; THE X VALUE (THE COLUMN OF THE PIECE ON THE BOARD)
; IS IN THE TOP HALF OF A
; THE Y VALUE (THE ROW OF THE PIECE ON THE BOARD)
; IS IN THE BOTTOM HALF OF A
;
CONVIT  PUSH    HL
        PUSH    DE              ; SAVE REGISTERS
        PUSH    BC
        LD      DE,BOARD        ; HL IS ADDRESS OF PIECE
        XOR     A               ; SO NEED TO SUBTRACT OUT
        SBC     HL,DE           ; ADDRESS OF BOARD TO GET
        DEC     A               ; OFFSET INTO BOARD
        LD      DE,9            ; LENGTH OF EACH ROW
CNVL    EQU     $
        INC     A               ; INCREMENT ROW NUMBER
        SBC     HL,DE           ; DECREMENT OFFSET
        JR      NC,CNVL         ; IF MORE ROWS CONTINUE
```

159

```
7DA4  47          01270
7DA5  19          01280
7DA6  7D          01290
7DA7  3C          01300
7DA8  07          01310
7DA9  07          01320
7DAA  07          01330
7DAB  07          01340
7DAC  80          01350
7DAD  C1          01360
7DAE  D1          01370
7DAF  E1          01380
7DB0  C9          01390
                  01400
                  01410
                  01420
7DB1  C0          01430
7DB2  0000        01440
7DB4  0000        01450
                  01460
                  01470
                  01480
7DB6  00          01490
7DB7  0000        01500
7DB9  0000        01510
                  01520
                  01530
                  01540
                  01550
                  01560
                  01570
                  01580
                  01590
                  01600
                  01610
                  01620
                  01630
                  01640
                  01650
                  01660
                  01670
                  01680
7DBB              01690
7DBB  CD137E      01700
7DBE  FEFF        01710
7DC0  C8          01720
7DC1  E67F        01730
7DC3  FE01        01740
7DC5  C8          01750
7DC6  FE02        01760
7DC8  284E        01770
                  01780
                  01790
                  01800
7DCA  E5          01810
7DCB  19          01820
7DCC  D5          01830
7DCD  11F6FF      01840
```

160

```
        LD      B,A         ; B = ROW NUMBER (Y)
        ADD     HL,DE       ; GET BACK COLUMN NUMBER
        LD      A,L         ; A = COLUMN NUMBER (X)
        INC     A           ; FIRST COL IS NUMBER 1
        RLCA
        RLCA                ; PUT IN TOP HALF OF REGISTER
        RLCA
        RLCA
        ADD     A,B         ; ADD IN Y
        POP     BC
        POP     DE          ; RESTORE REGISTERS
        POP     HL
        RET
;
; DATA AREA FOR NORMAL MOVES
;
MOVE    DB      0 ; FLAG TO INDICATE IF A MOVE WAS FOUND
FROM    DW      0 ; BOARD ADDRESS OF PIECE TO MOVE
DIR     DW      0 ; DIRECTION TO MOVE IT
;
; DATA AREA FOR CAPTURES
;
CAPT    DB      0 ; FLAG
CAPTF   DW      0 ; BOARD ADDRESS OF PIECE
CAPTD   DW      0 ; DIRECTION TO MOVE
;
;
;
; TEST  TYPE OF MOVE POSSIBLE FOR PEICE AT POS (HL)
;       MOVING TO POS (HL)+(DE)
;
;       IF A LEGAL MOVE IS POSSIBLE IT IS STORED
;       IN THE DATA AREA FOR A NORMAL MOVE
;
;       IF A PIECE CAN CAPTURE ITS MOVE IS PUT
;       IN THE CAPTURE DATA AREA
;
;       LEGAL NORMAL MOVES WHICH WOULD RESULT
;       IN POSSIBLE TRAPS (IMMEDIATE CAPTURE)
;       ARE SAVED ONLY IF NO OTHER MOVE HAS
;       BEEN FOUND TO DATE
;
TEST    EQU     *
        CALL    BRDFCE
        CP      NULL        ; CHECK FOR MOVE OFF BOARD
        RET     Z           ; NO MOVE IF SO
        AND     07FH
        CP      BLACK       ; OR ONTO OWN MAN
        RET     Z
        CP      WHITE       ; CHECK FOR A CAPTURE
        JR      Z,EVALCAPT  ; YOE => CHECK IF VALID
;
; EVALUATE A NORMAL MOVE
;
        PUSH    HL
        ADD     HL,DE
        PUSH    DE
        LD      DE,-10      ; CHECK FOR TRAPS
```

161

```
7DD0 CD0D7E    01850          CALL
7DD3 2827      01860          JR
7DD5 11F8FF    01870          LD
7DD8 CD0D7E    01880          CALL
7DDB 281F      01890          JR
7DDD 110800    01900          LD
7DE0 CD057E    01910          CALL
7DE3 2817      01920          JR
7DE5 110A00    01930          LD
7DE8 CD057E    01940          CALL
7DEB 280F      01950          JR
               01960 :
7DED D1        01970 SAVI1    POP
7DEE E1        01980          POP
7DEF 22B27D    01990          LD
7DF2 ED53B47D  02000          LD
7DF6 3E01      02010          LD
7DF8 32B17D    02020          LD
7DFB C9        02030          RET
               02040 :
7DFC           02050 TRAP     EQU
7DFC 3AB17D    02060          LD
7DFF A7        02070          AND
7E00 28EB      02080          JR
7E02 D1        02090          POP
7E03 E1        02100          POP
7E04 C9        02110          RET
               02120 :
7E05           02130 GETPC1   EQU
7E05 CD137E    02140          CALL
7E08 E67F      02150          AND
7E0A FE02      02160          CP
7E0C C9        02170          RET
               02180 :
7E0D           02190 GETPCE   EQU
7E0D CD137E    02200          CALL
7E10 FE82      02210          CP
7E12 C9        02220          RET
               02230 :
7E13 E5        02240 BRDPCE   PUSH
7E14 19        02250          ADD
7E15 7E        02260          LD
7E16 E1        02270          POP
7E17 C9        02280          RET
               02290 :
7E18           02300 EVALCAPT EQU
7E18 E5        02310          PUSH
7E19 19        02320          ADD
7E1A CD137E    02330          CALL
7E1D E1        02340          POP
7E1E FE00      02350          CP
7E20 C0        02360          RET
7E21 3E01      02370          LD
7E23 32B67D    02380          LD
7E26 22B77D    02390          LD
7E29 ED53897D  02400          LD
7E2D C9        02410          RET
               02420 :
```

162

```
        GETPCE      ; IS THERE A KING BEHIND PIECE
        Z,TRAP      ; YES A TRAP
        DE,-8
        GETPCE
        Z,TRAP
        DE,8        ; IS THERE ANY PIECE IN FRONT
        GETPC1      ; OF COMPUTERS MAN
        Z,TRAP      ; YES => A TRAP
        DE,10
        GETPC1
        Z,TRAP


        DE          ; NO TRAP SO SAVE MOVE
        HL
        (FROM),HL
        (DIR),DE
        A,1
        (MOVE),A    ; SET FLAG TO SAY MOVE FOUND



        *
        A,(MOVE)    ; WAS A TRAP SO SEE IF ANY
        A           ; OTHER MOVES
        Z,SAVIT     ; NO => SAVE THIS ONE
        DE          ; ELES IGNORE IT
        HL



        *           ; CHECK IF PIECE AT (HL)+(DE)
        BRDPCE
        07FH        ; IS ANY WHITE PIECE
        WHITE



        *           ; CHECK IF PIECE AT (HL)+(DE)
        BRDPCE
        WHITE+KING  ; IS A WHITE KING



        HL          ; RETURN PIECE AT (HL)+(DE)
        HL,DE
        A,(HL)
        HL



        *           ; CHECK FOR A VALID CAPTURE
        HL
        HL,DE
        BRDPCE      ; GET PIECE ON OTHERSIDE
        HL          ; OF PIECE TO CAPTURE
        BLANK       ; IS IT EMPTY
        NZ          ; NO => NO CAPTURE
        A,1         ; YES => SAVE CAPTURE
        (CAPT),A
        (CAPTF),HL
        (CAPTD),DE
```

# Adventure

An adventure is a program that allows you to
enter and explore strange new worlds, find treasures
and battle fierce monsters. As an adventurer you must
solve the riddles and problems of the world you will
enter if you are ever to leave alive.

This program allows you to have an adventure
on your SPECTRUM. The computer will describe the locations
you will visit and the things you will see. Also it
will prompt you to tell it want you want to do. The
commands you may use consist of one or two words. You
must always supply a verb (i.e the action you wish to do)
and often you will need a noun (i.e the object you wish
to perform the action on).

Some examples are :
'north' - move north and have a look around
'take axe ' - if there is an axe where you
are this will tell the computer
to try and pick it up for you
In a few cases you will be asked for more
information after you have given the computer a command.
For example if you say
'kill dragon' the computer will ask you what
you wish to kill it with. In this case just enter the
name of the weapon you wish to use or nothing (just hit
enter) if you want to use your bare hands.

As well as giving you an adventure to play this
program also allows you to easily create your own worlds
for yourself or a friend to adventure in.

How to play

The computer will display a description of the
location that you are in and it will describe any objects
that you can see. It will then ask you what you want to do.
You must then answer with a command as descibed above.
The computer will try to perform your command and if all
goes well it will go back and do this all over again.
If however your command does not work - perhaps because
of a spelling mistake - or if you are not able to do
the command yet the computer will print an appropriate
message, go back and try again.

Some of the commands you can use are
north, south, east, west, up and down
These allow you to move around.
inventory - lists everything you are carrying
take - picks up objects
drop - drops objects
etc
If an object description has an adjective in it
- e.g 'mean troll', then you cannot say 'kill troll'. You
must use 'kill mean troll' or just 'kill mean'.

Note most words may be abbreviated to one or two
letters; provided this does not cause any ambiguity
between words. If an abbreviation would match more than

one word the computer uses the first one it finds

When playing an adventure it is usually a good idea to draw a map of the world you are exploring. Since many adventures contain mazes it is almost impossible to find your way around unless you have a good map showing you which way to go.

## How the program works

This program consists of two distinct parts Firstly there is the data base that is in effect the game. It contains all the descriptions, objects and actions that make up the game. Secondly there is the program needed to allow the player to interact with the data base. This consists of the initialization for the game, getting the users input and performing the desired action.

## The data base

The fundamental parts of this adventure are the locations that make up the world, a map describing how these locations are connected, the objects that exist in this world and all of the actions that the player may perform. The way that each of these is built up will now be described in more detail

### Locations

For each location we need a description to give the player to tell him where he is and a list of the locations he can get to from where he is. As well as these it is often useful to have some sort of condition that can be applied upon entering a location. These can be anything from, making sure the player has a source of light before allowing him to enter, to performing some action when he enters (such as making a monster attack him if he is not carrying a particular object).

In this program each location has a unique number that the computer uses to access that location. The numbers start at 1 and increase in increments of 1 up to the last location. For example this adventure has 30 locations.

The locations exist in the program in data statements in the format
line number DATA "string",N,S,E,W,U,D,condition
The line number is the location number plus some constant (9000 in this game).
The "string" is the description of the location.
The values N,S,E,W,U,D are the locations that the player will end up in if he tries to go in the appropiate direction (north,south,..,up,down). A value of 0 means there is nowhere to go in that direction.
The condition is the number of the condition to be performed upon entry to THIS location.
Conditions consist of short pieces of program

located at the condition number plus a constant (7100 in this program)

Objects

The information we need for each object consists of its description, where it is, what type of object it is (i.e a treasure or a monster etc), how strong it is and to allow greater flexibility a condition to be performed if the player tries to pick up this object. These conditions may be one that always fails to stop people from taking things like tables, or one to kill the player if he tries to take a forbidden object

The computer knows about each object by its number just like locations.

The format of the data for objects is slightly different than that of locations. Each object has two lines in the program describing it

The first is:

line number DATA "string"

where

line number = object number + a constant (8000 in this adventure)

and "string" is the description of the object

The second is :

line number DATA type,strength,condition

where

line number = object number + a constant (8500)

the type is 0 for an ordinary object

)0 for a treasure and this value is the score for this treasure

(0 for a monster

strength   this is used in two ways

for a weapon it is the value added to the player strength if he uses it in a fight

and for a monster it is its strength that is matched against the player in battle

condition   is the condition to be done if the player tries to take this object

Lastly we need the location for each object and this is stored in an array. The initial locations for each object (as well as the number of objects) are stored in a DATA statment (at line 8000 in this program) and the location array is built from this.

The values used for these locations are

-1 - is used for objects that you cannot see or use, such as dead animals or treasures that have been returned to the first location.

0 - is for objects being carried by the player

) 0 - all other objects and this value is the location number of the object

166

The list of verbs that the player may use is
placed in data statements (starting at 7001 in this program)
Whenever a player types in a verb this list is searched
to find a match. Each verb also has a number which
the program uses to find the subroutine that performs
the action of the verb. The verb number is equal to
its position in the list (i.e the first verb is number 1)
and the subroutine to perform the verb is found at
a constant + 20 * the verb number (the constant is 1480
in this program so the first subroutine is at 1500 and
the others every 20 lines after that).

The following is a breakdown of the program

| LINES | FUNCTION |
|-------|----------|

5 - 40          initialization
                fixed value variables, screen parameters
                and variables peculiar to this particular
                adventure are set up here

50 - 110        control loop for the program
                it consists of

            1 print location description
              print any visible objects
            2 get the users input command
              perform the action the player wants
              if the action failed goto 2
              goto 1

900 - 940       initialization of the variables
                peculiar to this adventure
                that is it sets up the number
                of actions and objects, builds
                the object location array and
                defines some strings which are
                common to a number of locations
                to save memory space.
                It also sets up some variables
                that are used as conditions for
                the game such as a door being
                locked or unlocked etc

1000 - 1100     inputs the players command
                upper case is converted to lower
                case and the first two words
                of what the player typed are put
                in the variables a$ and n$ (a word
                is any sequence of characters ending
                in a space).
                The verb list is then searched for
                a$ and if it is found this subroutine
                returns the verb number to the main
                program, otherwise the player is
                prompted to try again

| | |
|---|---|
| 1200 - 1260 | This subroutine searches a given list for a given word. It is used to search the verbs for an action and the object descriptions for an object |
| 1300 - 1311 | searches the object descriptions for the variable n$ (the second word typed in by the player) If it is found it returns the description found in the list, the object number and a flag to indicate that the search was successful, otherwise the flag is set to indicate failure |
| 1500 - 1802 | This set of subroutines is used to perform the actions required by each verb |
| 1987 | This line is jumped to if some action fails. It prints the message "You can't" and sets the flag to indicate failure |
| 1988 | This line is jumped to if an action fails and the above message should not be printed, it just sets the flag |
| 1999 | This line is jumped to if an action succeeds, it sets the flag to indicate success |
| 2000 - 2050 | lists all the objects whose location is equal to the variable '1'. If none are found it prints "nothing". |
| 7000 - 7004 | This area contains the verb list line 7000 contains the number of verbs |
| 7100 - 7160 | These are the conditions that are done for taking objects or entering locations Note condition 0 always succeeds so if an object or location does not need a condition it is given this one |
| 8000 - 8525 | this is the data for the objects |
| 9001 - 9030 | this is the data for the locations |
| 9980 - 9981 | These lines are jumped to at the end of the game if the player has found all the treasures successfully |
| 9990 - 9992 | This section is used at the end of the game (either after the player has been killed or if he finished the game) it prints the score and asks if the game is to be replayed |

How to create your own adventure

Firstly you need a world to explore. This involves building into the data base the descriptions of all the locations to be visited along with the connections between them. Along with this you will need to decide what if any conditions will be applied to entering the locations.

As an example let us build a world with two locations. These will be

A hall stretching as far as the eye can see.

and   A small cavern.

The hall is north of the cavern and going south from the hall ends up in the cavern. No other directions are allowed. As a condition there will be a door between the two locations that will be locked. The player can only pass between the two if the door has been unlocked.

So we have

9001 DATA "in a hall stretching as far as the eye can see",0,2,0,0,0,0,0

9002 DATA "in a small cavern",1,0,0,0,0,0,1

Note doors are only one way so that entering the hall has no condition while entering the cavern requires that the the door be unlocked.

Since the hall is the first location this will be where the player starts and treasures must be put.

Now we need some objects. We already need a locked door and an unlocked door (at the start the locked door will exist between the locations but when the door is unlocked we will put the locked door in location −1 to get rid of it and replace it with the unlocked one). Obviously we also need a key to unlock the door. For a treasure let us have an emerald in the cavern. As well there will be a sword in the hall and a snake guarding the emerald.

So we have

| object | type, | strength, | condition | location |
|---|---|---|---|---|
| locked door | 0 | 0 | fail | 1 |
| unlocked door | 0 | 0 | fail | −1 |
| key | 0 | 0 | 0 | 1 |
| sword | 0 | 10 | 0 | 1 |
| snake | −1 | 100 | fail | 2 |
| emerald | 30 | 0 | 2 | 2 |

This means that the player cannot take either door or the snake, and the emerald can only be taken if condition 2 is met. We will write condition as a test for the snake being alive.

The sword has a strength of 10 and the snake 100 so if the player starts with a strength of 100 the fight between them should be fairly matched with a slight advantage to the player.

The emerald has a score of 30, the snake is a monster and all else are just objects.

In the program this would be

169

```
8000 DATA 6,1,-1,1,1,2,2
8001 DATA "locked door"
8002 DATA "unlocked door"
8003 DATA "key"
8004 DATA "sword"
8005 DATA "snake"
8006 DATA "emerald"
8501 DATA 0,0,fa-cs        (fa is the address of
8502 DATA 0,0,fa-cs        failure routine and cs
8503 DATA 0,0,0            is the address of the
8504 DATA 0,10,0           conditions so fa-cs is
8505 DATA -1,100,fa-cs     a condition that fails)
8506 DATA 30,0,2
```

Now we need the actions to perform. The movements
and their subroutines as well as 'inventory', 'take',
'drop' and 'kill' are fairly standard and will probably
be used in all your adventures so look at the program for
these. The other action we will have will be 'unlock' for
the door, so the verb list will be

```
7000 11                (this is the number of actions)
7001 DATA "north","south","east","west"
7002 DATA "up","down","take","drop"
7003 DATA "kill","inventory","unlock"
```

The only routine we need write is for unlock.
This needs to check if the player is in the hall and
is carrying the key and the door is still locked. We
now need a variable to indicate if the door is locked
or not say 'lu' (remember this must be initialized at
the start or the door may be unlocked when we thought
it was locked).

Unlocking, then will consist of
```
1700 IF lu = 1 OR 1 () 1 OR o(3) () 0
        THEN GO TO fa    (check conditions)
1701 LET o(1) = -1       (get rid of locked door)
1702 LET o(2) = 1        (replace it with other one)
1703 LET lu = 1          (set variable)
1704 GO TO tr            (success)
```

Now we need the conditions, we only have two
and they are
```
     1  is door unlocked
and  2  is the snake dead
```
In the program these will be
```
7101 GO TO fa+lu    (if lu=0 this will go to fa
                     and fail, if lu=1 this will
                     goto tr and succeed)
7102 GO TO fa+(o(5)=-1)
```
The second of these may need some explanation
What it means is IF o(5)=-1 THEN GO TO tr
        else IF o(5)()-1 THEN GO TO fa
It works because the statement   (o(5)=-1)
will be equal to 1 if o(5)=-1 and it will equal
0 if o(5) () -1.

So now we have an adventure even though it
is pretty small. Good luck writing your own.

Adventure

```
   5 LET tr = 1999 : LET fa = 1998 : LET Ls = 9000 :
       LET os = 8000 : LET oz = 8500 : LET vs = 7000
       : LET cs = 7100 : LET sc = 0
   6 LET vr = 1480 : LET z = 0 : LET ct = 1997 :
       LET dr = 1601 : LET cx = 6 : LET st = 100
  10 BORDER 5 : PAPER 7 : INK 0 : CLS
  30 LET L = 1
  40 GO SUB 900
  50 POKE 23692, 255 : RESTORE L+Ls : READ m$ :
       PRINT "You▲are▲"; m$ : LET q$ = "You▲see" :
       GO SUB 2000
  60 BEEP .2, 12 : PRINT
  70 GO SUB 1000
  80 PRINT v$; "▲";
  90 GO SUB vr+vn*20
 100 IF f = 0 THEN GO TO 60
 110 PRINT : GO TO 50
 900 RESTORE os : READ oc : DIM o(oc)
 910 FOR i = 1 TO oc : READ o(i) : NEXT i
 920 RESTORE vs : READ vc
 930 LET be = 0 : LET Lu = 0 : LET gu = 0 :
       LET e$ = "in▲an▲endless▲desert" :
       LET p$ = "in▲a▲passage"
 940 RETURN
1000 INPUT "Tell▲me▲what▲to▲do▲"; s$ :
       IF LEN s$ = 0 THEN GO TO 1000
1010 LET a$ = "" : LET n$ = ""
1020 LET x = 0 : FOR i = 1 TO LEN s$
1030 LET i$ = s$(i TO i)
1040 IF i$ >= "A" AND i$ <= "Z" THEN
       LET i$ = CHR$ (32+ CODE i$)
1050 IF i$ = "▲" AND x = 1 THEN LET i = LEN s$ :
       GO TO 1080
1051 IF i$ = "▲" THEN LET x = 1 : GO TO 1080
1060 IF x = 0 THEN LET a$ = a$+i$
1070 IF x = 1 THEN LET n$ = n$+i$
1080 NEXT i : LET w$ = a$ : LET c = vc : LET d = vs+1
       : GO SUB 1200
1090 IF vn = 0 THEN PRINT
       "▲INV I▲don't▲understand ▲IBU ▲"; a$ : GO TO 1000
1100 LET v$ = y$ : RETURN
1200 LET vn = 0
1210 RESTORE d
1220 FOR i = 1 TO c : READ m$ : LET x = LEN m$ :
       IF x > LEN w$ THEN LET x = LEN w$
1240 IF w$( TO x) = m$( TO x) THEN LET vn = i :
       LET y$ = m$ : LET i = c
1260 NEXT i : RETURN
1300 IF n$ = "" THEN GO TO 1311
1301 LET w$ = n$ : LET c = oc : LET d = os+1 :
       GO SUB 1200 : IF vn = 0 THEN GO TO 1311
1310 PRINT y$ : GO TO tr
1311 PRINT "▲INV I▲don't▲understand ▲IBU ▲"; n$ :
```

```
          GO TO fa
1500 LET d = 1 : GO TO dr
1520 LET d = 2 : GO TO dr
1540 LET d = 3 : GO TO dr
1560 LET d = 4 : GO TO dr
1580 LET d = 5 : GO TO dr
1600 LET d = 6
1601 PRINT : RESTORE L+Ls : READ m$ : FOR i = 1 TO d
     : READ nL : NEXT i
1602 IF nL = 0 THEN PRINT "You can't go that way"
     : GO TO fa
1603 RESTORE nL+Ls : READ m$, s, s, s, s, s, s
1604 READ s
1605 GO SUB cs+s : IF f = 0 THEN GO TO 1611
1610 IF o(1) = 0 THEN LET L = nL : GO TO tr
1611 PRINT "Something stops you" : GO TO fa
1620 GO SUB 1300 : IF f = 0 THEN RETURN
1621 IF o(vn) <> L THEN PRINT "It's not here" :
     GO TO fa
1622 RESTORE oz+vn : READ s : IF s < 0 THEN GO TO ct
1624 READ s
1625 READ s
1626 GO SUB cs+s : IF f = 0 THEN GO TO ct
1630 IF cx <> 0 THEN LET cx = cx-1 : LET o(vn) = 0 :
     RETURN
1631 PRINT "You are carrying too much" : GO TO fa
1640 GO SUB 1300 : IF f = 0 THEN RETURN
1641 IF o(vn) <> 0 THEN PRINT "You don't have it"
     : GO TO fa
1642 RESTORE oz+vn : READ s
1643 LET o(vn) = L : IF L = 1 AND s <> 0 THEN
     LET sc = sc+s : LET o(vn) = -1 :
     PRINT "The "; y$; " vanishes"
1644 LET cx = cx+1 : IF sc = 220 THEN GO TO 9980
1645 RETURN
1660 GO SUB 1300 : IF f = 0 THEN RETURN
1661 LET t$ = y$ : LET mn = vn : RESTORE oz+vn :
     READ s, ms : IF s >= 0 THEN GO TO ct
1662 LET s = 0 : BEEP .1, 20 :
     INPUT "kill with what ?"; w$ : IF w$ = ""
     THEN GO TO 1670
1663 LET c = oc : LET d = os+1 : GO SUB 1200 :
     IF vn = 0 THEN GO TO 1662
1664 IF o(vn) <> 0 THEN GO TO 1662
1665 RESTORE oz+vn : READ s, s : IF s = 0 THEN
     GO TO 1662
1666 PRINT " with "; y$;
1670 PRINT : LET s = s+st : IF ms > s+ RND *20 THEN
     GO TO 1679
1671 IF s > ms+ RND *15 THEN GO TO 1678
1672 PRINT "The "; t$; " fights back.
      You feel weaker"
1673 LET st = st- RND *5 : GO TO tr
1678 PRINT "You have killed the "; t$ :
     PRINT "The body vanishes in a cloud of
      smoke" : LET o(mn) = -1 : GO TO tr
```

172

```
1679 PRINT "The "; t$; " has killed you" :
     GO TO 9990
1680 LET L1 = L : LET L = 0 : LET q$ = "You are
      carrying" : GO SUB 2000 : LET L = L1 :
     GO TO tr
1700 PRINT sc : GO TO tr
1720 GO SUB 1300 : IF f = 0 THEN RETURN
1721 IF vn <> 20 OR o(2) <> 0 THEN GO TO ct
1722 LET o(14) = o(vn) : LET o(vn) = -1 :
     PRINT "An ivory key falls from the
          ceiling" : RETURN
1740 IF L <> 11 AND L <> 29 THEN GO TO ct
1741 IF L = 11 AND o(3) <> 0 THEN PRINT "You sink
      to the bottom of the   lake and
      drown" : GO TO 9990
1742 IF L = 11 THEN LET L = 29 : GO TO tr
1743 LET L = 11 : GO TO tr
1760 GO SUB 1300 : IF f = 0 THEN RETURN
1761 IF L = 1 AND o(4) = 0 THEN LET o(22) = -1 :
     LET o(23) = L : LET Lu = 1 : RETURN
1762 IF L = 13 AND o(14) = 0 THEN LET o(24) = -1 :
     LET o(25) = L : LET gu = 1 : RETURN
1763 GO TO ct
1780 IF o(16) <> 0 OR L < 3 OR L > 10 THEN GO TO ct
1781 PRINT "You find ";
1782 IF L = 6 AND o(4) = -1 THEN LET o(4) = L :
     PRINT "something" : GO TO tr
1783 PRINT "nothing" : GO TO tr
1800 GO SUB 1300 : IF f = 0 THEN RETURN
1801 RESTORE oz+vn : READ s, s1, s1
1802 IF s < 0 THEN GO TO ct
1803 GO SUB cs+s1 : IF f = 0 THEN GO TO ct
1804 PRINT "That hits the spot" : LET o(vn) = -1 :
     RETURN
1820 GO SUB 1300 : IF f = 0 THEN RETURN
1821 IF L <> 24 OR vn <> 7 THEN GO TO 1830
1822 PRINT "A bridge appears across the
          chasm" : LET o(15) = L : LET be = 1
     : GO TO tr
1830 PRINT "Nothing happens" : GO TO fa
1840 IF L = 24 OR L = 26 THEN PRINT "The fall has
      broken your neck" : GO TO 9990
1841 GO TO 1830
1860 GO SUB 1300 : IF f = 0 THEN RETURN
1861 IF vn <> 18 THEN GO TO ct
1862 PRINT "That was delicious" : LET o(19) = o(vn)
     : LET o(vn) = -1 : RETURN
1997 PRINT "You can't"
1998 LET f = 0 : RETURN
1999 LET f = 1 : RETURN
2000 LET x = 0 : PRINT q$
2010 RESTORE os+1 : FOR i = 1 TO oc : READ m$
2020 IF L <> o(i) THEN GO TO 2030
2021 LET x = 1 : PRINT "  a";
2022 LET z$ = m$(1 TO 1) : IF z$ = "a" OR z$ = "e"
     OR z$ = "i" OR z$ = "o" OR z$ = "u" THEN
```

173

```
            PRINT "n";
2024 PRINT ".."; m$
2030 NEXT i
2040 IF x = 0 THEN PRINT "..nothing"
2050 RETURN
7000 DATA 19
7001 DATA "north", "south", "east", "west", "up",
        "down"
7002 DATA "take", "drop", "kill", "inventory",
        "score"
7003 DATA "cut", "swim", "unlock", "dig"
7004 DATA "eat", "wave", "jump", "drink"
7100 GO TO tr
7101 GO TO fa+Lu
7102 GO TO fa+gu
7103 GO TO fa+be
7104 GO TO fa+(o(3) = 0)
7105 GO TO fa+(o(11) = -1)
7106 GO TO fa+(o(12) = -1)
7107 GO TO fa+(o(10) = -1)
7150 IF o(18) <> 0 THEN GO TO tr
7151 LET o(18) = -1 : LET o(12) = -1 : PRINT "As.you
        .enter.a.pirate.steals....your.rum
        .and.runs.off.laughing" : GO TO tr
7160 PRINT "The.devil.kills.you" : GO TO 9990
8000 DATA 25, 1, 12, 27, -1, 14, 17, 21, 25, 29, 12,
        14, 17, 20, -1, -1, 11, 2, 2, -1, 19, 11, 1,
        -1, 13, -1
8001 DATA "brass.lamp"
8002 DATA "sword"
8003 DATA "snorkel"
8004 DATA "large.key"
8005 DATA "persian.rug"
8006 DATA "gold.coin"
8007 DATA "silver.wand"
8008 DATA "ruby"
8009 DATA "diamond"
8010 DATA "mean.troll"
8011 DATA "green.dragon"
8012 DATA "pirate"
8013 DATA "devil"
8014 DATA "ivory.key"
8015 DATA "crystal.bridge"
8016 DATA "shovel"
8017 DATA "kitchen.table"
8018 DATA "bottle.of.rum"
8019 DATA "empty.bottle"
8020 DATA "rope.tied.between.the.floor.and
        .ceiling"
8021 DATA "small.lake"
8022 DATA "locked.door"
8023 DATA "door"
8024 DATA "padlocked.gate"
8025 DATA "gate"
8501 DATA z, z, z
8502 DATA z, 20, 7
```

```
8503 DATA z, z, z
8504 DATA z, z, z
8505 DATA 10, 7, 5
8506 DATA 50, z, 6
8507 DATA 20, z, z
8508 DATA 30, z, z
8509 DATA 100, z, z
8510 DATA -1, 87, z
8511 DATA -1, 110, z
8512 DATA -1, 200, z
8513 DATA -1, 200, z
8514 DATA 10, z, z
8515 DATA z, z, z
8516 DATA z, z, z
8517 DATA z, z, fa-cs
8518 DATA z, z, z
8519 DATA z, z, z
8520 DATA z, z, fa-cs
8521 DATA z, z, fa-cs
8522 DATA z, z, fa-cs
8523 DATA z, z, fa-cs
8524 DATA z, z, fa-cs
8525 DATA z, z, fa-cs
9001 DATA "in.the.living.room.of.a.large
     .house..A.sign.says.Return.all
     .treasures.here.", 2, z, z, z, z, 12, z
9002 DATA "in.the.kitchen", z, 1, 3, z, z, z, z, z
9003 DATA e$, z, 4, 5, 2, z, z, z
9004 DATA e$, 3, 7, 6, z, z, z, z
9005 DATA e$, z, 6, 7, 3, z, z, z
9006 DATA e$, 5, 8, z, 4, z, z, z
9007 DATA e$, z, z, z, 4, z, z, z
9008 DATA e$, 6, 9, z, z, z, z, z
9009 DATA e$, 8, z, 10, z, z, z, z
9010 DATA e$, 11, z, z, 9, z, z, z
9011 DATA "at.an.oasis", z, 10, z, z, z, z, z
9012 DATA "in.a.cellar", z, 16, 13, z, 1, z, 1
9013 DATA "at.the. EXI SHI 2GATES.OF.HELL EXI SHI 0", z, z,
     z, 12, z, 20, z
9014 DATA "in.a. INV blackened.cavern IRU ", z, 15, z,
     z, z, z, z
9015 DATA p$, 14, 18, z, 16, z, z, z
9016 DATA p$, 12, z, 15, z, z, 17, z
9017 DATA "in.the.pirates.lair", z, z, z, z, 16,
     z, 50
9018 DATA p$, 15, 19, z, z, z, z, z
9019 DATA p$, 18, z, z, z, z, z, z
9020 DATA "in.HELL....A.devil.says.'Find.the
     .right.direction.and..live.-. EXI SHI 2else
     .die EXI SHI 0'", 30, 30, 30, 21, 30, 30, 2
9021 DATA p$, z, 24, 22, 20, z, z, z
9022 DATA "in.a.dead.end", z, z, z, 21, z, z, z
9023 DATA " EXI 0 EXI SHI 2DEAD.IN.HELL EXI 7 EXI SHI 0", z, z
     z, z, z, z
9024 DATA "at.the.brink.of.a.deep..chasm", 21,
     25, z, z, z, z, z
```

175

```
9025 DATA "in a beautiful jewelled hall", 24, z,
     27, z, z, z, 3
9026 DATA "at the brink of a deep  pit. There
      are traces of  EXI SHI 2fire EXI SHI 0   and
      EXI 6brimstone EXI 7 here.", z, 27, z, z, z, 23,
     z
9027 DATA p$, 26, z, z, 25, z, 28, z
9028 DATA p$, z, z, z, z, 27, 18, z
9029 DATA " EXI SHI 1swimming in a small lake EXI SHI 0",
     z, z, z, z, z, z, 4
9030 DATA "", z, z, z, z, z, z, 60
9980 PRINT : PRINT : PRINT : PRINT
9981 PRINT "CONGRATULATIONS   This adventure is
      over  and you have returned   safely
      with all the treasures."
9990 PRINT : PRINT "SCORE "; sc : PRINT "Do you
      wish to play again ?"
9991 LET m$ = INKEY$ : IF m$ = "" THEN GO TO 9991
9992 IF m$( TO 1) = "y" THEN GO TO 5
```

Hints for playing the ADVENTURE program

(1)  Lost in the desert?
      Do not despair the desert is not really endless
and if you strategically drop objects in the desert you
should be able to make a map of the desert. You will
need this map to find the oasis.

(2)  Can't get through the living room door?
      You will need the key that is buried somewhere in
the desert. To dig up the key you will of course need a
shovel which is also outside the house - somewhere.

(3)  Stuck in HELL?
      Do what the devil says.

(4)  Can't get past the pirate?
      Try the rum.

(5)  Can't kill the dragon?
      Keep trying.

(6)  Can't find the key to the gate?
      Try the rope.

(7)  Can't cross the chasm?
      Maybe a magic wand would be of assistance.

(8)  Can't find the last treasure?
      Go swimming.

You may also enjoy...

Printed in Great Britain
by Amazon

47301362R00108